Beyond Reality

Leyland Bus
- the twilight years

ISBN 1 898432 02 3

Front Cover Illustration

The final production Leyland Bus chassis was the Olympian – which ironically started life
as a Bristol model. This view is evocative of the changes in the industry which culminated
in the demise of the Company.
　　When the Leyland National first entered production, would anyone have believed that an
erstwhile Tilling Company or its successor in name would be running a yellow, Northern
Counties bodied double-decker built at Workington?
　　F175LBL of Berks and Bucks, heads into the night, on its way to Reading.

Typeset and produced electronically for the Publishers by
Mopok Graphics, 128, Pikes Lane, Glossop, Derbyshire
Printed and bound in Great Britain

Beyond Reality

Leyland Bus
- the twilight years

by

Doug Jack

Venture *publications*

CONTENTS

CONTENTS

FOREWORD

by

Marcus Smith

first Director & General Manager
Leyland National Company Ltd

I was fortunate to be associated with the Cumberland project almost from its inception all the way through the creative phase which established Workington as a fully rounded manufacturing organisation in its own right. This was indeed a challenging, heady experience that despite the subsequent years of decline will remain rewarding and memorable years in the working lives of those who dedicated themselves to the Workington Plant.

Doug Jack's tireless research into the darker corners of the Workington story revealed to me, and I am sure will to many others, much that was new concerning those years which I call the second phase of the plant's history – a phase of diversification, of politics both internal and external, personality clashes, and not least unforeseen economic pressures.

I, as the gamekeeper turned poacher, saw the outward signs of the inward sickness. As it happened I was involved from within London Transport in prolonging its life when, during the 1980s, LT took batches of Nationals and agreed to the transfer of the Titan from Park Royal to Workington. I am not so sure we knew just how serious the position was becoming at that time. The scale of the effort undertaken to try and survive during the latter half of Workington's 24 years life came as a surprise. I found it a fascinating story.

The Cumberland Project, the National Bus, Leyland National Ltd, the Workington Plant, by whatever name it was known at each stage of its development, became a legend in its own lifetime. There were so many adventurous initiatives which ultimately came together at Workington that friends, competitors, and just the plain curious from all walks of life, beat a pathway to its doors from all over the globe. They came to stand and stare and went away, with hardly an exception, excited and stimulated by the breadth of innovation in so many facets of automotive manufacture.

It is great credit to everyone involved that the National itself, the factory, the manufacturing processes, and above all the Cumbrian workforce, stood the test of time and coped with changed technology, and a variety of vehicle design far beyond that envisaged at the beginning.

The danger of becoming a legend is the emergence of myths but the story of the Workington Plant needs no help from mythology, for leaving aside the underlying effects of political dogma and personalities in its later years it achieved its objectives on time, on cost, and built a product of first class quality. That is the reality of the Workington Story – beyond that reality is the rest of the story so ably brought together by the author.

He has been careful in naming names. To me the abiding satisfaction was the building of a team of ordinary men and women drawn from many backgrounds to make the successes which is at the heart of this story. They are the 'golden thread' which winds its way through the rich tapestry of Workington's history. They were blessed with the dedication, and the tenacity in adversity, needed to achieve success in so many 'pastures new'! The Bus, the plant, the workforce, the location, – nearly all were untrodden paths.

The severe strictures on not poaching manpower from within the already stretched resources of the Leyland Motor Corporation challenged us to form the management team and the workforce around a small group of under a dozen that came North from Lancashire and the Midlands. A group of four young graduates, at the start of their careers, formed the nucleus of middle management. They matured rapidly and I am sure look back on their Workington days with satisfaction from the senior posts a number of them now hold in the automotive industry.

There are two names who I think are typical of the characters that made Workington – an import from Lancashire, and a homespun product from the shores of the Solway – John Clarke and David Ratsey. Involved in quite different ways, they were full of respect for each other, and were well respected by colleagues and customers alike.

John Clarke as Works Manager was dedicated to the Leyland National even before Workington was dreamt about, having been responsible to Joe McGowan for building the prototypes down at

Leyland. A Lancastrian from the Leyland village, a hands-on-man, he earned the not easily won respect of the Cumbrian, and on a different plane, the respect of our hard to please customers for his honesty and forthrightness.

The inborn natural ability of David Ratsey, as a roving Service Engineer, became the face of Leyland National in many parts of the world. Language difficulties were swept aside with impunity as he established a working rapport with his hands and the skills they held. His 'stubby' pencilled reports on any odd piece of paper written as he flew home were works of art covering technical problems alongside his own special view of local politics and personalities!

They are but two names and I am sure that all those not mentioned will be happy to have them as their representatives in my tribute to those who really made the Leyland National project an achievement without precedent in the UK bus building industry.

The role of the National Bus Company in Leyland National must never be underestimated. The part which fell to me to play as the bridge in the relationship between NBC and Leyland taught me a lot. A 50-50 ownership is fairly unique and demanded much diplomacy and negotiation. The level of satisfaction and enjoyment in working between the two organisations of LMC and NBC remains a 'high' in my memories of the Workington saga. The ears of such names as Robert Brook and George McKay were always ready to listen. It was essential that we took well prepared papers to a Leyland National board meeting, and I feel sure that the term 'shuttle diplomacy' was invented to meet the needs of such an unusual relationship!

There were tough characters on both sides – not to say the least Ron Ellis – who had their own partisan views and these had to be reconciled for the relationship to survive and to prosper. We faced our critics in the NBC operating companies but they never failed to treat us with courtesy and constructive support.

I have perhaps over emphasised the two-phase nature of the Workington Story as I perceive it. From a 'once removed' level in the Passenger Vehicle Division of Leyland Truck and Bus I was involved in the early stages of diversification into railway work – not then as a lifeline – but as a natural expansion of the technology of the National as a vehicle, and the emerging flexibility of the production process.

Towards the end of my association with Leyland there were clouds on the horizon – no bigger than a man's hand – but nevertheless signs of impending change. The appearance of personalities remote from the product and from man management experience imposed styles that were arrogant and crude to say the least.

The story of Workington's latter years I find fascinating with the repeated misjudgments, the waste

of human endeavour by the mishandling of individuals, and the manipulation of the facts and figures. One wonders if the truth had been known when it was first perceived whether 'a stitch in time might have saved nine'!

At some point in time the end became inevitable but the record of Workington's achievement, and of its tasks fulfilled, is a fitting memorial to those whose lives were dedicated to the Workington Plant. That there are sad parts of the story, or even black parts, can in no way detract from an imaginative concept turned into a well executed reality.

Marcus Smith
South Brenton
Devon
September 1993

AUTHOR'S INTRODUCTION

Leyland was one of the greatest names of the British motor industry, and the world's largest exporter of commercial vehicles, before the Government of the day arranged the marriage with BMC and its problems of poor management obsolescent models and rampant restrictive trade unionism.

The cost of trying to resolve those problems diverted vital funding from the commercial vehicle operations, but not before the creation of a fabulous factory at Workington to build a new generation of single-deck city buses.

There is an old saying in the motor industry to the effect that you can change a product, or a workforce, or a factory, but never change more than one at a time. Putting a totally new product into a brand new factory, with a workforce which had never before built buses, was considered risky to the extent of recklessness.

Yet, a small team of dedicated people succeeded. The first, and best known product, the Leyland National, set new standards in the world's bus industry. 'The world' is not an exaggeration – that is the measure of the technology employed. Workington's contribution stood the test of time magnificently. It was only the engine, which was beyond Workington's control, which let the National down originally.

I joined Leyland Motors as a graduate trainee in 1964, probably the only one with a Scottish law degree. As Legal Advisor to the Truck & Bus Division from 1968, and additionally Company Secretary from 1970, I saw the Workington project rise up from a bare Cumbrian heath.

When output exceeded thirty buses a week in 1975/76, it was a truly impressive plant. Many a visitor stood transfixed at the giant jigs and orderly conveyors carrying partly built buses from station to station. It was a showpiece which was viewed with envy by Leyland's international competitors.

The factory was built in one political climate and went onto its deathbed in another. Harold Wilson's Labour Party was right in its attempt to develop a long term industrial strategy for the country, but was so deeply into bed with the trade unions that it had no hope of killing the restrictive practices which made much of British industry uncompetitive. However, I hasten to add that Workington was not afflicted by that problem and had an excellent workforce.

A decade later, Margaret Thatcher's Conservative Party championed free market forces. The Tories and their friends in the City of London, an overhead not carried by German or Japanese industry, were in for short term opportunism. Two of the legacies of Margaret Thatcher's strategy for industry are the oldest bus fleet, and the weakest bus building industry, in any major nation.

This book tells how, as a result of her Government's policies, or rather a lack of them, a highly automated plant, built for one product, was forced to diversify into chassis, bodywork, coaches and railbuses. A management buy-out of Leyland Bus was soon followed by a management sell-out to Volvo.

I am very grateful for the tremendous help given by many people when researching and writing the Workington story. If the others will excuse me, three men deserve special mention. Joe McGowan was the brilliant engineer who conceived the project, and it is to his credit that operators are still finding it economic to rebuild his bus after up to twenty years service.

Marcus Smith was the man who set up the factory and got it into production. I spent several very enjoyable hours reminiscing with him in Bristol last summer, and am delighted that he has written the Foreword. Marcus was the leading personality in the British bus manufacturing industry in the 1970s.

It is therefore appropriate that great help also came from Sandy Glennie, who took over that mantle in the 1980s and holds it to this day, having taken Volvo to nearly 60% of the British market for heavy duty buses and coaches.

There are those who have criticised Volvo for the demise of Workington and Leyland Bus, but they will be better informed by the end of the last Chapter. Volvo hastily picked up a baby with a very dirty nappy and it is to the great credit of the Swedish company that it not only carried out the enormous cost of reworking defective railbuses, but also kept the Workington factory open in the rapidly declining market, probably three to four years longer than any other owner might have done.

Volvo has also taken on the considerable responsibility for supplying parts and service for the thousands of Leyland buses which are still operational, and that should not be forgotten.

Among the many others who freely gave John Senior and me help and advice were David Quainton, Ken Hargreaves, David Burnicle, Stewart Brown, Jim McKnight, Alan Townsin, Peter Dawson, Steve Dewhurst, Ian Lister, Eddie Brown, Bob Smith, Andrew Huddleston, Chris George, Barry Wills, Alan Jackson, Rodney Swarbrick, Bill Dixon, Selwyn Scott, John Arkell, John Broadley, Brian Cherry, Colin Hardman, Derek Lowe, Ken Haines, and last but by no means least, Ron McCullock, who lives in Workington and kept me supplied with a regular steam of information.

While the Workington plant went through its traumas, so unfortunately did my publisher, with whom I had worked on 'The Leyland Bus'. Venture Publications was formed in 1993 to pick up the mantle of producing quality books about the industry and I wish the new team every success. John Senior and Alan Townsin continue in their roles and I greatly appreciated their contributions. Neil MacDonald and Duncan Roberts, directors of the new company, were also very helpful.

We debated the layout of this book at length. John Senior and I have accumulated many photographs over the years, partly for an earlier official history of the plant which never saw the light of day, and partly for our on-going Leyland research. They were nearly all black and white, but we were keen to include colour where possible. By happy coincidence, Chapter 10 mentions most of the products made during Workington's lifetime. We therefore balanced cost and availability of material against the added impact of colour and hope that you like the results.

Most of the photographs have come from John and me, but several people or organisations loaned interesting material to fill gaps. We have not credited each photograph individually, but thanks go to Alexander (Belfast), David Cole, Ken Hargreaves, Stuart Jones, Bill Luke, Neil MacDonald, Roy Marshall, Duncan Roberts, Mark Senior, David Stanier, Alan Townsin, Ulsterbus, Volvo Bus and Reg Wilson.

Then there are those who worked so hard behind the scenes. My wife Jan typed all the text from tape to disc, and Margaret Davies put it onto the systems at Glossop. The pritt stick and the galley proof are as out of date as the half cab bus!

It is difficult to condense more than twenty years of recent history into a concise volume. If there are any omissions or errors, I apologise to those concerned, but please let me know, through my publisher.

Above all, I hope that the earnest endeavour and very real achievement of those who knew what they were doing, and who played a constructive part in the Workington story, outshines and outlives the role of those who contributed, directly or indirectly, to the decline of Leyland's commercial vehicle operations, especially in the late 1970s and early 1980s, when the real damage was done!

Ashby St Ledgers, Rugby   January 1994

CHAPTER ONE
Moving Fast In A Fast Moving World

In the mid-1960s, the Leyland Motor Corporation was a dynamic organisation and a world leader in the manufacture and export of commercial vehicles. Before recounting the Workington story and the associated events of the final quarter century of the company's existance, it might be helpful to go back in time and review the main events leading to the construction of the world's most highly automated bus factory.

Leyland's origins can be traced to the Lancashire Steam Motor Company Ltd, which commenced business in 1896 in that county, in the small town of Leyland. Within eight years, the first petrol engined models were produced. The company changed its name to Leyland Motors Ltd in 1907. Like many manufacturers Leyland had to expand facilities to meet the demand for military vehicles in the First World War. While one can never forget the personal sufferings caused by war, it was a stimulus to creative design and production. War also spawned factories which had to be utilised after hostilities ceased.

In the early 1920s Leyland barely survived a long national recession. Design was generally by evolution, rather than revolution, but the company's fortunes started to improve following the introduction in 1927 of the TD1 Titan, Britain's first truly versatile double-deck bus. Leyland produced an extensive range of bus and coach models, as well as trucks, or lorries as they were then called. Some other companies in the British market concentrated, in some cases exclusively, on lorries or, like Daimler, on buses and cars.

The wartime 'RAF' type vehicle formed the basis of the post-war bus and lorry range. In addition to new production there was also a major programme of rehabilitation of ex-military vehicles.

The First World War created a demand for motorised transport and Leyland produced many thousands of vehicles to help meet that need. These early armoured vehicles were rudimentary, especially when compared to the sophisticated tanks Leyland designed and built for the Second War.

A Leyland double-decker of the early 1920s for Todmorden clearly showing the high straight frame. The chassis could be used for passenger or haulage work. Shortly afterwards designs started to cater for two separate needs.

Lorry production always formed a substantial part of Leyland's output. This Hippo, built in June 1930, was one of the largest lorries of the period.

The Titan TD1 introduced in 1927 was a landmark in British bus design. The combination of a frame cranked low between the axles and a sunken gangway on the offside for access to the upper deck seats reduced the overall height to about 13ft. This, with more refinement and performance than many single-deckers of the period, and excellent reliability, made it the first 'universal' double-decker to be found all over Britain.

The growth of the large company bus fleets, many of whose intake was almost exclusively of Leyland manufacture, produced a steady flow of orders. This line of Tigers of the late 1930s belonged to East Kent. In the 1950s it was Leyland's proud boast that in addition to the company fleets over 60% of the municipal bus fleets were Leyland users.

Leyland's double-decker bus body designed by Colin Bailey and introduced in 1936 made the Titan of that period the quintessential British bus. It represented a classic design copied by other builders but, in many people's opinion, never bettered.

The operating side of the bus industry changed from the rough and tumble pioneering of the 'twenties to the consolidation of large groups during the 'thirties, following the introduction of route licensing. Leyland built strong links with these groups which, in the passage of time, helped to lay the foundations for the Workington factory. A whole series of popular and well-engineered models came out of the Lancashire factories in the 'thirties. The main development in this period was the widespread adoption of diesel engines in larger buses and lorries. Further substantial expansion came during the Second World War.

Leyland pulled ahead of the rest of the pack in the late 1940s. New and durable models came on stream, powered by a range of very reliable diesel engines. These varied in size and power, depending on gross weight requirements. Leyland and some of its competitors at that time designated engines according to capacity in cubic inches, rather than litres. A series of advertisements quoted bus operators whose O.600 (9.8 litre) engines achieved half a million miles, without major overhaul. Although traffic was much lighter, there was less knowledge about materials able to withstand the wear and tear of daily use in a bus engine. Lubricating oils had improved, but they were not comparable with those available today, therefore the O.600 acquired and deserved its very special reputation. The larger 11.1 litre O.680 engine, first introduced in 1951, and basically a bored-out O.600, was highly regarded internationally and became the basis for engine ranges produced by Scania, DAF, Mack and Pegaso.

From the earliest days Leyland and other British manufacturers had been active in export markets, principally in the old British Empire. After the Second World War the Labour Government of the day actively encouraged export business, to help pay off huge war debts. An aggressive young team at Leyland, led by Donald Stokes, went all over the world in search of business. The majority of British manufacturers confined their activities to the Empire, but Leyland opened up many new markets.

Facing – A selection of Leyland vehicles posed outside South Works (right), in 1953. Thurston Road, with some of the company's offices, is behind the two double-deckers, whilst in the distance the smoking chimney belongs to North Works.

Left – One of an attractive series of advertisements placed by Leyland in the railway trade press in the mid 1930s.

Above – The high mileage achieved by the O.600 engines owed much to the Centurian tank development during the Second World War.

The first significant acquisition came in 1951. Leyland took over the old established Albion Motors Ltd of Glasgow. A fair percentage of models was complementary, with Albion adding light and medium weight commercial vehicles to the generally heavier Leyland range. Where there was direct competition the Albion model soon disappeared, particularly at the heavier end, and considerable rationalisation was achieved between the two companies. Leyland supplied the majority of Albion's engine requirements while Albion back-loaded gearboxes and axles in the opposite direction. Albion had been more prominent than Leyland in central and southern Africa, India and Malaysia, therefore this was an important acquisition in export terms. Export strategy was a vital part of Leyland's plans in this period and was a dominant theme right up to the establishment of the Workington factory, and for some years thereafter.

In 1955 Scammell Lorries Ltd of Watford was added to the fold. Scammell's expertise lay in heavy trucks, including enormous tractor units for hauling indivisible loads, and for military applications. Another factory at Watford produced a wide range of semi-trailers. A third product line was a small three wheeled articulated tractor unit for local delivery – the 'mechanical horse'.

The introduction and fairly rapid adoption of air brakes on heavier commercial vehicles required an engine-driven compressor and air reservoirs. Leyland and Self Changing Gears Ltd, (SCG), of Coventry, used the availability of an air system to adapt the design of the SCG gearbox to air operation, putting it into volume production in 1954, with the name 'Pneumocyclic'. Leyland bought SCG in 1956. The company had been established to commercialise the Wilson gearbox which was originally developed as a transmission for tanks in the First World War. It was adapted to pre-selective operation and taken up by Daimler and AEC as a city bus transmission from 1930/31 onwards. Leyland had installed this gearbox in the large fleet of Titans supplied to London Transport from 1948 onwards, with air operation of the preselective system, and the direct acting air operated version was a logical development.

Both systems differed from current automatic gearboxes in having manual operation. On the preselective gearbox, the driver had to move the lever into the next slot in anticipation of the next change, which did not take place until after he put his left foot firmly on the gear-change pedal, located in place of the usual clutch pedal. On the direct system, the driver moved a miniaturised lever when he wanted to change gear. There was no clutch or change pedal. All he was expected to do was lift his foot off the accelerator while the change was made.

There was a surprising change of direction in 1961, with the acquisition of Standard-Triumph, which built a range of saloon and sports cars. It was to be Leyland's first experience of the Midlands car industry. By all accounts Standard-Triumph was rather loosely controlled, with tales of staff having two and three company cars each. This was simply not acceptable to the thrifty Lancastrians, and so Stanley Markland, the authoritarian director in charge of Leyland's factories, was sent south to knock Standard-Triumph into shape. At first it was one way traffic, with Leyland putting disciplines and ideas into the car company. Within a few years, however, a small group of Standard-Triumph engineers had an important part to play in the Workington story.

Some feel that the acquisition of Standard-Triumph was a disastrous move, because it diverted money and attention from more crucial needs at Leyland. Alan Townsin, at that time a transport journalist, but nowadays Editor-in-Chief of Venture Publications Ltd, has suggested that the relationship between Leyland and some leading domestic bus operators started to decline from this point. He cited problems with early Atlanteans, the first rear-engined double-decker in Britain, and shortages of spare parts as shortcomings which failed to receive sufficient attention.

Leyland corporate advertising sought to promote the advantages of the acquisition of Standard-Triumph – some people say that far from being a Triumph it marked the start of Leyland's decline.

Albion complemented Leyland in many ways, bringing generally lighter models to the range, and some loyal export markets. This timber framed Victor bus entered service in Penang around 1955.

Scammell brought a variety of products to Leyland, ranging from the diminuative Mechanical Horse, right, through to the large tractor units of the type seen below. The railway carriage was part of a Park Royal export order.

The acquisitive pace started to quicken. In June 1962 it was announced that Leyland would merge with the Associated Commercial Vehicles Group (ACV). The latter had been built around its principal subsidiary, AEC. Other members included Maudslay, Crossley, Thornycroft and two bus bodybuilders, Park Royal Vehicles of London and Charles H Roe of Leeds. The merger was presented as being necessary to meet the increased levels of competition in overseas markets. The emphasis on export was interesting and said much about attitudes in Britain at that time. Many parts of the country were dependant on manufacturing industry and exporting was seen to be not only essential, but also quite glamorous. Companies would release details of export orders, however small, and the national press would print them with pride.

Companies with proven export experience were able to attract good managers and Leyland and ACV were no exception. Donald Stokes was rapidly rising to the top at Leyland, though Sir Henry Spurrier, a member of one of the founding families, was Chairman at the time of the merger. Jim Slater, essentially a financial man, was a powerful personality in the ACV ranks, where Sir William Black was Chairman.

By putting the emphasis on export as the primary reason, it was then difficult for anyone to protest about restriction of choice in the home market. The prevailing political climate was not averse to mergers. The two main parties were generally in favour, as were the trade unions, in the belief that mergers increased their powers. The laws on competition were nothing like as strict as they are now. Indeed, they were not introduced until after Government concern about a proposed merger between ICI and Courtaulds.

(It is peculiar that the attitude to mergers has changed so much. There was no suggestion that there should be a law preventing Leyland and AEC getting together, nor even the events described later in this Chapter. Yet, in a bus industry context, in 1989, when South Yorkshire Transport took over two small bus companies, each with abysmal maintenance records, they faced the great expense of prolonged legal action to determine whether their purchases were monopolistic! The matter was not finally resolved until 1993, when the Minister for Trade and Industry in effect over-ruled the Monopolies and Mergers Commission.)

In order to allay fears among domestic customers, the merger statement promised that Leyland and AEC would continue to develop their respective model ranges and would sell in competition in the United Kingdom. Although the combined enterprise became known in 1963 as the Leyland Motor Corporation, and Leyland was clearly in the driving seat, the AEC influence should not be under-estimated. Several senior people from ACV subsequently held very high positions in the Corporation. Jim Slater has already been mentioned. Jack Plane, ACV's importer in South Africa, later became head of the international operations. Other promotions from AEC included Arthur Fogg (production), George Francis (international projects), Bob Fryars (engineering) and Brian Shepherd (sales and marketing). Competition between Leyland and AEC in the domestic market was intense. It took some time before it was realised that the two were sometimes still in the ring, slogging it out for an order, when the real competition had retired!

While AEC was the principal supplier to London Transport right up to the early 1970s, Leyland also received a major share in the post-war period. The Titan on the right was built to LT's specification and was one of 500 which were the first London buses built to an overall width of 8ft. They were fitted with London's preferred air-operated pre-selective gearbox, as almost universally used on London's AECs, like the one on the left.

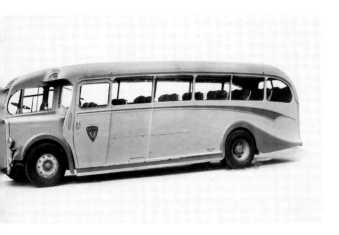

Steps were taken to rationalise the product range. The introduction of the Ergomatic cab on trucks was an early and very noticeable move. This was one of the first truck cabs which could be tilted to permit much easier access to the engine and gearbox. It was also a significant advance over contemporary cabs in terms of driver comfort, visibility, and access to controls. The cancellation of the rear-engined Routemaster bus, due to be exhibited at the 1966 Earls Court Show, was another example of rationalisation, taken not out of emotion, but for the valid reason that London Transport had indicated its intention to switch to large capacity single-deckers. Overall, and with the benefit of hindsight, the pace of rationalisation was too slow, but that was the nature of the industry in that era.

Concurrently several developing countries were starting to set up their own motor industries. The ability to build vehicles locally not only saved valuable foreign exchange, but was a matter of intense national prestige. The normal method was to start with assembly of imported kits, then progressively set up the local manufacture of components under licence from an established manufacturer. Many overseas assembly operations started with trucks and buses, for two important reasons. Firstly, the need for public and freight transport was usually greater than the relative luxury of private cars. Secondly, the assembly of cars required heavy investment in tools and paint booths, whereas trucks and buses could be built by more simple traditional methods.

The major international manufacturers competed for this business, because the successful bidder usually gained a strong market advantage through immunity from local import taxes. These were levied against built-up imports in order to protect the local industry and let it develop. In some cases, the import of built-up vehicles was excluded. Tariff barriers were widespread, even within Europe, though they have subsequently fallen or been abolished inside economic groupings, like the European Community. While Leyland was very active in this field, entering into a whole series of licence and assembly agreements, Mercedes-Benz and the two rising Swedish builders, Volvo and Scania, were also securing important areas of the world. The end result was to reduce the number of truly open markets, but the repercussions did not become clear until well after the Workington factory was established.

In Britain Leyland was regularly in the news and, at that time, for all the right reasons. In 1964 Harold Wilson's Labour Party had been elected with a small majority and Stokes had shown that he was one of the relatively few industrial leaders who was prepared to work with a Labour Government. One significant sign of this policy came late in 1965 when the Leyland Motor Corporation acquired 25% of the shares of Bristol Commercial Vehicles and Eastern Coach Works (ECW) from the state owned Transport Holding Company (THC). This organisation ran the former Tilling and Balfour Beatty bus companies in England and Wales and the former SMT Group of operators in Scotland, all of which were nationalised as a result of the Transport Act 1948.

The first Bristol ECW buses to be sold outside the state owned sector after the 1965 deal were supplied to Coventry in 1967. This ECW body on a Leyland Leopard chassis was supplied to West Hartlepool at the same time.

Bristol as chassis manufacturer and ECW as bodybuilder worked very closely, supplying the THC subsidiaries, which at that time represented roughly half the major non-municipal bus fleets in England and Wales. They also had access to the Scottish fleets, mainly with double-deckers. In turn, THC acquired 29% of Park Royal Vehicles, which included Charles Roe. This little nudge towards 'privatisation' was assisted by Anthony Wedgwood (later Tony) Benn, at that time Member of Parliament for one of the Bristol constituencies. The purpose of this transaction was to give Leyland additional bus manufacturing capacity and to free Bristol and ECW from the previous restriction of selling only to THC bus companies. Leyland provided Bristol and ECW with sales and service experience, especially in overseas markets. At home there were loud complaints in the old Leyland headquarters when Eddie Brown, seconded from there, succeeded in selling fleets of Bristol-ECW products to Ribble, a major bus company, right on Leyland's doorstep!

This transaction also brought Leyland into direct contact with Marcus Smith, who had been appointed Deputy General Manager of Bristol at the beginning of 1965, and General Manager from the middle of that year. He was later to become the single most important person in the Workington story. His career had started as a 'sandwich' apprentice with Brush in Loughborough in 1942. He took a degree in mechanical engineering at Bristol University, then worked for three years at what was then the Bristol Tramways & Carriage Co as an assistant experimental engineer in the bus chassis manufacturing works, at the time the revolutionary Lodekka was being developed. This was the first volume production double-decker to employ a drop centre, or portal, rear axle, enabling a lower floor line.

This configuration provided greater interior headroom within a given overall height and gradually replaced Leyland's patent of 1927 for a low height double-deck bus with a sunken gangway on the offside of the upper deck. It is only in very recent years that certain continental manufacturers have adopted the drop centre axle to facilitate lower floor heights in single-deck buses. Reverting to Marcus Smith, he left Bristol and spent fourteen years rising through the engineering ranks of three THC bus fleets, before returning to the company which had meantime become Bristol Commercial Vehicles.

Sir Donald, later Lord, Stokes.

In 1966 the Labour Government was re-elected with a larger majority. Anthony Wedgwood Benn was appointed Minister of Technology. Within two years he set up the Industrial Re-organisation Corporation, which had as its objective the long term modernisation of British manufacturing industries. Sir Donald Stokes, recently knighted, became one of the first members. It was now becoming clear that there was a race to rationalise the British motor industry. Leyland promoted a vigorous corporate image, one of the favourite slogans being: 'Moving Fast in a Fast Moving World.'

Leyland was regularly in the news in the 1960s and here Trevor Webster (left) describes extensions to the Spurrier plant where Leyland's drawing office, engine factory, frame shop, power house, engineering centre and vehicle test centre were located. Lancaster House, the Company's headquarters, was located in relation to the model where HRH the Duke of Edinburgh is standing and the test track is located in the foreground. At the time of going to press this once-thriving complex was being offered to let in small units.

Right – The arrival of a batch of Bristol RE single-decker buses in the local Ribble fleet certainly did not escape Leyland's notice. The ever-popular RE was eventually sacrificed in an attempt to increase sales of the Leyland National. Ulsterbus was able to continue taking the RE because local body content was part of its policy and Leyland might otherwise have lost body and chassis orders in a contract which ran to some 650 vehicles.

Bottom right – Daimler gave Leyland a good run for its money. The Fleetline was a very popular machine, so much so that Leyland continued production (in Lancashire) until 1980. Coventry, naturally, was a good customer for Daimler buses and this vehicle carried ECW bodywork, another instance of work going to that company as a result of the Leyland shareholding.

Below – Guy had a reputation for building a rugged no-frills vehicle like this classic Arab double-decker. The disastrous Wulfrunian chassis and problems in South Africa brought the company to insolvency.

By far the largest domestic competitor, across the automotive range, was British Motor Holdings. BMC, itself an amalgamation of Austin, Morris, Wolseley, Riley, MG and Morris Commercial, plus the Pressed Steel Fisher metal-pressing subsidiary, had merged with Jaguar Cars in December 1966 to form British Motor Holdings. Jaguar had previously acquired Guy and Daimler and was therefore Leyland's main competitor in the domestic bus market. In terms of share capital, British Motor Holdings was still slightly larger than the Leyland Motor Corporation, but that started to change in March 1967 when Rover was acquired by the Leyland Motor Corporation. In those days, Rover was a medium-sized builder of higher quality cars and the utility Land Rover, based at Solihull, near Birmingham. Once again official statements were intriguing, with a heavy emphasis on export. A press release at the time said: 'The two

Land Rover became an extremely hot potato in later years, as described in Chapter 11.

organisations have much to offer each other and by joining forces can face the threat of foreign competition in all markets with greater effect, confident of success.'

Leyland was still riding the crest of the wave, and Rover was a prestigious name in its own right. There was a limited amount of direct competition, for instance between Rover and Triumph 2000 cars, but the Land Rover had an enviable reputation and was a worthy addition to the corporate range. Rover also brought with it Alvis, which had been a low volume manufacturer of prestigious cars, but was by that time concentrating on light armoured vehicles. The pace of rationalisation continued unabated. Early in 1968 Leyland acquired Aveling-Barford of Grantham, best known for its extensive range of road-rollers, construction equipment and heavy-duty dump trucks, many of which used Leyland engines. The significance of this transaction was that, for the first time, the share capital of the Leyland Motor Corporation became greater than that of BMH.

The Government was becoming increasingly concerned about the dismal performance of British Motor Holdings. It had an ageing product range and a poor reputation in the market. It was losing market share not only to Ford and Vauxhall, but also to imported cars which were starting to appear on Britain's roads in much greater numbers. Harold Wilson invited Stokes and Sir George Harriman, Chairman of BMH, to Chequers. Wilson persuaded the two leaders to merge their companies, with the incentive of a £50 million Government grant towards reorganisation. Harold Wilson must have had remarkable powers. He sold Stokes, a great salesman, a dying company. The severity of BMH's financial problems only came to light after the merger, but it had been within weeks of bankruptcy. The merger with BMH eventually caused Stokes to lose his position as one of the media's favourite captains of industry, and ultimately, despite great effort, to lose his job. Poor man – never has a British Prime Minister sold anyone a bigger pup!

The new company became known as the British Leyland Motor Corporation, with former Leyland people very much in command. At Leyland itself Ron Ellis, then Managing Director of Leyland Motors Ltd, called the senior staff together and told them of the latest development, just as it was being announced to the world at large. Ellis, a big man with a great sense of occasion, read out a statement to the assembled management. He said that a Truck and Bus Division would be formed, with himself as Managing Director, and that it would also take over responsibility for the former BMC commercial vehicle operations, including Daimler, Guy, and the BMC truck and tractor factory at Bathgate, Scotland. He then asked for questions. After a number had been raised the late Bernard Pickup, then Truck Sales Director for the home market, spoke up. Pickup was an amazing character, not unlike Tony Hancock in stature and humour, with a great reputation for earthy wit. He said: "BMC stands for Build More Crap. Does that mean BLMC will Build Lots More Crap?" The question raised lots of laughs, but it was amazingly prophetic. The people in that room were proud of their company, but were well aware of the poor reputation of Bathgate's products.

BMH also brought with it Pressed Steel Fisher, Europe's largest car body specialist. In addition to supplying all BMH requirements, and also Rolls Royce, PSF offered a

Ron Ellis, Managing Director of Leyland Motors 1964-1967; Leyland Truck & Bus 1968-1975; Chairman Leyland National Ltd 1969-1975. In the opinion of many he was the last head of Leyland who really understood the industry.

One of Leyland's later Bathgate tractors.

complete engineering and tooling service to the motor industry at home and overseas, including the manufacture of press tools, jigs and fixtures. In the high volume car industry, bodies were, and still are, made out of pressed metal. The expensive part of the process is making the dies, especially those for panels with complicated shapes. The alternative at that time was low volume panel-beating and shaping by hand, or glass fibre mouldings, which had been used by bodybuilders in the truck, bus and coach industries, on non-load bearing panels and the like, for about fifteen years.

They were heady days back in 1968. The old Leyland team dominated the Truck and Bus Division, but strengthened by some good people from acquired companies. It took time to rationalise the various product ranges, partly because sales and service networks, including dealers and overseas agents, had to be sorted out. On the home market the merger all but eliminated competition in the premium (non truck-derived) bus and coach chassis sector, putting the company in a position which nowadays would be seen as far too monopolistic, but the export potential outweighed any domestic market objections. On the engineering side it was possible to start planning ahead. Commercial vehicle engineering was centred in the town of Leyland, but with a clear brief to look at other facilities available within the greatly expanded Corporation.

Any story which refers to Leyland in the late 'sixties must not become confused with subsequent events. The car range which came from BMC had some quite advanced technology for its time, like transverse engines driving the front wheels, but unit production costs were high and quality was poor. The most popular model, the Mini, was already ten years old and, as for new designs, the cupboard was all but bare. The car business was riddled with all that was bad with British trade union practices at that time, especially job demarcation.

In 1968 the implications of buying BMH had probably not sunk in. The Corporation strode the world stage, winning order after order for trucks and buses. Competitors respected, indeed feared, Leyland as a very powerful opponent, especially in international tenders. It was different on the car side. Poor quality, late deliveries, indifferent dealers and other problems contributed to a steady loss of domestic and export market share. Morale at the Truck & Bus Division was high. The management was very visible, frequently being seen in the sprawling factory complex at Leyland, often with visitors. Outside the Divisional headquarters, there was a flagpole, which could carry three flags. For years, it had been the custom to fly the national flags of overseas visitors when they came to Leyland. More often than not, at least one foreign flag was flying. That was the picture in the late 'sixties. Leyland was indeed moving fast in a fast moving world.

Lancaster House, Leyland, the impressive headquarters of the Truck and Bus Division.

21

CHAPTER TWO

Castle In The Air

Following the election in October 1964 Harold Wilson's first Labour Government, with its very slender majority, was under pressure from the trade unions. They had been clamouring for a much bigger say in the running of many sectors of British life. One of their ambitions was the creation of a nationalised public transport industry.

Wilson's first Minister of Transport had been Tom Fraser, who appears to have done little during his term in office. In response to pressure from the Labour Party Wilson called for Barbara Castle shortly before Christmas 1965 and persuaded her to take over the Transport portfolio.

Barbara Castle might not like the comparison, but she was as determined in her views and actions on the left of her party as Margaret Thatcher was later to become on the right of her party. Her diaries show her to be straight to the point, but with a distinct sense of humour, which was lacking in the Iron Lady. Her constituency of Blackburn was only a few miles from the main Leyland factories in Lancashire. Stokes and Ellis quickly realised that her ideas could lead to a resurgence in demand for buses, and they made sure that she was kept well aware of new developments.

For instance, Leyland had won a prestigious contract to supply 200 Panthers and 50 Atlanteans to Stockholm, in time for Sweden's change in September 1967 from left to right hand rule of the road. These buses had many advanced features, including what was probably the first British application of sensitive edges in the entrance and exit doors. Leyland diverted two of the buses from the Park Royal bodyworks so that they could be shown to the Minister of Transport, before crossing the North Sea.

Back in 1964 Leyland and AEC had respectively introduced the Panther and Swift low-floor rear-engined single-deck bus chassis, with common main frames, which were designed in the traditional way, for bodying by external builders. Although bus fleet engineers complained about poor mechanical reliability, compared with front and mid-underfloor engined layouts, traffic managers appreciated the lower floor levels ahead of the rear axle. They enabled passengers to get on and off more quickly. The low-floor rear-engined configuration was the most logical for local service buses. The Americans had largely standardised on a rear engine location, shortly before the Second World War, but had conspicuously failed to combine the rear engine with a low-floor layout.

Leyland had kept in touch with developments in the American commercial vehicle industry for many years, indeed more closely than many industry observers realised. There were occasional well-publicised events, like persuading John Rackham to return to Britain from the Yellow Coach Company to develop the original Titan TD1, which was launched in 1927. (Rackham had previously been one of the team responsible for the London General Omnibus Company's 'B' type bus in 1910.) Most of the contact was regular and much lower profile. The Americans were important suppliers of machine tools, but there were also transfers of technology in both directions, and sales of loose engines from Leyland. In the 'sixties and 'seventies, there were some strong friendships with American manufacturers at senior executive level.

In Britain the Leyland Atlantean and Daimler Fleetline had firmly established the supremacy of the rear-engined double-decker over alternative layouts. On the continent, the trend was also moving rearward. The mid-underfloor engined Mercedes 0317 lost much of its popularity as a city bus after the rear-engined 0305 was launched in 1967.

Barbara Castle, Minister of Transport in the first Wilson Government, visited the Earls Court Show in 1966 and took the wheel of a Stockholm Panther. Visible on this bus are the public address system, the integral power steering and the tachograph, still not a legal requirement in buses used on local services in Britain.

The 11 metre Panther was a typical first-generation low floor British city bus chassis. Note the high frame rising rearward, just ahead of the rear axle, and the ease with which a second doorway could be accommodated. The large lump of engine and gearbox behind the rear axle caused these chassis to flex and bodybuilders had to allow for this in their structures.

This 10 metre Panther Cub demonstrator was built in 1966 and shows the raised seating behind the centre entrance and the low steps to both entrances.

The development of transit buses in the United States went straight from front to rear engines. This Yellow Coach double-decker entered service with the Chicago Motor Coach Company in 1938, about six years after the first rear-engined transit buses had appeared.

Bottom right - On the continent too, the trend was towards low floor rear-engined city buses. This Mercedes O.305 (below right) was at the Frankfurt Motor Show in 1969.

Facing page centre
Leyland prepared thoroughly for major tenders and put great effort into winning prestigious business like the Stockholm contract. Before Sweden changed from left to right-hand rule of the road, a Park Royal bodied Panther demonstrator was sent to the Swedish capital for evaluation trials. It later returned to Leyland and was used as an engineering vehicle for several years.

Facing page lower
By 1968, it was known that the first generation of rear-engined single-deck buses could suffer from failure of the body structure, particularly when centre exits were fitted. One of the production batch of Stockholm Panthers is seen undergoing deflection testing in the Leyland Experimental Department.

Berliet was taking the same route in France, although both Berliet and Saviem continued to build a bus with a horizontal engine beneath the driver, mainly for the requirements of Paris. All the more developed countries with good road systems were looking at rear-engined single-deckers. Leyland had to start thinking about a product which would benefit from the lessons learned with the Panther, Swift, and other first generation rear-engined single-deckers, such as the Bristol RE.

In great secrecy, therefore, a small engineering team under Joe McGowan started a project to see how low a floor height could be achieved on a city bus. Although the Panther and Swift could have a fairly low floor ahead of the rear axle, the intrusion of the front wheelboxes was considerable and there were awkward boxes over the front springs. Joe McGowan opted for integral construction, built in modular form, so that various alternative lengths could be offered.

By 1967 a full size mock-up was completed. It was usually described as the 'Commutabus', but was also called the 'International'. In order to get the floor level as low as possible four axles were employed, two behind the front entrance and two behind the centre doorway, ahead of the rear-mounted power pack, which consisted of the tried and trusted O.600 coupled to a Pneumocyclic gearbox. The mock-up had smaller wheels and tyres than anything previously seen on a British bus, including the Bedford VAL chassis with its novel twin-steer layout on 16 inch wheels. Entry and exit was very easy, even for elderly and infirm passengers.

The interior was exceptionally light and airy, thanks to side windows which were deeper than those normally used on buses at that time. Both doorways were very wide, and passengers were free to circulate between them without stumbling over internal steps or wheelboxes. There was only one internal step, rearward of the centre exit, just ahead of the rear axles. The driver and passenger environments were years ahead of anything else on the market.

Leyland showed the Commutabus to Barbara Castle at a most opportune time. She was preparing the Transport Policy White Paper which led to the Transport Act 1968. The Commutabus was just the kind of vehicle to attract motorists out of their cars and onto public transport.

The prototype was also shown in confidence to a number of important customers, who were then asked to complete a brief questionnaire. Although the spacious layout met with universal approval several operators were distinctly unimpressed with the complexity of the driveline and the number of axles.

Indeed, one or two told Leyland quite bluntly that they had enough problems maintaining brakes on two axles and they certainly did not want double the trouble! There were complaints about short brake drum and lining life on the Bedford VAL. There was also concern about the risk of grounding a fully laden bus with such a low floor. For those and various other reasons the Commutabus project did not proceed, but it was a very important marker in the ground. Leyland took out several patents on the structure and went back to the drawing board.

Looking back, the Commutabus was two decades ahead of its time, and was less of a compromise in design than the first generation of ultra low floor buses (around 330 mm height) produced by certain German manufacturers in the early 1980s.

Even the twin steering concept was to appear again, on the Volvo stand at the UITP Conference and Exhibition in Stockholm in June 1991. (UITP is the Union Internationale des Transports Publics, the international body which represents the interests of the world's major bus and light rail operators. It has its headquarters in Brussels.)

The Commutabus prototype of 1967. The concept of such easy access from the kerb to the bus was far ahead of its time.

Joe McGowan, Engineering Director and leader of the new bus project.

Small wheels and tyres were one way of reducing internal floor height. Volvo showed this front end mock-up at the UITP Conference and Exhibition in Stockholm in June 1991. The similarity to the 1967 Commutabus is obvious.

In the mid-1960s the British trade union movement had much greater power than it enjoys now. Although bus crews were by no means the most militant members of the nation's workforce they frequently took a tough stance with their employers in national negotiations. Employment levels were high, which helped to strengthen the bargaining position of the crews.

Operators were becoming concerned about rising costs and falling revenues, and wanted to introduce one man operation on a very wide scale. The unions resisted this, but by the early 1960s reached a temporary compromise, namely that they would be willing to accept one man operated single-deckers with up to 45 seats, provided drivers received higher wages for one man working.

The unions realised that one man operation would in due course halve their membership but, faced with the inevitable, accepted a solution which would give them a smaller number of better paid members. They were not prepared to accept one man double-deckers which, in any case, were not legal at that stage. Also, double-deckers at that time outnumbered single-deckers by about three to one.

Many fleets were buying 36ft. long single-deck buses, which became legally permissible from 1961. They had a carrying capacity very similar to the old 53 and 56 seat double-deckers which they were replacing. It looked as though the operating industry was going to switch to large one man single-decker buses, and that the two man double-decker would become a dying breed.

London Transport was one of the first to start the ball rolling, placing very large orders with AEC for Merlin single-deckers, built to the maximum 36ft. limit. The Merlin was basically a heavy duty version of the Swift. London's actions and forecasts played a very important role in the new project. The capital's fleet in 1966 consisted of around 8,000 buses, with a planned twelve year life. That amounted to an annual requirement for 600-700 buses.

The high capacity of the 36ft-long single-decker posed a threat to the traditional double-decker. Examples such as this one on a Leopard PSU3 chassis for Caerphilly Council Transport seated 53 passengers.

In 1967, it looked as if London Transport would replace its double-deckers with large high capacity one-man-operated single-deckers. The 36ft long versions of the AEC Swift were known as the Merlin in London; the example shown had been transferred from LT's country bus department to London Country, a newly-created NBC subsidiary.

One-man-operated double-deckers appeared in numbers on various Leyland group stands at the 1968 Earls Court Motor Show. The Park Royal bodied example for Sheffield Corporation (left) was built on the optional longer Atlantean PDR2.1 chassis, with an overall length of 33ft. The Manchester vehicle (right) represented manager Ralph Bennett's influence in producing a more attractive vehicle for that city. Strangely the significance of this congregation of high capacity one-man double-decked vehicles did not appear to carry weight with Leyland's policy makers. Bennett had seen the possibilities of the one-man double-decker in 1966, obtaining Manchester City Council approval for such vehicles in October of that year.

The move to one man operation was welcomed by the bus companies, mainly because of the savings in wages. In many areas they were suffering staff shortages, because low unemployment levels were compounded by the fact that people preferred jobs without anti-social hours.

The development of a new bus is not something which is done overnight. There is a series of important stages, from product planning through to design and development, the construction of prototypes, and the tooling of a factory, before volume production can commence. The average cycle for a totally new product can be four to five years.

In 1967 Leyland foresaw a domestic demand for up to 3,000 large single-deck buses per annum, together with substantial on-going export business. Consequently, approval was given to develop a new generation of single-deck city service buses. A very clear part of the brief was to look at technology available in other parts of the Corporation, especially the car companies.

One has to be careful that hindsight does not distort a story, but it has to be said that this forecast was over-optimistic. One man operation of double-deckers became acceptable and legal by July 1966. Most operators were slow to react, probably because of local union agreements, but, within one month, Manchester Corporation placed an order for one man double-deckers.

Within a year several other cities followed Manchester's lead, prompting Alan Townsin, by then Editor of the principal trade journal, *Bus & Coach*, to write in the November 1967 issue: 'It may well be that 1968 will prove to be the year of the double-decker's renaissance.'

He was proved right. In 1968 the Earls Court Show featured several high capacity one man double-deckers. As they were all on Leyland group chassis it seems in retrospect very surprising that there were apparently no second thoughts about the new single-deck project and, in particular, the forecast volumes.

Around the same time the important Australian market was having second thoughts about double-deckers, which were faced with extinction, despite being popular with passengers. The Department of Government Transport in New South Wales noted that rear-engined double-deckers

Australian Atlanteans had unique styling. After a lifetime in Sydney, a small number were shipped to Tokyo for promotional services. True to form, the Japanese authorities soon found regulations which prevented their continuing use.

could be suitable for one man operated services on longer suburban routes, and 200 Leyland Atlanteans were ordered in June 1968. When they entered service there were bitter battles with the Australian Tramway and Motor Omnibus Employees' Association, resulting in a compromise whereby one man operation was permitted on the quieter sections of routes.

Meanwhile, Barbara Castle had been busy on other parts of her transport strategy. Most bus services in England and Wales were run by THC, BET, and those municipalities which had their own fleets. The THC companies were already nationalised. In numbers of buses, the BET Group was roughly equivalent in size to THC, but generally speaking was stronger in the more industrialised areas.

In the White Paper which led up to the Transport Act 1968, Barbara Castle let it be known that she was considering establishing Passenger Transport Authorities (PTAs) which would be responsible for co-ordinating all public passenger transport operations in major conurbations. The first four were planned for Manchester, Liverpool, Newcastle and Birmingham, and their respective satellite towns. In all those areas BET had substantial bus fleets.

Alan Townsin reported the political manoeuvrings of the time in *The British Bus Story – Turbulent Times* **(see Bibliography)**. Barbara Castle had been unsuccessful in her attempts to persuade BET to sell out its bus fleets voluntarily. One of the problems was a personality clash between John Spencer Wills, Chairman of BET, and Sir Reginald Wilson, Deputy Chairman and Managing Director of THC.

Alan Townsin recorded the next step: 'Mrs Castle invited them both to lunch in May (1967) and proceeded to 'frighten' Wills by saying that the PTAs would have powers of compulsory acquisition and could cut some of his profitable services in half, but said that she would prefer that the BET's assets be sold as a going concern. Wills said he was appalled but showed no sign of caving in at that stage.'

Despite strong protests, including anti-nationalisation slogans on many of its buses, BET eventually came to the negotiating table and, in November 1967, agreed to sell its bus interests to THC with effective transfer in March 1968. Shortly after that the Transport Bill was published, proposing the setting up of the National Bus Company, and the PTAs, of which there were initially four.

The Bill also introduced another very important element. The Labour Party was anxious to make public transport more attractive and therefore introduced the concept of a new bus grant, in effect a capital subsidy of 25% on the ex-works price. This grant was only to be payable on buses which met certain design standards, including the ability to be one man operated.

Significantly the concept included double-deckers, not long after the trade unions gave up their resistance to one man operation of double-deck buses. Barbara Castle might have been influenced by Albert Neal, who retired as General Manager of Manchester Corporation Transport in March 1965, and had then been appointed by her as a Special Advisor.

The Transport Act 1968 received the Royal Assent on 25 October that year and the National Bus Company became operational on 1 January 1969. It took over the former THC and BET companies, and West Riding Automobile Co Ltd, an independent which had sold out to THC on 1 January 1968. On the same date, the THC shareholdings in Bristol, ECW and Park Royal Vehicles were transferred to the National Bus Company, whilst the nationalised bus companies in Scotland became members of the newly created Scottish Bus Group (SBG).

The Leyland Motor Corporation Board had been strengthened in 1965 by the appointment of Dr Albert Fogg, a distinguished engineer whose previous post was Director of the Motor Industry Research Association at Nuneaton. He brought very wide experience to Leyland, but sometimes came up with unconventional solutions to technical problems. Looking back, he somehow did not quite fit at Leyland, but, as a former colleague said: "Nobody ever defied him."

The key to any commercial vehicle is a reliable engine. Leyland had set the pace with units like the O.600 and O.680, although the latter was prone to cylinder head gasket failures at higher power ratings, above 200bhp. AEC also had some excellent engines but they had a similar, if not worse, reputation for cylinder head gasket weaknesses, particularly if driven hard. These problems were not so prevalent on buses as trucks, which generally required higher power ratings. Although the basic core of the engine was common to trucks and buses, some of the auxiliaries were different and were relocated, not that this normally caused problems. The most obvious example was on rear-engined double-deckers, where all the auxiliaries had to be located on one side, accessible from the rear, because a steel bulkhead separated the other side of the engine from the lower deck.

Dr Albert Fogg came to Leyland from the Motor Industry Research Association, as the Corporate Director responsible for Engineering.

The truck range had required more power since 1964, when a change in the British Construction and Use Regulations permitted an increase in maximum gross weight of articulated trucks from 24 to 32 tons.

Within a couple of years imported trucks started to appear on British roads. Scania, Volvo, DAF and Mercedes all entered the market, but the early pace was set by Volvo's legendary F86. For a maximum capacity truck it had what was then considered to be a tiny engine of only 6.7 litres, but turbocharged to produce almost 200bhp. The equivalent normally-aspirated Leyland O.400 engine of 6.54 litres produced 125bhp, and was fitted in medium trucks.

The Corporation had to proceed with the development of a new generation of engines, with the design teams at Leyland and AEC taking quite different approaches. AEC opted for a normally-aspirated V8 engine with optional power ratings of 252 and 272bhp, comfortably ahead of the market at that time. It soon proved to be under-developed and hence unreliable. It was later abandoned after a comparatively short life. Leyland went in a most novel direction, intending to produce an engine which had ample scope for development and uprating right through the 1970s. It was Dr Fogg who drew on his broad experience of the industry and suggested the development of an engine marginally larger than the 11.1 litre O.680, but without a separate cylinder head. It was certainly a one hundred per cent guaranteed cure for cylinder head gasket problems! It also ensured water flow right round the hottest part of the engine, at the piston crowns.

The idea was not new, having been used on Bentley and many other cars in the 1920s. The obvious drawback was the inaccessibility of the valves, but this was not too great a problem when the cylinder block and crankcase could be separated.

Because of improvements in materials, many components in existing Leyland engines were proving to have a much longer life. For example, Stellite valves were lasting up to 300,000 miles. This was one of the factors which encouraged Leyland to follow the headless route, even though replacement valves had to be inserted from the bottom end of the engine.

The fixed head concept had a number of other notable features. The choice of an overhead camshaft layout not only reduced the number of moving parts in the valve operation, but also resulted in a very slim engine. Several prototype engines were built, to a capacity of 700cu in, or 11.4 litres, and plans were put in hand for production.

At a critical stage, the programme was changed, to a smaller unit, built in exactly the same way, but of 500cu in, or 8.2 litres, capacity. One of the reasons was the desire to produce an engine weighing less than 1,000 kg.

Maybe this was a crucial mistake, from a bus point of view, where the saving in weight did not translate directly to increased payload. An 11.4 litre engine would not have needed to work so hard and was more in line with contemporary bus industry opinion. Demand was for a big engine, working well within its capacity, like the 11.1 litre O.680 or the 10.45 litre Gardner 6LXB.

Another proposed member of the fixed head family, which never saw the light of day was a V12 version, intended for military applications. It had two 500cu in blocks set at an angle of 60 degrees, driving a common crankshaft!

The horizontal version of the 500 series engine was remarkably slim, and therefore ideal for locating under the floor at the rear of a single-deck bus. This example is seen coupled to the Pneumo-cyclic gearbox on the right hand side of the picture whilst the turbocharger os visible at the top left.

When the 500 series was announced in 1969 the standard power rating was 170bhp at 2,600rpm, with a torque of 375lbf.ft. at 1,800rpm. There was option of turbocharged versions, up to 260bhp at 2,600rpm.

Some years later, around 1974, the Board of Leyland Truck and Bus Division was having a heated argument about the 500 engine, which was proving particularly troublesome, especially at the higher power ratings for trucks. Warranty costs were enormous. Someone recalled the by then departed Dr Fogg's remarks about Bentley and the fixed head concept and was promptly told: "And it didn't work in't blooday Bentley neither!"

There were good grounds for recrimination about the 500 series engine. Other manufacturers had successfully taken the O.680 concept and developed it to produce well over 300bhp in turbocharged form, and without cylinder head gasket troubles. That kind of research would have cost much less than developing a totally new engine.

Even then the Corporation fell between two stools. Parts of the 500 series suffered from inadequate development. Because of the late decision to scale it down in size, corners were cut. Some of the production tooling, especially in the first year or two, was erratic, therefore some 500 series engines worked very well, whereas others failed at comparatively low mileages.

When there was a problem with a 500 series engine it usually meant that it had to be removed and repaired on a bench. As Engineering strove to cure the problems it took two or three years for test engines to reach a sufficiently high mileage to be confident of solutions.

The saga of the 500 engine highlights the dilemma facing a motor manufacturer. It takes time to develop a product, usually three to four years. Concurrently, the last two years of that period can be spent in tooling up. It can then take up to two years for a serious problem to come to light and a couple of years to develop and introduce an effective cure.

During this prolonged time management faces great difficulties and dilemmas. One cannot stop production, unless a suitable replacement is available in the right volume and at the right price. One has to soldier on, in the hope of reaching a solution but, in the intervening period, loyal customers can become dissatisfied and place their orders elsewhere.

Again, there is the risk that hindsight can distort the recording of events, but there were those in Leyland who felt that the AEC designed V8 engine should have been developed further. Although V8 engines can be difficult to get right, Mercedes-Benz has followed this route very successfully, as have Iveco, Mack and Scania with their largest truck engines.

It was very unfortunate that so much time and effort went into the 500 series engine because, in the first half of the Workington story, it became the enduring weakness in an otherwise superb first product.

The AEC V8 engine

The powerful AEC V8 engine was mounted in-line at the rear of a coach chassis called the Sabre. ECW built the luxury coachwork on this show example built in 1970 – it never went into production.

CHAPTER THREE

Designed Like An Aircraft:
Built Like A Car

In 1968 the entire British bus industry, including independent operators, was buying British built buses and coaches. There was only a handful of foreign vehicles in the country. Caetano, at that time Leyland's agent in Portugal, had supplied its first luxury coach bodies to British specification, but on Ford chassis, and Mercedes had tried unsuccessfully to interest British operators in the integral O302 coach, which became a runaway success in several other markets. Admittedly it was very expensive by British standards.

When one looks nowadays at the fleets of imported buses and coaches it is hard to realise how solidly British the market was at that time. Alan Townsin summarised the reasons in *The British Bus Story – Late 'Seventies* **(see Bibliography)** when he wrote: 'The virtually complete reliance on British manufacturers that had been accepted practice was based not so much on patriotism as the British industry's previously undisputed ability both to produce vehicles suitable for the operating conditions and meeting the specification often peculiar to this country at prices often well below those ruling in Europe.'

Furthermore, the transport systems in many major cities around the world were heavily dependant on buses produced by the British Leyland Motor Corporation, whether of Leyland, Albion, AEC, Daimler or Guy origin. It was for all those reasons that the Corporation felt confident about an exciting new project.

Marcus Smith had left Bristol in the summer of 1967 to become the executive responsible for engineering matters with United Transport Overseas, a British company which had extensive bus operations in southern and eastern Africa. The trade press suggested that he left because he was not permitted to go ahead with a proposed new range of Bristol chassis, but that was only part of the reason. He found it extremely difficult to develop new markets for Bristol, when Leyland was sitting on the Board.

At that time, United Transport had its London offices on the second floor of Berkeley Square House. Leyland, and subsequently BLMC, had its head office on the fifth floor of the same building. One day in May 1968 Marcus Smith returned from an overseas trip to find a personal and confidential letter from Stokes, inviting him to come up for a talk. When they met on the following Friday Stokes gave Smith a copy of a highly confidential report about the new single-deck bus project and asked him to read it over the weekend. Stokes was a shrewd and persuasive personality, and by Monday morning had his man!

Berkeley Square House

United Transport was a major operator of bus services in Southern and Eastern Africa. This Albion Clydesdale operated in Salisbury, Rhodesia, now the city of Harare in Zimbabwe. The bodywork was built locally by Zambesi Coachworks.

Wind tunnel testing was carried out on scale models at the Motor Industry Research Association. This highlighted an unfortunate feature of the National – in wet weather substantial quantities of dirt were deposited on the back of the vehicle, being drawn in by the vortex.

The real reason for recruiting Smith could not be revealed. Therefore, a few weeks later, it was announced that he would be appointed to the newly created post of Deputy General Manager of Leyland Motors Ltd, which remained the largest company in the Truck and Bus Division. That was good cover, because Ron Ellis was heavily involved with Divisional business and the Leyland site needed strong senior management.

Alan Townsin, then Editor of *Bus & Coach*, welcomed his appointment with the words: 'I am sure I was not alone in hoping that his flair for getting things done would not remain hidden, comparatively speaking, for long.' He went on to write: 'I will be surprised if Mr Smith's arrival does not have some noticeable effect before long.'

Around this time, the new bus project was given the code name 'FPB7', standing for 'Forward Project Bus 7', usually somewhat irreverently and more frequently known within Leyland as 'Fogg's Perfect Bus'! If one looks at the timing of FPB7 and the 500 series engine, the two programmes were running almost concurrently in Engineering. The flat profile of the 500 series engine made it an ideal candidate for horizontal underfloor installation at the rear of a bus, in a version known as the 510.

The 510 engine seemed to get the best results when running in smaller fleets which had good daily checks. Even the best run fleets, however, could not cure the 510's habit of puffing out smoke when starting from rest, due to a lag in response from the turbocharger. It was a serious shortcoming in a bus intended for stop-start work.

Plans for the rest of FPB7's design took shape rapidly. The traditional separation between chassis and bodywork was abandoned in favour of a totally integral structure. In theory integral structures should save weight, without any loss of strength. In practice, they are often considerably heavier, as was the case with FPB7. It proved, however, to be one of the strongest buses ever built. New techniques were used to install electrical, heating and other systems.

From the outset FPB7 was designed and built totally to metric dimensions. There was a general swing to metric about this time, mainly because the British Government wanted the country to become a member of the European Economic Community. Many British firms, including AEC, had previously used metric but adopted imperial measurements around 1950/51, in response to Government policy and American influence.

FPB7 was to be available in right and left hand drive, with one or two doorways. As the early literature said: '(it) was designed like an aircraft and built like a car'.

The original plan was to work with three overall lengths, namely 10, 11 and 12 metres. All the more complicated pressed panels, particularly at the front and rear, were to be common to all three lengths. Similarly, other expensive components, like the entrance and optional centre exit, front and rear wheelarches, and the framework, were to be standardised. Using the modular principle, the only variable panels and sections would be low cost ones, along the sides and roof of the bus.

Each bay would have been 1,175 mm, 1,375 mm, or 1,575 mm, on the 10, 11 and 12 metre models respectively. The standard door modules would have had a clear width of 1,156 mm. Just as these design concepts were being hardened, the influential UITP recommended a minimum clear width of 1,200 mm on city bus doorways. The engineering team took a further look at current and proposed legislation in all the main world markets and then decided to build the new bus to overall lengths of 10.3 or 11.3 metres.

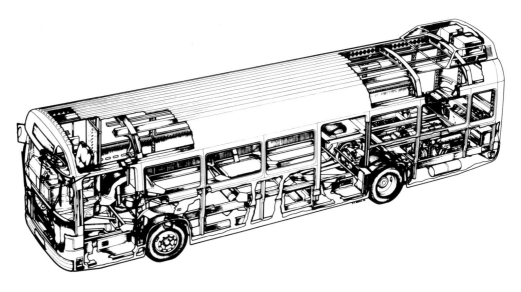

Sectioned drawing of FPB7.

External Dimensions of Standard Models

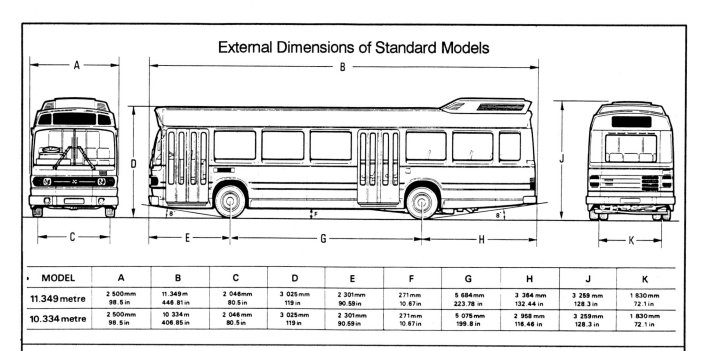

MODEL	A	B	C	D	E	F	G	H	J	K
11.349 metre	2 500mm 98.5 in	11.349 m 446.81 in	2 046mm 80.5 in	3 025mm 119 in	2 301mm 90.59 in	271mm 10.67 in	5 684mm 223.78 in	3 364 mm 132.44 in	3 259 mm 128.3 in	1 830mm 72.1 in
10.334 metre	2 500mm 98.5 in	10 334 m 406.85 in	2 046mm 80.5 in	3 025mm 119 in	2 301mm 90.59 in	271mm 10.67 in	5 075mm 199.8 in	2 958 mm 116.46 in	3 259mm 128.3 in	1 830mm 72.1 in

Construction areas common to varying lengths of vehicle

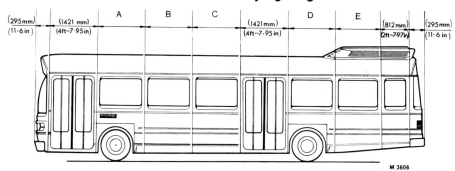

MODEL	A	B	C	D	E
10.3M	1218mm	1218mm	1218mm	1218mm	1218mm
11.3M	1421mm	1421mm	1421mm	1421mm	1421mm
10.9M	1421mm	1421mm	1421mm	1218mm	1218mm

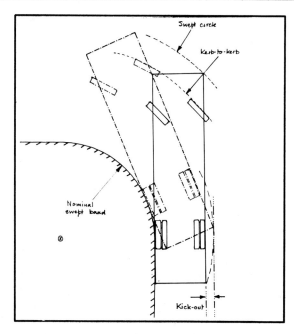

Diagram showing "kick-out" of a turning vehicle on full steering lock.

The computer drawn front wheelarch assembly.

The concept of standardising on all except the simple side modules was retained. The longer and more popular 11.3 metre model consisted entirely of 1,421 mm modules, including door apertures, with the exception of a short rear module of 812 mm, to accommodate an emergency exit on the offside.

Starting from the front, the shorter 10.3 metre model had a 1,421 mm door module, followed by three bays each of 1,218 mm, then another module of 1,421 mm, whether a centre exit was fitted or not. That in turn was followed by two bays of 1,218 mm and the short rearmost module of 812 mm. The precise dimension of each module was set by rivct pitch.

Seven prototypes were built at Leyland in 1969/70 and were used on extensive proving trials. These included continuous running over Belgian pavé, considered so uneven that one mile on that surface was equivalent to 100 miles on ordinary roads. Pavé was, and remains, an accelerated form of endurance testing which will show up any faults much quicker than ordinary road running. Other prototypes were tested in extreme cold in Finland and in the hottest part of Spain.

When testing prototypes any manufacturer is faced with a dilemma. If it is simply an update, like a newer engine, pre-production units can usually be installed in operators' vehicles to gain practical in-service experience. With a radically new product like FPB7, there was a natural desire to keep the design and development process secret for as long as possible. As a result all the testing was carried out by highly skilled development drivers. They were an élite group, to whom driving was a matter of pride, and so prototypes sometimes failed to exhibit weaknesses which can occur within days of handing production models to drivers of lesser skill and sympathy. FPB7 bristled with new ideas, many of which were proved and refined on the prototypes over the following months.

The first prototype FPB7 taking shape. The corrugations in the roof added considerably to the overall strength.

It was the first bus to use a new kind of tyre, known as low profile. The Commutabus prototype of 1967 had used four axles with small wheels and tyres, to bring down floor and step heights, but, as mentioned earlier, there was strong customer reaction against the complexity of four axles.

Goodyear worked closely with Leyland to develop a tubeless radial tyre, designated 11/70 (11 inch section width, 70% aspect ratio). The purpose of this tyre was to give a smaller rolling radius than normal, but with the same load carrying capacity. The smaller radius was only partly used to reduce step and floor heights. The main benefit was in reducing the size and intrusion of the wheel boxes into the passenger space.

Hot climate testing was carried out in the height of summer in southern Spain; arctic weather testing took place in northern Finland, north of the Arctic Circle; road testing took place in Belgium and pavé testing on the MIRA test track.

The low profile tyres were heavily criticised in early operation for being non-standard and not giving as good mileage as standard tyres. Times change, however, and low profile tyres are now standard on low floor city buses.

Another early decision was to build almost entirely in steel, even though aluminium was becoming popular on grounds of lighter weight and resistance to corrosion. Part of the reasoning was that projected volumes of 2,000 units per year justified investment in car type manufacturing techniques.

Steel was less expensive than aluminium. It was easier to work, and could be pressed into a variety of shapes. There was also a widespread belief that steel structures were easier to repair, especially in overseas markets, because some aluminium structures were difficult to handle.

The use of new technology was most graphically illustrated by the front wheelarch assembly. At one time it would have taken several man weeks of drawing office time to design this complicated part of the bus. Computers were starting to be more widely used.

Engineers fed in all the critical dimensions, such as maximum steering angles, the new low profile tyre sizes, and the maximum travel of the wheels, both vertically and on full lock. It was said that the very complicated front wheel pan assembly (ie, the two wheelarches and the floor in between) was drawn by computer in under twenty minutes!

The end result was a marked improvement in the width of the gangway between the front wheelboxes. They were practically concealed beneath two inward facing bench seats, leaving a completely flat floor in between.

Steel structures, and particularly bodywork, had a reputation for suffering from corrosion. The engineers examined various anti-corrosion systems. They had to be capable of being applied to galvanised steel and of accepting external painting. The only other user of galvanised, or zinc-coated, steel at that time was Rolls Royce. Among its properties, it was self-healing, repairing the edges of holes as they were drilled. This was a very important point.

Eventually the engineers decided on epoxy powder coating, which had never previously been used on a large scale in the motor industry. In fact, at the time, the normal application of epoxy power coating was as a semi-decorative finish on steel office furniture.

It was soon found that decorative quality epoxy powder was hopelessly inadequate, but Arthur Holden & Sons of Birmingham produced 'Duraplast' corrosion resistant epoxy powder, which was specially formulated for the FPB7 project. The plant will be described in the next Chapter, but it has to be said that the decision to use epoxy powder coating was inspired. It has proved highly resistant to corrosion, even on buses which have been in service for around twenty years.

At the end of the 'sixties bodybuilding was still a very traditional business in the United Kingdom. The two biggest builders of luxury

The first running prototype had been completed by the autumn of 1969. The recessed cove panels were not retained on production models, and the front end was still to benefit from styling by Michelotti.

Goodyear developed the 11/70 tubeless tyre specially for the National. Note the new lower profile on the right in the diagram.

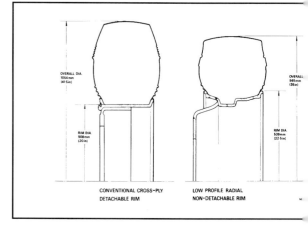

The ring frame structure of the National was enormously strong. It has proved almost indestructible and still forms the basis for re-skinned and refurbished models produced by East Lancashire Coachbuilders (see photograph on page 157).

coaches, Plaxton and Duple, were using timber framing, with some steel reinforcement. Roe built the last of its famous teak framed double-deck bus bodies in 1968. Even where steel or aluminium was used the process was very basic and needed a large number of man hours, usually with more expensive skilled tradesmen.

The same was true of continental bodybuilding. Some of the larger companies, like Mercedes and Van Hool, had developed jigs which facilitated more rapid welding and fabrication, and Mercedes was making use of pressed metal panels at the front and rear ends. Smaller builders used a fair degree of welding with jigs. Even so, all the continentals remained heavily dependant on skilled labour, and a complete bus was taking around 1,000 man hours.

FPB7 gave the engineers the opportunity to take a completely different look at bus assembly methods. By introducing the kind of tooling normally only associated with the car industry, man hours could be very substantially reduced. A great deal of care and thought was given to the assembly process, with an important role being played by Neville Brownlow, who had transferred from Standard-Triumph.

In order to give the bus strength, continuous ring frame construction was adopted, using pillars and roof sticks supplied by Pressed Steel Fisher. They imparted enormous transverse strength to the body. The one piece corrugated aluminium roof also made a remarkable contribution to the overall rigidity.

David Burnicle, later Engineering Director for buses, gathered evidence of several serious accidents and reckoned that the strength of the structure would have been responsible for saving the lives and limbs of many passengers.

Service buses tend to suffer from localised bumps and scrapes, therefore ease of repair was another important consideration. The body panels were attached to the structure by specially developed rivets. This was another new idea, first tried out on FPB7, but again, it has stood the test of time extremely well.

The design project set many new standards. Priority was to be given to driver and passenger comfort. Ergonomics, the study of the relationship between a person and his or her working environment, had been used in the development of Leyland's Ergomatic truck cab, which was launched at the 1964 Motor Show. That technology was used to good advantage in FPB7.

The driver's compartment was designed from scratch. Certain controls had to be situated in predetermined positions, such as the steering wheel and foot controls. The power assisted steering was controlled by an 18 in. wheel, which was much easier to use than the 20 or 22 in. wheels then customary on buses and coaches.

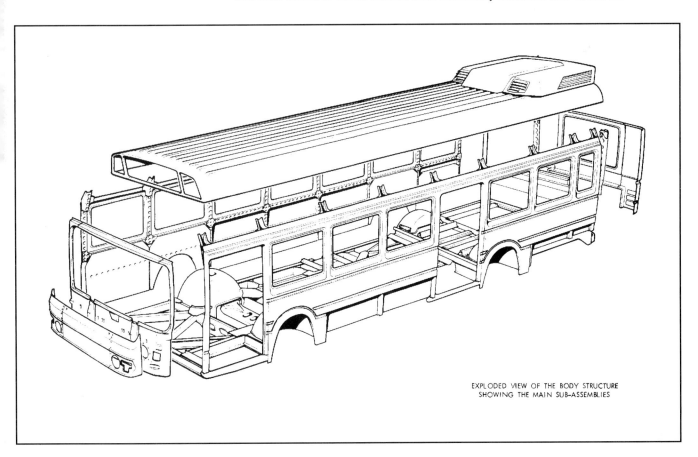

EXPLODED VIEW OF THE BODY STRUCTURE
SHOWING THE MAIN SUB-ASSEMBLIES

Similarly, the pedals were smaller and more comfortable, especially the air-operated accelerator. Unlike previous Leylands and most continental buses however, the accelerator and brake pedals were almost identical. When the driver turned back from collecting fares, it was possible for him to find the wrong pedal, and this may well have been the cause of some of the mysterious accidents which happened to early models. The location of every other instrument, control and switch was assessed on the number of times it was likely to be used during a normal driving roster. Everything had to be light enough for a female driver to work a full shift. The controls which were used most frequently had to be nearest to hand.

On a standard right hand drive model the area to the left of the steering wheel was kept clear for ticket issuing equipment. The direction indicators, horn and headlamp dipper/flash controls were mounted on two stalks on the steering column. This feature had first been introduced on Triumph cars and was soon copied, almost universally. To the driver's right hand side there was a ledge, running beneath the side window. Towards the front of this, within easy reach of the steering wheel, was a miniaturised gear selector unit, controlling the Pneumocyclic gearbox. Just behind it was the small lever for the air-operated parking brake.

Behind them came other switches. Nearest the front were those which the driver might use more frequently during a shift. Further back, and out of normal sight line, were those only used occasionally during a shift, such as the heater controls. The instrument panel was built into a binnacle which sat just beneath the steering wheel, comfortably within the driver's sight line.

The door operating switches were on this panel, as were an array of warning lights. They were colour coded, so that a red light warned the driver of a serious problem, such as loss of water, and a yellow one warned of something which would require attention on the vehicle's return to the depot. The end result was probably the biggest single improvement ever made in driver's compartment layout. Every detail was considered, right down to the size and position of the coat hook.

Another major innovation was the heating and ventilation system. Contemporary buses relied on under-seat heaters which were supplied by hot water from the engine cooling system. They required extensive piping, connected by rubber hoses clamped with clips to the piping. The failure of one hose could lead to the loss of water, and, if the driver failed to heed the warning, the engine could seize and be ruined.

Distribution from the under-seat heaters was patchy and they were difficult to maintain, because pipes could be both above and below floor level. On FPB7, the heating and ventilation system was mounted in a pod on the rear of the roof, where the outside air was reckoned to be relatively clean. Air passed into the front of the pod and over a heat exchanger. It was then blown along either side at roof level and ducted down into the passenger area, over the windows. Extra air was blown over the door apertures, forming a hot air curtain.

This system completely cured the problem of windows streaming with condensation on a wet day. As hot air tends to rise, however, or at least is reluctant to fall, there were complaints from passengers about cold feet.

A mock up of the driver's compartment above, and the actual location, below, showing the strength of the structure around the driving compartment.

The strength of the National was legendary. Even when crashed at 20mph into a solid concrete block, deformation was not serious.

Ken Hargreaves, one of the first men into Workington and very definitely the last man out, is seen here at the wheel of the first National to be completed at the Workington factory.

Ken Hargreaves, at that time a young development engineer at Leyland, tested the system on one of the seven prototypes in extreme Arctic winter conditions in the north of Finland. The bus was fitted with twin heaters which worked perfectly, well below zero, but between that time and the start of volume production, one of the heaters was removed from the domestic specification, as part of a cost cutting exercise.

Hargreaves told an amusing story from the Finnish test programme. Marcus Smith had come out to see how the bus performed. He was renowned for cutting his time to catch planes and trains to the last minute. Hargreaves had to drive the valuable prototype at top speed, over packed snow and sheet ice, covering the 100 km to Rovaniemi airport, just inside the Arctic Circle, with minutes to spare!

The interior lighting consisted of fluorescent tubes, concealed by a translucent panel in the centre of the roof, starting just behind the driving compartment, and running the length of the bus. Although it could cause reflections on the windscreen this arrangement not only gave excellent illumination, but was also quite restful. Mechanically the project demanded that FPB7 should have a better performance than its competitors and be capable of keeping up with traffic, which in the late 'sixties generally flowed much more smoothly than nowadays!

Air suspension was fitted as standard, in a system which was cleverly designed to prevent the common tendency for buses to 'dive' when braking. It was the first fully successful air suspension system on a British bus. The levelling valves were carefully and properly developed and were one of the main reasons for the success of the suspension system.

There had been a limited number of previous British air suspension systems but they were troublesome and tended to make many passengers queasy. Some fleet engineers expected problems with the FPB7 system and had to be reassured with consignment stocks of spare parts. After two to three years experience, most were returned unused. FPB7 overcame the resistance of British bus fleet engineers to air suspension.

In July 1969 it was announced that the new bus would be built in a joint venture with the National Bus Company. According to press releases at the time the decision was made in the belief that the pooling of knowledge between the biggest bus operator in the world and the major British manufacturer of buses should be of benefit to other operators, and provide a bridgehead to develop further world markets.

British Leyland increased its shareholding in Bristol and ECW to 50%. A new company, Bus Manufacturers (Holdings) Ltd (BMH), was incorporated on 4 February 1970, owned equally by British Leyland and National Bus Company. BMH then acquired 100% of the share capital of Bristol Commercial Vehicles, Eastern Coach Works, and the newly formed Leyland National Company, which was to build FPB7.

The actual legal entity of Leyland National Co Ltd was formed by changing the name and altering the Memorandum and Articles of Association of Crossley Motors Ltd, which had originally been formed on 13 December 1910. Crossley had been dormant since the late 1950s and had come as part of the ACV Group. The new Leyland National Company needed to have a substantial share capital, which Crossley had. The device of changing the name on 4 September 1969 was perfectly legal and saved considerable costs, compared with forming a new company.

By all accounts, it was an initiative by Sir Donald Stokes and Ron Ellis to involve NBC. They were clearly worried that acceptance of one man operated double-deckers by the main cities and trade unions would have an adverse effect on production forecasts for the new single-decker.

Several major operators had already announced large double-deck orders. London Transport was starting to rethink its policies, having found that long single-deckers were having difficulty on some routes. Double-deck buses, based on Daimler Fleetline chassis, were ordered by London, very soon after Ralph Bennett's move from Manchester to become a full time member of London's Board.

There are often two sides to a story. In *National Bus Company 1968-1989*, **(see Bibliography)**, there is a record of an interview held in 1988 with George McKay, who was Director of Technical Services on NBC's formation in 1969.

He said that NBC had been presented with a *fait accompli*, in that Norman Todd, then the Chairman of NBC, had been present at a dinner with Stokes when the latter had 'persuaded' Todd that NBC and Leyland should combine to produce a new single-deck vehicle. The approach had followed a complaint made by Todd that AEC and Daimler had been swallowed up by Leyland and he was faced with a monopoly supplier situation – to which Stokes replied that he now had a monopoly purchaser!!

McKay, a forthright Scot, went on to say that, had London Transport not had an interest in developing single-deckers, the new project would not have materialised! When a view is expressed twenty years after the event there is often the risk of distortion by hindsight but, in McKay's defence, NBC had only a limited number of urban routes for which the new bus was best suited. He was also remarkably accurate in his forecast, in 1969, that demand from NBC would not exceed around 500 units per annum. Even so, NBC was persuaded to take a bus which owed more to London Transport than any other operator group.

When the Leyland National Company was established, British Leyland Truck and Bus Division Ltd was given management responsibility. That was reinforced by the appointment of Ron Ellis as Chairman of Leyland National Co Ltd, but to some extent balanced by the appointment of Marcus Smith with his THC experience as Director and General Manager of the Company in September 1969. At the same time it was announced that construction of a totally new factory would be financed by Government grants and loans, and also by loans from British Leyland and National Bus Company.

In the Foreword, Marcus Smith has referred to the 'shuttle diplomacy' in the management of the project, and the plant, after it was opened. He has said that: "it had to be managed day in, day out." Many of us in Leyland tended to forget this point. To us it was simply another plant in the Division, producing part of a wide range of trucks and buses. One of his best aids was a large scale model of the plant which was housed in the Butec electrical factory in Leyland. It kept the partners visually involved in the project and they knew what to expect.

In 1969 there were around 35,000 double-deckers and 10,000 single-deck service buses running in the United Kingdom. When the market looked as though it would move largely to single-deckers it had been perfectly reasonable for Leyland to forecast that operators might require 2,500-3,000 new buses each year. As the largest producer by far, it was also reasonable to forecast that the new Leyland project would take up to 75% of the domestic market, with much of the remaining share being supplied by other Leyland Group models.

It was always accepted that some operators might prefer mid engined buses and could have preference for existing bodybuilders. This was especially true of the Scottish Bus Group. The balance of the new factory's capacity would be available for export.

When the trade unions accepted one man operation of double-deckers, following legislation accepting the concept, the forecasts changed dramatically. Registrations of new double-deckers would probably out-number those of new single-deckers by two to one, even allowing for some switching from double-deckers on less heavily trafficked routes. While the newly introduced Bus Grant was likely to stimulate demand for new vehicles, there was no way in which it would make up for the forecast shortfall in the single-deck sector.

Leyland must therefore have faced the very difficult decision of whether to scale down or even abandon the FPB7 project. The former option would have meant abandoning the advanced construction techniques, which were a fundamental part of the project's costings. The latter option would have been difficult, because Leyland would have had to walk away from a growing market sector. There was demand for low floor rear-engined single-deckers, but first generation models like the Leyland Panther and AEC Swift were incurring high warranty and running costs.

Ron Ellis, Prime Minister Harold Wilson and Sir Donald Stokes with a model of the Leyland National Factory in February 1970.

George McKay, Director of Technical Services, NBC.

The large-scale model of Workington which became one of Marcus Smith's most useful tools.

Ralph Bennett's move to London was soon followed by a return to ordering double-deckers. Large numbers of Daimler Fleetlines were ordered instead of the Nationals which Leyland had built into its projections. In a double irony, London's inability to operate the Fleetlines satisfactorily resulted in wholesale premature withdrawal. The effect of placing such a vast quantity of generally sound vehicles onto the second-hand market severely depressed new bus sales for some time.

The Scottish Bus Group remained loyal to Alexander for its bodywork and continued to take mid-engined chassis from Leyland and, simultaneously for five years, from Seddon. Neither of these chassis allowed the easy entrance low-step facility of the National to be incorporated into the construction, but SBG favoured vehicles with all-forward-facing seats for its many long routes. Alexander's Y-type body was produced from 1963 to 1983.

The rugged Olympic integral bus was assembled by MCW, using Leyland running units. Here a batch for Cuba waits to board at Dagenham docks, ironically right next to the huge Ford car factory.

ideas on pricing and margins." The high volume concept of FPB7 looked like offering significant savings.

By joining up with the National Bus Company, Leyland did its best to try to secure a customer base for the new vehicle, but the decision to press ahead with a plant with a capacity of 2,000 units per annum was, with hindsight, over optimistic.

Maybe there is a reason. In an interview with *Motor Transport* in November 1969, Ron Ellis said that the joint effort between Leyland and the bus industry would not have been 'a runner' ten years previously, but it had become possible because bus fleet operations were now 'in very large pieces', meaning London, NBC, SBG and the four large PTAs. "Fortunately there has been full consultation about what sort of bus Leyland National should make." He concluded the interview by saying: "We are going through a transitional period in which we are reorganising very large chunks of the industry. We might fall short of targets we have set, but this is certain. Lots of energy will be applied and industry will see the effects of this in the next year or so."

Ellis was a strategic thinker. He had the amazing capacity to deal equally with grand plans and fine detail. FPB7 was just one of the projects on his plate at the time, but it had strong Government support, backed by generous grants. It fitted the concept of re-organising a chunk of the industry, and it would have been very difficult to change part of the Government's strategic plan.

With hindsight, it could be said that the factory was created in artificial circumstances, beyond the reality of the market. Having said that, nothing should detract from the tremendous personal efforts which went into its creation and operation.

The threat imposed by the formation of Leyland National was not lost on bodybuilders in the British market. Leyland had enjoyed a successful relationship with MCW, building the integral Olympic for overseas markets. Almost as soon as the Leyland National project became public, the relationship between Leyland and MCW became fraught, culminating in a serious dispute in 1970, when MCW was building 115 inter-urban coach versions of the Olympic for Cuba.

In the summer of 1969, MCW had found an alternative partner in Scania-Vabis AB of Sweden and there were fears at Leyland that MCW might secure former Olympic business with Scania running units. As it happened not one single MCW Scania product was sold outside the United Kingdom, but the development of the Metropolitan double-decker, and later the more acceptable Metrobus, can be traced to this time.

MCW was not in a position to have an outright fight with Leyland, because Bus Grant stimulated demand for double-deckers. For most of the 1970s, about half of MCW's output continued to be traditional double-deck bodywork on Daimler chassis for London and West Midlands, also some smaller contracts on Leyland Atlanteans.

All through this time, the new single-deck project was still known as FPB7, but the name of the joint venture company gave the game away. It soon became clear that the new bus would be known as the 'Leyland National'.

No secret about the name now as the Leyland National directors pose for the photographer. Left to right - Marcus Smith, two officials from Cumberland County Council, Sir Frank Schon, Norman Todd, Sir Donald Stokes, Ron Ellis and Tony Gailey.

CHAPTER FOUR
A Unique Manufacturing Facility

In the late 1950s, the interventionist Conservative Government of Harold Macmillan started the practice of persuading manufacturers to locate new factories in areas where old traditional industries were declining. The motor industry had been concentrated in the West Midlands, but there was also considerable long-established activity in other areas, notably Oxford, Luton and Dagenham.

Under this new policy BMC built its truck and tractor factory at Bathgate, about 17 miles west of Edinburgh. Chrysler and Pressed Steel set up a car manufacturing facility at Linwood, just west of Paisley. Ford and Standard-Triumph built factories at Halewood and Speke respectively, in adjacent suburbs of Liverpool, and Vauxhall went just across the Mersey to Ellesmere Port.

The Labour Government of 1964-70 pursued this policy vigorously and gave attractive financial incentives to companies which were prepared to move to development areas. The FPB7 project was known in Government circles certainly no later than the last quarter of 1967. It would have been difficult to set up the new plant in the Leyland area, partly because of Government policy, but also because there was a low rate of unemployment.

There was growing awareness by manufacturing industry that large factory complexes could be more vulnerable to trade union activity, though in my personal experience of the Leyland commercial vehicle operations the trade unions were usually but not always more reasonable, and certainly more knowledgeable about the business, than the Personnel Department.

Having said that, there was a difficult period around the time that British Leyland was formed when the newly appointed convenor at Leyland, Len Brindle, led a series of disputes to demand parity with other Group factories. That happened at a critical time and was enough, in the words of Marcus Smith, to confirm that: ".. the (new bus) factory should be far enough from Leyland not to catch Leyland measles!" This philosophy was in line with the prevailing practice which was, where possible, to divide and rule, with a series of smaller manufacturing units.

There had previously been extensive bodybuilding facilities at Leyland, which had literally grown with the company. In 1954 a bitter dispute with the coachbuilders' trade union caused Leyland to cease bodybuilding, apart from truck cabs. At the time of closure the output included truck cabs, a very attractive and popular double deck body, a rather plain single-deck bus body, and a sturdy but quite stylish coach. The closure of that factory, while hardly fresh in the mind, was evidently a factor in deciding to design FPB7 so that it could be built and repaired by semi-skilled labour.

Word about the new project soon reached some of the development councils. Cumberland assembled a powerful team, headed by Sir Frank Schon. He had

One of the last bus bodies built by Leyland at the main factory complex in Lancashire. This was regarded by many as a classic double-deck design, even in low-bridge form as here. It was capable of meeting the requirements of most of Leyland's customers with only minor modifications.

Sir Frank Schon (left) and Lord Stokes look pretty pleased with themselves on the occasion of a visit to the Workington site. The creation of such a prime factory was clearly going to benefit the depressed area with its high unemployment rate. The conviction that the work force would rise to the challenge and that a strife-free environment would be created proved to be correct and was one of the happier aspects of what Leyland called 'the Cumberland project'. There must have been some within BL who had reservations and an interesting pair of maps produced at the time showed the disposition of the suppliers to be involved in the production of the Leyland National together with likely customer outlets. The former is reproduced below and it must be obvious to anyone – even with the benefit of hindsight – that of all the potential sites for the new factory Workington had little to commend it geographically.

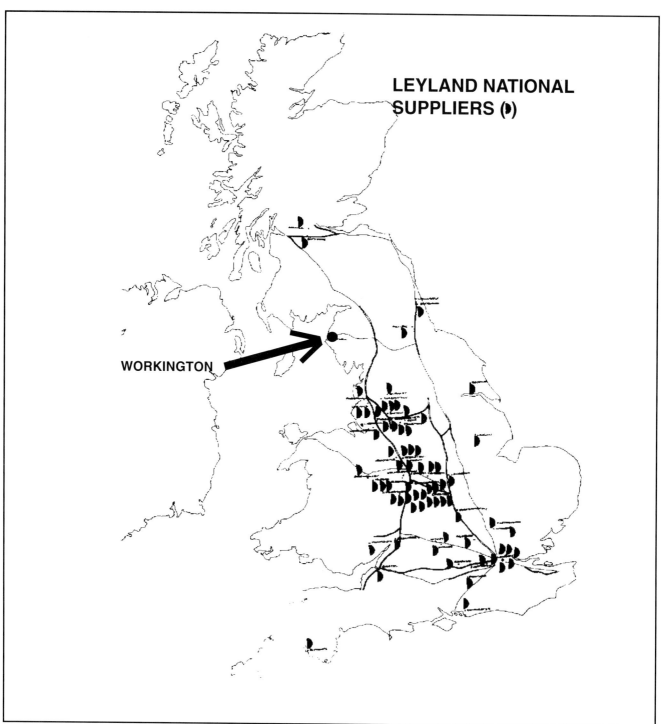

previously been a senior executive with Albright & Wilson, which had a major chemical factory trading as 'Marchon' in Whitehaven. Schon was a friend of Stokes, but he also had powerful backing from senior civil servants, and Fred Peart, the long-sitting Labour Member of Parliament for Workington. Another influential political figure was William (later Lord) Whitelaw, Conservative MP for Penrith.

One of the attractions to the Cumberland team was the high capital expenditure in the new project. It was seen as putting down roots, and was different from the mainly low cost labour intensive investment then being attracted to the area.

At that time Cumberland was the larger northern part of what is now known as Cumbria. The M6 motorway had almost been completed, by-passing the notorious old main road over Shap Fell, and running round Penrith and Carlisle to finish a few miles short of the Scottish border. The central part of the county was largely hill farming land, on the northern edge of the Lake District.

Further west there was an industrial area, centred on Workington and Whitehaven. The main industries had been coal and steel, both of which were declining, especially the former. There was the chemical plant at Whitehaven, and a growing atomic industry at Windscale, later to be known as Sellafield.

In the *Castle Diaries 1964-70*, the Minister of Transport referred to an *ad hoc* meeting which she had attended at the Board of Trade on 29 January 1968. 'Leylands (sic) have been induced to consider seriously putting their Park Royal factory into this Special Development Area (West Cumberland) with the help of every conceivable grant in the spectrum. In fact they are going to get something like three quarters of the capital cost met under these schemes.'

The Cumberland Development Council offered a choice of three prime sites. One was quite close to Workington town centre, but was rejected because it was on low lying land close to the sea wall. Another was a former airfield a few miles north, and the third was at Lillyhall, about three miles south east of Workington, on high ground, with clear views out over the Irish Sea and the Solway Firth towards the hills of southern Scotland.

There was strong competition from several other parts of the country, but eventually the decision went to Cumberland and the Lillyhall site, in preference to the Forest of Dean, which had been the second choice. Another possibility was part of the Triumph car factory site at Speke, Liverpool.

The selection of Lillyhall caused considerable surprise at Leyland and had some people looking at their maps. It was so remote, a word frequently connected with the plant throughout its life. I remember being sent there to check out some details for the conveyancing of the land. Standing on that barren windswept scrubland, it was hard to imagine why Lillyhall was chosen and that there would ever be a thriving bus factory.

Barbara's Castle's Diary entry for 29 January 1968 also recorded that the grants offered to Leyland were not enough. 'Rightly in my view, they are insisting on having proper communications created as well and that means the building of the West Cumberland road: cost £10 million.' She referred to arguments with colleagues who were insisting that the cost be met from her Transport Department's budget and she prepared herself to fight the issue in the Cabinet if need be.

About a year later Harold Wilson said that work would begin on upgrading the A66 trunk road between West Cumberland and the M6 motorway at Penrith. At that time it was a tortuous drive of over 40 miles, through busy little towns like Keswick and Cockermouth, and several smaller villages. Even in those days they tended to become jammed with tourist traffic in summer.

On 20 February 1970 Harold Wilson stood at a bench-mark, hewn out of Lakeland green slate, to inaugurate the building of the Leyland National factory at Lillyhall. The Prime Minister said at the time: "Today's achievement represents a tremendous job of teamwork between industrialists and the public services."

At the ceremony Wilson referred to the A66, when he said: "We all look forward to the contribution this road will make to existing industry in the area and bring in new industries. Among the first evidence of this will be the supply lorries driving along this road into Workington to feed the new Leyland National factory, and the convoys of buses going in the opposite direction, whether for British bus operators or to Britain's principal exporting ports."

While this might be dismissed as typical exaggeration by a politician, it was positive and encouraging, compared to anything likely to be said nowadays by a cabinet minister about manufacturing industry.

In fact considerable preparatory work had been done on the upgrading of the A66, but it had been held up by protests from some powerful groups of objectors. The

The Lakeland stone bench-mark which stood outside the Lillyhall factory and which is now preserved.

Conservative Government of Edward Heath came to power in June 1970, but did not interfere with the policies of the previous Labour administration, either on the construction of the Workington factory or, to any extent, on the ownership and regulation of the bus industry. Indeed, the Conservatives increased new Bus Grant to 50% in 1971.

The improvements to the A66 did not fare so well, although Marcus Smith recalled that Cumberland County Council kept him in regular contact, for instance by coming to see him and rolling out long drawings of proposed new sections of road. Eventually, after several delays, a public enquiry was held before an independent inspector, Sir Robert Scott, in Penrith from 25 January to 17 March 1972. There was general consensus for the need to divert through truck traffic off the narrow hilly Windermere to Keswick road, which could be very busy in the tourist season.

The objectors were particularly concerned about plans to take the road through a new hillside cutting, by-passing Keswick on the north side. There were also strong objections about proposed changes along the west side of Bassenthwaite Lake. One vociferous lobby called for the A66 improvement scheme to be abandoned and replaced by a more northerly route, about six or seven miles longer, following the line of an existing B road through the village of Sebergham to join an upgraded Carlisle to Cockermouth road.

A handful of witnesses gave evidence on behalf of industry in west Cumberland, among them Marcus Smith, who spoke eloquently about the problems of delivering "an exposed product along narrow Lakeland roads". He also produced a map showing the widespread distribution of Leyland National's suppliers. There was a heavy concentration in the West Midlands, and all the main running units came from Leyland, which was over 100 miles away.

The Inspector duly approved the plans for the A66. Work started fairly quickly and the completed road was not the eyesore which many objectors predicted. Marcus Smith reflected that it was a wonderful example of what an enquiry can achieve in terms of proper landscaping and minimal intrusion. Once completed, no other significant improvement was subsequently made to the A66 west of Penrith.

Early in 1970 work commenced on the factory. Leyland's regular architects were Harry S Fairhurst & Son of Manchester. Pat Barry was the partner and Arthur Higginbottom the site architect. They designed the plant in conjunction with Leyland's own in-house architect, David Laraway. Other specialists advised on structural engineering and landscaping.

Because the site was on exposed high ground, the structure had to be capable of withstanding wind speeds of up to 120 mph. Soil which was removed when the site was levelled was used in a perimeter embankment which partly sheltered the factory from prevailing winds and minimised the visual intrusion in an area on the edge of a National Park.

Construction of the factory was carried out by George Wimpey Ltd. The main buildings consisted of a large span steel-framed assembly shop, vehicle testing shop, boiler house, offices and separate canteen, covering a total area of approximately 39,000sq m. Daily weather reports were obtained from St Bees lighthouse, about 10 miles to the south, and the roof was put on between major storms.

Apart from the two storey office block, everything else was on one level. The main factory unit was almost rectangular, except for one corner which accommodated the office block. It was just over 300 metres long and 108 metres wide. The clear working space, from the floor to the roof structure, was a uniform 7.5 metres. It was a deliberate decision to build the factory, including the entry and exit doors, high enough to take double-deckers and to allow for full 12 metre vehicles between the pillars. It was recognition that it might be necessary at some future stage to extend the range beyond the single-decker to get extra volume.

The whole factory was windowless, apart from twin vertical full height windows at the end of each bay. Frequently it was quite reassuring to be cocooned in the warmth of the factory, almost blissfully unaware of the wild Cumbrian weather outside. The factory and its assembly lines were designed so that they could be expanded in the longer term to double capacity with the minimum of disruption.

The assembly lines did not run longitudinally down the factory, but to and fro across in short lines, for two reasons. Firstly, it facilitated delivery of components closest to their point of use. Secondly, a vehicle which required extra or remedial work could be taken out of line without disrupting the whole carefully timed production process.

When the land was bought an option was taken on an equally large plot of adjacent land. The theory was that any extension could be built alongside the original plant and that the lines could simply be extended across. It was ten years before any extension

By August 1970, construction of the factory was well under way. An idea of the height can be given by the size of the men working at various levels on the scaffolding.

The Leyland National factory, shortly after completion. The production process started with the powder coating plant at the far end of the building, gradually working down the factory, to end in the Test Centre which was some way behind the photographer's left shoulder. From the windows of the two storey office block on the front of the main building there were magnificent views over the Solway Firth.

The Vehicle Test Centre was modern, light and airy. The bus on the extreme right was one of the first batch for Jamaica Omnibus Services.

was made to the plant, but it was 'L' shaped and did not follow the theory.

A vehicle testing shop was built, as a separate unit, at one end of the main factory, but in such a way that it fitted into the overall planning grid so that the open space between it and the main factory could be enclosed and roofed over in the future. One side of the test shop had a sunken workshop area, leading directly into vehicle inspection pits. The idea was very modern for its time, but has since been copied quite widely.

The boiler house was also on a separate site, supplying services by way of an overhead bridge into the main factory complex. Heating, electrical, water and compressed air circuits were all designed on a ring-main principle, with expansion in mind. Supplies were brought down pillars and walls at regular intervals, and all were colour coded.

This feature was particularly noticeable. It was possible to walk round the factory with a party of visitors, without having to warn them about the cables, pipes and other floor level obstructions which were endemic in older factories at that time.

The new plant comfortably exceeded pollution standards from the outset. This was long before the current level of concern about environmental matters, but there was sensitivity in the area, because of Windscale, and Strathclyde University regularly sampled local waste levels.

The office block was largely open plan, with a small suite for the Managing (later Plant) Director, boardroom and visitors. This block had an interesting combination of features. On the one hand, it was fully air conditioned, which was unusual for that time and that part of the country. Heat from the fluorescent lighting system was recovered and re-used. On the other hand there were very attractive local features, like the green Cumberland slate tiling in the foyer and entrance area.

The Director's office was superbly located on one corner of the building. On a clear day there were excellent views across the Solway Firth to southern Scotland, sweeping round as far south as the Isle of Man. There was also a commanding view of everything entering and leaving the site, including staff, visitors, inward goods, and buses going to the test centre or leaving on delivery.

The January 1973 edition of *Design* magazine, published by the Design Council, described the Workington plant as 'the most impressive combination of industrial design and functional architecture that had ever been put together in Britain over the last twenty-five years'. That was very fulsome praise. Certainly it was a joy to go into the factory, but then it was mainly an assembly operation. The traditional noisy and dirty work, like casting, machining and cutting, was done elsewhere.

Concurrent with the building of the structure the management team was busy ordering plant and equipment. The advanced design of the National required automated production tooling, to assemble the vehicle to very fine tolerances.

It had been decided to use a rivetted structure which meant that the body panels could be primed before assembly. This would have been impossible with a welded structure. Because the panels were primed individually, it was possible to introduce an automated plant of the kind only previously seen in the volume car business.

At one end of the factory an area was set aside for pre-treatment of the body parts. These were delivered direct by truck to adjacent storage areas and loaded manually onto carriers on which they were transported through the pre-treatment and powder coating plants.

There were seven stages of corrosion resistant pre-treatment, each in a tank of approximately 13,000 litres capacity. Overhead cranes dipped the components into a sequence of tanks, on a pre-programmed schedule of one to five minutes. This applied even to steel members which had been made from galvanised or zinc coated steel sheets.

From the pre-treatment line structural components, and those exposed to corrosion, were transferred automatically to the powder coating plant, which consisted of drying booths, powder booths and ovens. In this section of the factory panels were carried on an overhead chain conveyor. The drying stage of the process took about twelve and a half minutes and was carefully controlled to ensure that panels were completely dry, but not too warm.

The next stage was the really interesting one. The components entered the powder coating booth, which had a manual compartment, followed by a much larger fully automated section. Both components and powder were electrically charged, so that, when the powder touched the metal, electrostatic action held it there. This action ensured that the layer of powder was of uniform thickness, including around edges, a notoriously difficult problem with liquid paints, which tend to retreat from edges.

In the first section, two men sprayed powder on sections which might not be reached during the automatic process. From there the conveyor passed into the second compartment which had eight automatic spray guns, four each side of the component. These moved up and down vertically, while continuously spraying powder. Therefore the compartment was like a dark grey sand storm and the parts were always well covered.

After leaving that process, the powder was converted into a tough coat by passing through a 30 metre long oven with an operating temperature of 180-200°C. After cooling they were ready to go to the assembly lines.

This process was frequently a source of amazement to visitors. By way of reinforcing the toughness of the finish a visitor would be given a coin or piece of sharp metal and be encouraged to 'break the skin' of the powder treatment. Despite some vigorous efforts the coin would simply skim across the surface, making no impression on the coating. It was a convincing demonstration.

A view over the finishing lines in the large and impressive factory. This was a new way of building buses. The layout, the tooling and the systems were so advanced that traditional bodyworks appeared hopelessly antiquated in comparison.

A nearly completed bodyshell has been lifted off the bogie by an overhead gantry, and will shortly receive its running units. Engines, gearboxes and axles were added near to the end of the production process, in order to minimise storage costs.

External panels, including the one piece roof, went through a separate priming process where they were degreased and then automatically sprayed with a wet etch primer. The automatic guns were controlled by photo-electric cells, which detected the presence of a component and actuated the spray guns accordingly. When sprayed, they passed into a 30 metre long gas fired oven and were ready for use after cooling. Body assembly was divided into sub-units which could be progressed simultaneously. At various stages, two or three sub-units were brought together, but it was only in the last two stages that all the units were involved.

The plant was laid out so that body shells passed through a number of stations during the assembly process. Work was arranged so that the time spent at each station was just under one hour. On the forty hour week at that time, it gave a capacity of 2,000 buses per annum. It was an impressive sight to watch the whole line move forward on the hour, in a blaze of yellow flashing lights. The movement was controlled by the foreman, using just one switch. At each station an emergency button could be pressed to delay movement of the track. The foreman could investigate and at his discretion either move the track or authorise a delay.

The whole assembly process was fascinating. A number of sub-assemblies came in from outside suppliers, such as pillars and roof sticks. They were put into jigs and drilled and rivetted together to make larger assemblies such as complete side frames, roofs, and so on. Panels were installed and clamped into jigs. In the major fixtures all the holes were drilled automatically.

When the drills retracted rivets were inserted and locked. The design specification called for a rivet which could be inserted quickly, give a constant clamping force, and be easily removable for repairs. It proved particularly difficult to find a rivet which could be removed easily. Therefore special tools were developed so that the unique Avdelok rivet could meet all these needs.

This rivet resembled a dome-headed bolt with a grooved shank. Insertion and clamping was a two man job. One inserted the rivet into the hole, from the outside or above, and the other operated a pneumatic tool which fed a collar onto the shank of the rivet, then clamped it tightly. Every one of the 5,000 rivets in each National was powder coated. For repairs, another special tool was used to split the collar from the rivet. This was far quicker and neater than the traditional method of drilling out the rivet.

The front and rear underframes, including wheelarches, were assembled in separate fixtures. A small fixture assembled the inner front structure, up to the base of the windscreen, but excluding the exterior skin panels. Each underframe was placed on a bogie, which was fundamental to the line concept of building. The bogie stayed with the bus until near the end of the assembly process. This revolutionary system was used not only on the National, but also on subsequent Workington models.

The bus started to take shape physically in the right and left hand body fixtures, in which complete body sides, excluding doors, were assembled. Another major fixture assembled the entire roof, except for the heater pod unit.

Next, the underframe, sides and roof were assembled together to make a rigid box structure. They were then brought together in a marry-up fixture, and joined up with the central portion of the underframe.

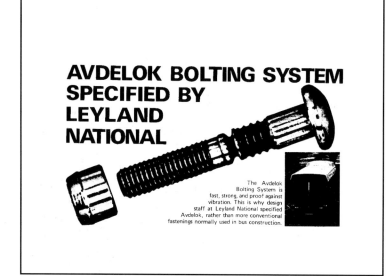

Reproduction of a trade advertisement for the Avdelok rivet together with explanatory diagram. The rivetting tool snapped off the longer part of the bolt, after the collar had been clamped in place.

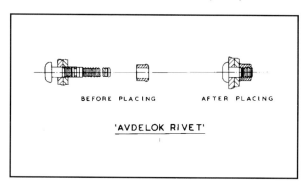

Body assembly was a simple process by virtue of the overhead gantry facility.

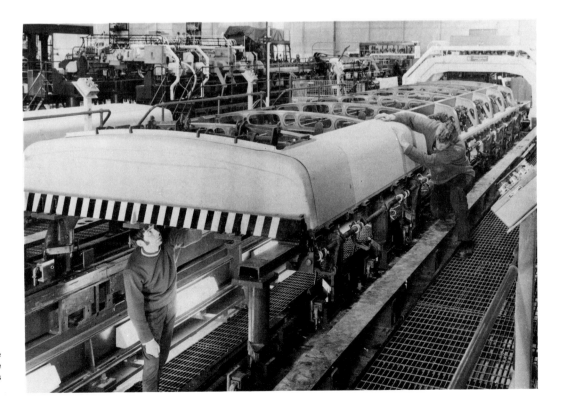

Roof assembly using the Pressed Steel Fisher jig. The great strength of the roof sticks can be seen clearly.

It was an amazing sight to see the huge automatic drilling carriages move along the fixture, drilling holes between the roof and the side, and the sides and underframe. In a second framing fixture, the driver's compartment and front and rear skin panels were added. Each of the processes described above took place inside one hour.

On all except the underframe fixtures, the drills were mounted on carriages which traversed automatically along the length of the fixture. The drill carriage could be automatically programmed, to move from stop to stop and drill a pre-requisite number of holes, for each different body specification. On some of the larger fixtures up to 400 holes were drilled and rivets inserted within the allotted hour.

Before the roof was married-up to the bodywork it was put into a 'turnover jig', then a layer of rigid polyurethane foam was applied to the underside. This flame-proof closed cell foam provided thermal insulation and prevented the roof from drumming. The insulation was necessary because warm air from the heating system was passed under the roof panel. It went on as a yellowy-orange liquid, but expanded to a uniform thickness of about 25 mm, looking for all the world like the texture of a 'Crunchie' bar.

When the last hole had been drilled and the last rivet inserted the bodies moved out of the assembly area into a small buffer store, usually of three to four bodies. From this point they were transferred to the next stage of the system, where they were towed along a series of conveyors, passing back and forth across the factory.

The first stage on this part of the build was the underseal line. The underframe was cleaned off and the lower portion of the body masked. Because this was a short operation entry exit and emergency doors were added at this stage. The body then went into an underseal booth where two lifts located into the front and rear cross-members. The complete body was then raised about 2 metres and rotated 60° to either side, like a joint on a spit.

Leyland's engineers had looked at a number of anti-corrosion systems and eventually settled on an epoxy pitch treatment which was used on the underside of the Cunard liner, *Queen Elizabeth 2*. The bodies were rotated to ensure that all sides of the underframe were reached and protected.

Unlike contemporary underseal treatments, which were soft and could be penetrated relatively easily, the epoxy pitch treatment bonded to the powder coating and set into a hard impenetrable skin. In retrospect, this also proved to be extremely effective and durable.

The next section in the operation was colour painting of the exterior, where the operation cycle times for preparation and painting/baking were 30 minutes. Within a year or so, the track was altered so that buses could pass back round the preparation

Spraying the underseal was an easy task on a raised body assembly. By rotating the body from side to side, it was easier to apply the underseal into every part of the underside.

Applying the cell foam insulation to the roof.

and paint line if they required a two colour paint finish. The body panels were all wiped with a special material which picked up dust, without depositing any particles on the panels.

Two coats of colour paint were then applied automatically to the top and sides of the bodywork, wet on wet. The front and rear panels and interior panels of the doors were sprayed manually. When the body entered the paint booth, a photo-electric cell actuated automatic spray guns, one on each side and another over the roof. The guns reciprocated continuously, so that the body effectively passed through a curtain of paint spray.

The body went through once, then the guns were arrested while the body passed back through the booth, before repeating the process with the second coat. This was applied while the first coat was still wet and achieved the required level of paint film. The use of automatically actuated spray guns was yet another example of equipment which was then at the leading edge of production technology.

After painting bodies passed slowly though a gas fired oven, with an internal temperature of 80-90°C. Having spent about 40 minutes in the oven single colour bodies moved on to final assembly, while those with two colour finishes repeated the cycle for the second colour.

In the first year or two at Workington there was great reluctance to do anything other than a very limited selection of mono colours – a policy which attracted criticism from several customers. The application of second colours was almost invariably sub-contracted, but later the plant became more flexible in its capabilities. After leaving the paint track the bodies were transferred to the trim and assembly tracks. In all there were twenty-five stations. Each operation continued to be completed within one hour.

The body remained on its bogie for the first eighteen stations, during which a wide number of operations were carried out, including installation of underfloor pipes, flooring, driving and operating controls, electrical harnesses, electrical fittings and lamps, door operating gear, heater pod assembly, glazing, hard trim panels, seat stanchions, internal screens, hand rails, seats and the driver's compartment.

At station 19 the body was transferred to an overhead cradle and the bogie went back to the beginning of the body assembly line. In the next three stations the engine, gearbox, axles, fuel tank and exhaust system were installed. At station 23 the complete bus was lowered to just above the floor, so that the radiator, cooling hoses and road wheels could be fitted. The air suspension was inflated and the bus then lowered to the factory floor.

At the last two stations, items like windscreen wipers and mirrors were fitted, and all the fuel, water and hydraulic systems filled. Batteries were installed and the engine was started. Then, after a final electrical test, the completed bus was driven out of the factory and across to the test centre. There, buses were given a thorough test, before final preparation and delivery. Brakes, steering, suspension and headlamps could be adjusted. Then every home market bus was ready to be tested by the Department of Transport. Initially, this meant the issue of a Certificate of Fitness, but the factory soon won the right to 'Type Approve' buses for the home market, because the highly tooled system guaranteed uniformity of construction.

The Workington factory was unlike anything seen before in the industry, anywhere in the world! It was designed to build a highly standardised bus by methods never previously applied to the bus industry. Very advanced tooling and production methods replaced much of the labour previously required in bus building. The factory was vast but also amazingly clean, orderly and relatively quiet. The hourly movement of the whole line was uncanny. Visitors came not only from the operating industry, but from Leyland's major competitors around the world. All were impressed – some were even speechless!

One, however, had seen it all before. A senior production man from Mercedes-Benz was shown round the plant. He was amazed that the jig system reminded him strongly of the Messerschmidt factory where he had worked on production of Bf 109 fighters during the Second World War. The allies had known that Messerschmidt had a significant advantage in man hours, and all was revealed to Marcus Smith when he was subsequently given a Bf 109 manual!

It was also proof of that early Leyland slogan that the National was designed like an aircraft...but built like a car!

CHAPTER FIVE

Production Commences

It was a courageous decision to consider building a totally new product, in a brand new factory, by completely new production methods, with a totally new workforce, in an area which had no previous motor industry experience!

There were sceptics among Leyland's competitors who thought, even hoped, that the whole project was too revolutionary to succeed. At the same time, they and others feared that, if Leyland National got it right, the new way of building buses might force them to think again. Even the best manufacturers could not get below 1,000 man hours for a full size single-deck city bus.

Consequently, if the Leyland National could get anywhere near the target of 300 man hours per bus – something totally unprecedented in the industry, anywhere in the world – it would represent a very serious threat, both at home and in export markets.

The enormous task of turning Leyland National from an engineering project into a volume production product fell principally on the shoulders of Marcus Smith. Having spent three years with Cumberland Motor Services earlier in his career, he was accepted as 'part of the family' in the community. He started recruiting his management team during 1970 and the pace quickened in 1971.

At first they worked from the Truck and Bus Division headquarters in Lancashire, in close proximity to the engineering team, and also able to draw on the expertise of the central staff, in functions like purchasing. His recruits included four young men from Leyland's graduate training scheme, one of whom was David Quainton, now Sales and Marketing Director at Plaxton. He also took on Ken Hargreaves, who moved from Development at Leyland, to start recruiting and training local people.

As the National factory neared completion they moved into a small advance unit at Lillyhall in the summer of 1971. The workforce was drawn principally from the mining, steel and fishing industries. A few months earlier, Leyland said that one of the main attractions to Cumberland was the availability of a steady and reliable workforce. That certainly proved to be the case. Several people worked at the factory almost from its opening until near the end.

Lord Stokes, by then ennobled following the 'merger' with BMH, commented in a wider vein: "We felt an instinctive welcome and desire to co-operate from everybody, which is so typical of this part of the world and which means so much to the mutual partnership which inevitably develops between industry and its local environment."

There was also a direct link between the choice of Cumberland and the trade union issue. Marcus Smith said that the new company wanted to be free to build buses without the restrictive practices and other restraints imposed at that time by skilled labour.

"We decided to go to Cumberland with a clean sheet of paper as far as the unions were concerned. There was a major trade union conference at York. We went along and gave some of the most senior people a presentation on our proposals. We told them that we wanted to start from scratch and that two of the major unions would be

The first pre-production National came down to Leyland along with the prototype in December 1971, and the two are seen on Leyland's test track. Although the completion of the vehicle was a landmark, morale was suffering, as recorded in the text, with the syphoning out of enormous sums of money from Truck and Bus profits to support the ailing car business.

The National, with its 300-hour target build, compared with a contemporary Northern Counties bodied Mercedes, built for evaluation by the then newly-formed SELNEC PTE. Like most city buses of the time, the Mercedes single-decker would have taken well over three times as many hours to build. On the right, one of the pre-production prototypes, driven hard on full lock, demonstrates the effectiveness of the suspension system.

permitted to compete for members. Our main concern was to get an agreement which gave us complete flexibility. The presentation was very well received and our relationship was excellent, right from the start."

There was another benefit. The Transport & General Workers Union divided the country horizontally into a number of areas. The new factory came within the area of the Newcastle office of the TGWU, well away from the Amalgamated Engineering Union's Manchester office, which covered the Leyland factories.

Because one of the hand-built prototype Nationals had been shown at Earls Court in 1970 there was no longer any secrecy about the project. On the other hand, it put pressure on everyone to take the project from launch to volume production. Operators and the technical press expected to see the new bus on the road.

Workington was responsible only for assembly. Not one single component was made there. Every part of the Leyland National came from outside suppliers. There were two kinds of suppliers at that stage. Some were required to design and manufacture the larger and more sophisticated pieces of tooling in the assembly plant, a process which took several months. Frequently this was taking place while Leyland engineers were still incorporating modifications as a result of proving trials.

The other suppliers were those who had won contracts to manufacture component parts of the National, once volume production got under way. Many had to install new tooling and equip their factories for the new bus, sometimes with last minute modifications.

All these activities were running in parallel, on an unprecedented scale. A minor but necessary design modification might necessitate quite significant tooling changes. Fortunately, much of the design was right first time.

Barrie Wills had been appointed Supplies Manager in September 1970 and within two months drew up the following annual purchase budget, based on 2,000 buses per annum:

		No of Items
LML/Electrics	£6,480,000	450
PSF/Sankey/Chassis	£2,532,000	300
Body Fittings/Trim/etc	£2,314,000	1,000
	£11,326,000	1,750

(LML = Leyland Motors Ltd). (PSF = Pressed Steel Fisher).

Finding and negotiating with suppliers of 1,750 items was no mean task and the map reproduced on page 42 of Chapter four shows how widely they were spread around the country. GKN Sankey supplied most of the underframe pressings, and the two sub-frames which held the front and rear axles.

Pressed Steel Fisher supplied many of the body pressings including pillars and roof sticks, which were initially delivered in a sub-assembled condition. Within a year, a small unit was added in Workington, for spot-welding and local sub-assembly.

By early 1971, the sourcing exercise was well under way, with Barrie Wills reporting to Marcus Smith that 'efforts to source within the Corporation are being held up by extreme delay in the submission of quotations by Leyland Motors'. That was partly because new and more sophisticated systems were being introduced so that product costs could be calculated more accurately. The prolonged postal strike early in 1971 was another headache.

The British motor industry was much more self sufficient in those days than it is now. Every part for the Leyland National could be sourced within the United Kingdom, although that soon changed, when the ZF fully automatic gearbox became available as an option, though the SCG unit remained much more usual.

The first pre-production National stands in splendid isolation in the new factory on November 9th 1971, little more than ten weeks after assembly began.

Marcus Smith was insistent on strict quality control and had Neville Brownlow set up a quality assessment system of the kind only previously found in the car industry. Although the system eventually worked well, delays in finalising the design of the National caused problems for the Supplies Department in the early days. At first it proved impossible for the inspection system to keep pace with deliveries into the factory.

The first few assembly workers were recruited in August 1971, when one of the seven prototypes was transferred to the incomplete factory. That prototype was dismantled and re-assembled many times, to give them practical experience.

It was then decided to build a series of ten pre-production (PP) models at Workington, prior to commencement of full scale production. Work started on PP1 in August 1971, and it was virtually complete by 14 November. That was only little more than the time cycle taken by a traditional bodybuilder, with no responsibility for the mechanical content.

Ken Hargreaves remembered that the team worked very long hours to complete this bus for the Scottish Show, but on driving it to Glasgow on a very stormy night, the wind blew the doors open. Also, some parts had been completed on soft tooling, and were not acceptable. Marcus Smith told Ron Ellis that he was not prepared to let it be exhibited, and there were no recriminations. A few customers were taken to see it at the rear of Kelvin Hall.

During the pre-production period, quite a number of parts had to be made on wooden jigs, including the underframe, because suppliers were not ready in time. Some of the more serious teething problems were encountered in the painting system. After the roof was sprayed and the body shell moved into the low bake oven, the sealer used for panel joint sealing seeped out, ruining the surrounding paint finish.

In fact painting of the bodywork highlighted serious faults in the condition and tolerance of some parts, notably in the form of slack metal on the upper and lower side panels. The problem was completely cured on the main body panels, but certain liveries continued to accentuate a slight ripple effect on the cove panels.

The design of the interior trim had never been successfully tested on a prototype. David Quainton recalled that the Earls Court Show model had trim which had been cobbled together from prototype components, then stripped out and used in PP1. This caused some major problems and gave rise to criticism from operators and the press,

New Street Square, London, was an unlikely venue for a bus, but it did house the NBC headquarters and this bus was waiting to be handed over as the first of the initial order for 498, in March 1972.

because this was part of the bus which they could easily see. Not one bus had been fully trimmed before volume production commenced.

Even so the pre-production exercise proved its worth, as other teething problems were identified and cured, for instance, door operation, air system leaks, and failures of some of the mechanical bracketry. This work was carried out despite some serious supply problems.

The National Bus Company had ordered 498 Nationals, with delivery to be spread among most of its subsidiaries in 1972 and early 1973. Cumberland Motor Services was the local NBC subsidiary and very appropriately, was the first customer to receive a National. PP5 was an 11.3 metre two door model, which was registered ERM 35K and handed over on 13 March 1972 at the then NBC headquarters in New Street Square, London.

Shortly after that NBC placed a second order, for 520 Nationals. Other business had been secured from municipalities and from the SELNEC and Tyneside PTEs. The Northern General group took a particularly large batch, putting buses simultaneously into service on several routes. Inevitably there were teething problems, exacerbated by the size of the batch, and prompting Marcus Smith to vow never again to put a mass of new buses into one fleet at the same time.

Production built up rapidly in the summer of 1972, and registrations had reached around 500 by the end of that year. It was a creditable performance, but still far short of the factory's capacity of 2,000 units per annum. The offer of 50% Bus Grant, however, was a strong incentive to operators to modernise their fleets, and the National quickly dominated the single-deck bus sector. Two bodybuilders, both major suppliers to BET before the merger into NBC, were particularly hard hit.

Marshalls of Cambridge practically gave up PSV construction and switched most

Marshalls of Cambridge lost a large number of bodybuilding contracts when the Leyland National was introduced. This Leopard, owned by Poole's of Alsager Bank, Staffordshire, carried a Marshall Camair body of the kind which Leyland tried to promote in overseas markets.

The National was shown overseas for the first time when PP7, the left-hand drive prototype, appeared at the 1972 Amsterdam Show.

of its resources to its aircraft division. Leyland tried to help by sub-contracting Marshalls on overseas contracts which called for less sophisticated front or mid engined buses, and also tried to interest two or three countries in setting up manufacturing projects for Worldmaster chassis with Marshalls' distinctive Camair body.

Willowbrook cut back sharply, concentrating on export markets and a limited number of coach bodies. Other domestic bodybuilders fared better. Park Royal, ECW and MCW were all heavily committed to production of double-deck bodywork, demand for which had also risen sharply under the impetus of Bus Grant. Several more years were to pass before those companies would feel the impact of the Workington factory.

Right from the concept stage it was planned to sell the National in export markets. The loss of forecast home market sales, because of the strong swing to one man operated double-deckers, meant that export business became all the more important. PP7 became the first left hand drive National, and made its debut at the Amsterdam Show in 1972.

Ron Ellis talked at that time about the problems of meeting European Economic Community regulations, particularly as there were high hopes of selling into EEC markets. For instance, the swing out at the rear of the Leyland National was not even 10 mm more than permitted under Dutch regulations. (When a long vehicle like a bus pulls away on full lock from a kerbside, the rear overhang 'kicks out' opposite to the direction of travel.) It was too small to illustrate on a graph, but prohibitively expensive to modify on such a highly tooled vehicle. The daughter companies of Netherlands Railways, which were good Leyland customers, were thus never able to take the longer 11.3 metre National.

Speaking to journalists around the time of the Amsterdam Show, Ron Ellis referred to the different regulations in each market about sight lines for drivers. In typically positive fashion, he said: "We put them all in a graph and it ended up looking like a spider's web. What is wanted is one set of regulations for the whole of the European Community and then we can meet their requirements.'

That observation was very telling. At that time, the United Kingdom was not even a member of the European Community therefore, at first glance, it read like a straightforward plea to the European Community to do something about harmonising regulations in the member states. Twenty years on considerable progress had been made, but a large number of anomalies remained. It may well take a further ten years to achieve a much higher degree of harmonisation.

The remark by Ron Ellis also said a lot about Leyland at that time. The company was sales led and was very good at going out and persuading customers to buy its products. The bus and coach range was very wide and there was invariably something which could meet specific overseas market requirements. This frequently meant working with local bodybuilders, who were then largely responsible for ensuring compliance with any local regulations. In the Netherlands, for instance, Leyland had supplied large numbers of Worldmaster chassis, which were bodied by Verheul and others. By the time the National was introduced orders had switched to sets of Worldmaster running units, which were incorporated in locally built integral buses.

The Verheul bodied Leyland Worldmaster was popular in the Netherlands. The National would have been a serious threat to Verheul and would have greatly reduced the Dutch content in the complete bus.

In the late 1960s, when the National was being developed, Leyland paid little more than lip service to marketing as we know it today. It was considered the back shop, supplying a limited amount of information which helped the salesmen in the front shop, so that they could win orders. Marketing was part of the Publicity Department and its activities centred on literature, including comparative analysis of the specifications of Leyland and competitive products.

There was no marketing in the sense of going out to ask customers what they expected in a new product, before it was designed and developed. That applied not just to Leyland, but to much of the European commercial vehicle industry. There was a strong engineering bias in Leyland. Sales and service staff had sufficiently close contact with customers to be aware of many of their needs, and these were reported faithfully to Engineering.

That type of contact worked well when it came to ensuring that any problems with existing products were rectified, and that modifications were introduced, where necessary. A Product Planning Department was established in the very early days of Truck and Bus Division, but it tended to be driven by legislation, which was becoming ever more voluminous, both nationally and internationally.

The lack of customer-directed marketing on the export side was a much more serious problem. For a start, there were only about 20 countries capable of building heavy duty bus chassis or complete integral buses. Another forty or so countries were capable of building bodywork on imported chassis, therefore they had an obvious incentive to save foreign currency and employ local labour. This was illustrated by PP6,

Roll-on roll-off facilities were seldom available for export orders in the 1970s and the vehicles were lifted on by crane as shown. Purpose made lifting brackets were attached to the road wheels, using the wheel studs. The brackets projected far enough beyond the bodywork to keep the slings clear.

which was demonstrated in South Africa, but not one order came from that country, because of the strong local bodybuilding industry. Another important factor was the tendency for countries to protect domestic industries, including vehicle and body building, by levying high import duties on competitive imports.

Of the remaining countries, which had neither chassis nor bodybuilding capabilities, there were only a few which had a need for sophisticated buses, and the money to pay for them. They were hotly contested markets, whenever they came out to tender.

There was a small number of wealthy countries, which might have looked good potential markets, but they considered buses as transport mainly for immigrant workers, and met the need by purchasing cheap truck derived products, including American school buses. This was particularly true in affluent parts of the Middle East.

Early press releases for the Leyland National mentioned how engineers had gone into export markets to talk to operators about their requirements. No doubt they contributed to the technical benefits of the National, like the ease of repair.

This type of research among friends and customers can be flawed. It is based largely on what has already been produced. It can fail to take into account the views of politicians, legislators and others whose decisions can be of vital importance to future product development. The collapse of trade union resistance to one man operated double-deckers, which affected projected sales for the National in Britain, is one such example.

Although a number of left and right hand drive demonstrators went abroad, two early orders graphically illustrated the problem of exporting the Leyland National, in two distinctly different ways. Jamaica Omnibus Services, a subsidiary of BET, ordered 10 early in 1973, soon followed by a major order for 90. All were 10.3 metre models, with a number of modifications, including raised suspension, additional ventilation, half drop windows and fibreglass seats.

Jamaica simply did not have the right terrain for a vehicle as sophisticated as the National. Even in the capital, Kingston, sudden tropical storms can turn roads into temporary rivers. Horizontal rear underfloor engines, remote from the driver, find it hard to live in such conditions. Within ten years, all the Nationals had disappeared, apart from one or two body shells, incongruously remounted on vertical front-engined Albion Clydesdale chassis.

An 11.3 metre demonstrator had been sent to Australia late in 1972. There, it was found that it could not carry a full load of seated and standing passengers, because the gross weight on the rear axle exceeded Australian legal limits. Melbourne ordered thirty 10.3 metre Nationals, and Canberra was extremely interested, but wanted maximum capacity. Leyland developed an interim 10.9 metre long model to meet Australian requirements. It consisted of 1,421 mm modules up to and including the centre exit, followed by two 1,218 mm modules, as used on the 10.3 metre National, and the final standard 812 mm module.

This compromise was not easy to accommodate in the highly automated Workington factory, and so Australian orders went through in batches of four. A further complication was Australia's requirement to have its buses delivered in a completely knocked down (CKD) condition.

In order to fulfil CKD orders the standard practice at Workington was to send the bus through all the body assembly stages. Every hole was drilled, but only every tenth rivet was inserted, until the bus came to the end of the body assembly section. It was then removed from the track. The rivets were broken and the parts were numbered and packed into containers for export.

The fact that all the holes were pre-drilled made overseas assembly extremely simple and foolproof. In that respect it was ideal for CKD markets. Unfortunately, Australian trade unions did not see it that way. They protested that there was much less local content and therefore a threat to their jobs. Similar objections were subsequently raised by other potential markets.

At home, the Local Government Act 1972 had resulted in the creation of two further Passenger Transport Authorities, covering South Yorkshire and West Yorkshire. The former acquired the previous municipal undertakings of Sheffield, Rotherham and Doncaster, while West Yorkshire took over Leeds, Bradford, Calderdale (which incorporated Halifax and Todmorden) and Huddersfield. The territories of the four original PTAs were also extended, in each case acquiring more former municipal fleets.

By 1973 the National was becoming a regular sight in NBC fleets, and was steadily picking up business from municipalities. Plymouth rapidly built up a fleet of sixty, and it was there that one of the more bizarre early incidents with Nationals occurred. The combination of relatively high power, light steering and air suspension seemed to encourage some fairly sporty driving in Plymouth.

As one particular National was driven in a lively manner into and out of a roundabout, a quantity of diesel surged up the neck of the fuel tank, forcing past the magnetic fuel filler cap, which had been designed for quick filling. The diesel spilled onto the road, creating an instant skid pan for a following motor cyclist. Fortunately he survived to tell the tale, but it caused an urgent re-design of fuel tanks, to incorporate internal baffles, and prevent a similar accident.

Although a very small number of Nationals went to independents in Scotland the Scottish Bus Group remained firmly in favour of Leyland's mid-underfloor engined Leopard, usually with a manual gearbox. The Group preferred to have all seats facing forward, because many routes were interurban and rural. Luggage lockers were necessary for parcels, newspaper deliveries and seasonal tourist traffic. That policy decision was a tremendous benefit to Scottish-based Alexander, which was much less affected by Workington than most other bus bodybuilders.

Alexander's aluminium alloy construction had proved itself very durable and resistant to the corrosive effects of the high quantities of salt spread on Scottish roads in winter. Also, there were powerful personalities in SBG who variously favoured front engines, or Gardner engines, and simple manual transmissions, all factors which conspired against the National. Several project vehicles then were created in an effort to broaden the National's appeal.

The Government organised a major transport symposium in April 1973 at the Transport and Road Research Laboratory at Crowthorne, Berkshire, under the theme

The Business Commuter was a design exercise to try to interest the Department of Transport in luxurious commuter coaches, with facilities which could enable an executive to work in comfort during the journey. Note the oversized air-conditioning pod on the rear of the roof, because there was no room to locate condensors and evaporators below floor level. The front section had eight work stations. In the raised rear section, above and behind the rear axle, there was comfortable perimeter seating and a small galley.

'Moving People in Cities'. The Minister of Transport himself was personally involved, along with operators and manufacturers. One of the most inspired exhibits from Leyland was a specially modified National, called the 'Business Commuter'. As the name implies, it was designed to tempt motorists to forsake their cars in favour of a highly personalised form of public transport.

A standard single door 11.3 metre National was equipped as a mobile office, or what later became known as an executive coach. A secretarial unit was fitted over the front wheelarches. The rest of the lower front half of the body was taken up by eight luxurious individual high backed seats, each located alongside a work station, where businessmen could dictate letters, read reports, and so on. The higher rear portion was laid out more sociably, as a lounge area for twelve passengers, with a small servery.

The idea behind the Business Commuter was that it would pick up a group of executives each morning on a regular circuit, alerting each to the imminent arrival of the coach by a paging system. Once they were all on board, the coach would run direct to a city centre, probably with the benefit of bus lanes, occupying far less space than the twenty cars which the businessmen might previously have occupied. It would travel round the city centre, dropping them at their office doors. The whole process would be reversed in the evening, at a cost estimated to be very competitive with a first class rail season ticket.

De-regulation of coach services has enabled some enterprising operators to establish high quality commuter services into London, an example being Kings Ferry of Gillingham, with this integral Mercedes O303.

A lot of clever thought went into the Business Commuter concept, but it failed to capture any political attention. It depended for its success on restricting the use of private cars in city centres, a nettle which no Government was likely to grasp. Secondly, as it would have abstracted business from British Rail, it would have been extremely difficult to win the necessary licences under the regulated route licensing system prevailing at that time.

The Business Commuter concept would be much more relevant today, even though the Government remains unlikely to grasp the much larger nettle of more than double the level of car ownership today. Deregulation of bus services has made it easier for entrants to the market, but operators have shown only limited interest in commuter traffic. The sums behind the Business Commuter project still make sound sense today.

The shining example must be Kings Ferry of Gillingham, which has built a solid business from north Kent towns into London, largely because of the discomfort and unreliability of the British Rail service compared with the high quality coaches offered by Kings Ferry. The coach might not compete with the train on station to station times, but the door to door timing is much more comparable.

Crosville was the first customer for the dual-purpose version of the National. High backed coach seats were fitted, and the normal transverse seats over the front axle could be folded down to form a luggage pen. The vehicle is seen on the 90 mile 'Cymru Coastliner' service, an ideal use.

The Business Commuter had a larger than normal pod on the rear of the roof, to house air-conditioning. When an operator subsequently expressed interest in buying it for PSV use, probably with a higher number of seats, it was found to be substantially over weight on the rear axle. It remained at Leyland and was used as an executive coach for several years.

At the Crowthorne Symposium Leyland also launched a dual-purpose version of the National. There had been criticism that the earliest versions had a very plain interior and that the low backed seats were awfully spartan. Even contemporary coach moquettes were fairly plain! The National had a lively performance and was capable of working on longer interurban routes. It was logical, therefore, to offer a version with high backed semi-luxury seats, while still retaining the standard floor layout.

In order to provide a limited amount of luggage capacity, a suitable pen was built over and around the nearside front wheelarch. The standard bench seat over the offside front was replaced by a modified version which could be folded down to provide additional capacity. The backs of the seats were mounted directly onto chequer-plate, which had a small raised rail round the perimeter. It was capable of carrying up to twenty suitcases without the risk of them falling onto the gangway floor.

Further luggage capacity was provided by overhead racks. They were mounted inboard, clear of the heating and demisting system. The base of the rack was open mesh, making it easy to see whether anything was sitting on the rack. A high 3.76:1 ratio rear axle gave the dual-purpose National a top speed of 64 mph. The anti-roll bar fitted to the front axle ensured a superior ride and handling.

The first examples of the dual-purpose National entered service with Crosville and were used on the lengthy routes linking Chester with North Wales towns. They were among the first buses to leave the Workington factory in a two tone livery, namely white from the windows upwards and a standard NBC green below.

Part of the objective of the Crowthorne Symposium was to make the Department of Transport aware of possible future trends. There were tantalising sketches of a 24 seat 6.7 metre midibus and a 12.8 metre model for airport use, both constructed entirely from standard National sections. A version of the shorter vehicle was actually built, under great secrecy, but never saw the light of day.

The 12.8 metre project would not have been legal on public roads, but offered potential to airlines and airports, at a time when larger capacity jet aircraft like the Boeing 747 were entering service. Because the strength of the National relied to a considerable extent on the ring structure, additional door apertures could be inserted without causing any weakness. Although the 12.8 metre project was never put into production, British Airways bought several batches of Nationals, with centre entry/exit doors on both sides of the vehicle.

By the second half of 1973 production of Nationals had settled down. The factory had cured the remarkably small number of teething problems and the National was attracting repeat orders, not only from NBC, but from several other customers.

During the winter of 1973/74, there was severe industrial unrest in the country, culminating in long and bitter disputes with power workers. Electricity was shut off for several hours a day, and much of industry went on to a three day week.

The main factory complex at Leyland was not seriously affected at first, because it had its own independent power station, installed when the Spurrier works had been built for the Ministry of Defence in preparation for the risk that the Korean war of 1951 could turn into another world wide conflict. Supplies into Leyland, however, soon became severely disrupted and deliveries slipped badly.

Edward Heath's Conservative Government resigned and sought re-election, hoping that the public would support its stand against union militancy. He was about one month late in going to the country. More of the electorate preferred heat and light to political argument and Harold Wilson's Labour Party was returned with a slender majority. In October 1974, Wilson went to the country and was re-elected with an increased and much more workable majority.

During this time British Leyland was running into serious financial troubles. All the profits from Truck and Bus Division were being used to prop up the volume car operations, but it was money down the drain. By December 1974, British Leyland was deeply in debt.

Even before the acquisition of BMH, John Barber had been recruited from Ford as Director of Finance, a position he held from the inception of British Leyland. Admittedly he had a genuine enthusiasm for cars, which was more than could be said for some of the former BMC directors, but he was also held responsible for introducing a bureaucracy which did not fit well with the traditional Leyland methods. Ford ran a business by expecting people to sit at desks and implement written policy instructions. A person who sat at a desk reading paperwork in Leyland was thought to be idling!

While British Leyland needed many of the financial disciplines which came from Ford, it did not need the other plague which came initially from the same place. Right up to 1968 Leyland Motors had an employment manager and a few clerical assistants, and the company prospered. Then British Leyland took on personnel managers who built an enormous empire and eventually disrupted the business to such an extent that decline was inevitable.

They should have served the company discretely and efficiently. Instead, they created a central role for themselves as an integral part of the business, totally above their station, yet remarkably ignorant of the operation of the industry. Every year or two, in order to justify their own positions, they re-organised the business, moving people around like pawns. A major international motor manufacturer was being driven onto the rocks by internal incompetence!

Many loyal and experienced managers in Truck & Bus failed to understand how this could be permitted. Time and time again, Personnel picked people, promoted them, moved them, and fired them, yet they themselves remained in power! As it happened, the Personnel Director was the only director to remain in power at the main Truck & Bus board level throughout the 1970s, and he went on, through Rover, to a senior post in British Aerospace!

A National heads south along 'the longest cul-de-sac' on delivery to PMT in Stoke-on-Trent.

Reverting to the disastrous events of December 1974, there was a great deal of bitterness in Truck & Bus Division. Annual profits in the region of £30-40 million, a sizeable sum in those days, had been diverted to support cars, rather than be re-invested in the business. Ron Ellis was given permission to persuade the Government to pay a nominal one penny for the volume car business, leaving the rest of the Corporation in private ownership.

It was turned down. The whole of British Leyland was nationalised in order to save the business from collapse, rather than for purely political reasons. Only a tiny shareholding, less than one per cent, remained with private holders. On a more positive note, a promise was made that each Division would be examined independently and given a greater degree of autonomy.

Leyland National was already half owned by the state, through National Bus Company, so it became almost 100% nationalised.

CHAPTER SIX

Searching for Markets

The transition of the Leyland National from an engineering project to regular volume production was remarkably smooth. Considering all the new technology and a totally new workforce, buses were soon coming off the line exactly as predicted.

The National was very heavily promoted, with both right and left-hand drive demonstrators. One of the latter was sent to the 21st International Week of the Bus at Nice, in May 1973. This event used to be held annually and was organised principally for coach and tour operators. Around 100 vehicles usually attended. Against much more glamorous opposition, the National carried off four major awards, including the Grand Prix for general safety, the first prize for technical innovation, the Grand Prix d'Honneur for bus bodywork, and a Prix d'Honneur in the technical tests. In the same year, the National became the first bus to receive the coveted Dewar Trophy, which is awarded annually by the Royal Automobile Club for design and safety.

These accolades were a help in promoting the National. It was recognised that the home market was not going to account for more than 800-850 sales per year and accordingly the rest of the factory's capacity would have to be filled by special projects and export sales.

Initially all Nationals had been built with the floor on two levels. The lower level ran from the front entrance to a point immediately ahead of the rear axle, where the optional central exit could be fitted. Then there was an internal step, up to the raised floor in the rear part of the bus, over the axle, engine and gearbox. It was decided to build a single-door prototype with a raised floor throughout, reached by a single step behind the driver's platform.

The prototype was fitted with 48 high backed coach seats, all forward facing, and had small luggage pens at the front. It was called the 'Suburban Express' and exhibited at the Scottish Show in November 1973. It was a deliberate attempt to woo the Scottish Bus Group, which was a committed user of dual-purpose buses. They were not persuaded, partly because of their deep suspicion of rear engines, but also because of the need for rear luggage lockers, mentioned earlier.

In March 1975, the 'Suburban Express' was re-fitted with standard bus seats and sent to CIE for extended evaluation. That was also doomed to failure, not because

The Suburban Express version of the Leyland National had two steps at the entrance and a flat floor throughout. It was originally equipped as shown below with forward facing fixed coach type high-backed seats. Note also the inswung overhead racks.

The vain attempt to interest the Scots in the Suburban Express, above, was followed by an equally unsuccessful attempt with the Irish!

The less attractive re-seated version of the National Suburban Express, photographed before its unsuccessful stay with CIE.

The Van Hool McArdle double-deck design was striking if not, perhaps, to everyone's taste.

of any product problem, but more because of an internal conflict of views within CIE. The Irish national transport operator had responsibility for trucks and trains, in addition to buses and coaches. On the rail side, there was a strong engineering bias towards General Motors, which had supplied quite a range of power units. Some of the rail executives pressed CIE to look at alternatives to Leyland as the main source of trucks and buses.

The troubles in Northern Ireland strained relationships between Britain and Irish Republic, and fuelled the growing pressure within CIE to have buses built entirely in Ireland. Eventually CIE sold its bodybuilding facilities to Van Hool, giving the Belgian company a contract which said that all CIE's buses would in future be bought from Van Hool McArdle, a joint venture, in Dublin. The contract, however, did not place any obligation on CIE to buy buses regularly each year! After three or four years CIE had no money to buy new vehicles and Van Hool had to close the factory, suffering substantial losses.

Leyland also looked at the possibility of increasing the appeal of the National by using the standard body shell and running units, but adapting the interior for special purposes. All these variants were known as 'Super Nationals'. Mike Cornish took on this task and one of the first results was the 'Lifeliner', exhibited at the 1974 Earls Court Show. It was designed as a mobile casualty and communication centre which could be rushed to the scene of any major accident. The interior was fitted out with sufficient medical equipment to enable staff to stabilise the condition of seriously injured people, before transferring them to hospital. It had the same high floor as the Suburban Express, and the space below was used to store oxygen bottles and other heavy equipment.

Mechanically the Lifeliner was completely standard, except that the driver had controls which enabled him to modify the air suspension. By adjusting the valves in each air bellow individually, he could ensure that the vehicle was completely level on rough or uneven ground. The Lifeliner created considerable interest, but was not practical. Health authorities were not willing to pay the substantial cost of a vehicle which would have only limited use at the time of a major incident. They preferred to buy cheap standard ambulances which could take patients straight to much better equipped hospitals.

(Dennis had gone through the same experience two years previously, when it developed an ambulance with a Jaguar 2.8 litre engine, automatic gearbox, independent suspension and a very low floor for loading patients. Ambulance drivers loved it, but the authorities would not pay for it.)

Mike Cornish was responsible for the Super Nationals, and, later, played a major part in the railcar derivitives.

The 'Lifeliner' was a fully equipped mobile medical emergency centre, based on the National. Heavy items like oxygen bottles were stored beneath the floor. Later this vehicle was refitted as a bus and delivered to Midland Red.

Several other Super National concepts were suggested, including mobile banks, libraries, shops, exhibition vehicles, and more specialised versions, like an outside broadcast unit, and a telephone exchange. In all cases, Workington was to be responsible only for the standard body shell and running units. Outside specialists were to be sub-contracted for fitting out the interior.

In fact only a small number of Super Nationals were actually built. Midland Bank bought two 10.3 metre mobile banks in 1975, and the Scottish Prison Service later bought two Nationals which where specially adapted to transport high security prisoners within Scotland. National Travel (South East) bought an executive version, very like the 'Business Commuter', on behalf of the National Bus Company. It was registered JMY 120M and subsequently passed to the Embassy of the USSR.

It was export business which offered the best potential for getting Workington towards its production capacity. There were efforts to sell not just complete vehicles, but even the technology. One such example came very early in the life of the Workington factory. Back in 1966 Leyland had entered into an agreement permitting a Polish company, ZPL, to build the O.400 and O.680 engines under licence. At that time it was thought that both engines were nearing the end of their production lives at Leyland and thus the Polish deal made sound sense. ZPL was an established builder of military equipment, based at Mielec, in the south of the country.

After that operation was up and running, another Polish company, Jelcz, sought technology to enable it to build complete city service buses. There was fierce competition between the Leyland National and the Berliet PR100, which had been launched in 1970. Eventually Jelcz selected the Berliet on the grounds that it had been longer in production and that the practical in-service experience of operators could be verified. Also, the Polish Government wanted some reciprocal trade. The British Government refused to help, but the French were willing to take Polish ham and corn!

Ironically, Berliet had to modify the PR100 to take the horizontal Polish built Leyland O.680 engine. That leads to an intriguing thought. If the Poles had selected the Leyland National, they would have required it to be suitable for the O.680. Had that happened, then the troublesome 510 engine might have gone much sooner than it did!

Another early attempt to sell National technology was equally fascinating. The United States Government was becoming increasingly concerned that cities were being choked by the private car – a familiar story! The Urban Mass Transit Administration was established, with a multi-million dollar budget, and charged with

The Scottish Prison Service Nationals.

AM General acquired rights to build the Canadian Flyer transit bus at South Bend, Indiana.

modernising America's public transport, especially some of the city fleets which had a high age profile and very poor image. UMTA sought tenders for the design of a new generation of city bus. It was made clear that the vehicles would have to be built in the United States, to a width of 8ft. 6in (2,590 mm), but it would have been prohibitively expensive to adapt the National factory to construct buses to different overall widths.

Ron Ellis had known Cruse Moss, the head of AM General, for a number of years. That company was the commercial vehicle arm of American Motors, the fourth and smallest of the American car manufacturers, having been formed in 1954 by the amalgamation of Nash and Hudson. The AM General Division was based in the former Studebaker factory at South Bend, Indiana. The main products were a range of military trucks dating from the Second World War, and local delivery vans, some of which were electrically powered. The principal customer for the vans was the US Post Office.

AM General had earlier reached agreement with Flyer Industries of Winnipeg, Canada, for manufacturing rights to Flyer's diesel and electric city transit buses. Production had started at South Bend in 1972, using body shells supplied from Canada. The Flyer was an old design which was incompatible with UMTA's desire for modern technology. AM General therefore asked Leyland for help and so drawings were prepared, based on the National and its technology.

UMTA reviewed this and several other bids, but was eventually pressed into accepting that low floor buses were unsuitable for American road conditions, particularly the adverse cambers and sharp ramps found in many city streets. ('Low floor', in UMTA terms, was around the 25in of the front section of the National, and not the 12-13in which has been developed more recently by several European manufacturers.) General Motors went on to develop the RTS2, which had some of the features proposed by UMTA, but other than that the project fizzled out.

France joined the export markets for built up Nationals, when six were delivered to Dijon Municipality at the end of 1973. Jamaica Omnibus Services ordered a further sixty 10.3 metre models, and the Australian capital, Canberra, took seventy to the intermediate length of 10.9 metres.

During 1974 a number of detailed improvements was made to the National. It had been found that the original full size roof pod was difficult for maintenance staff to handle, so it was replaced by one which was approximately half the size. The interior trim was modified to reduce windscreen glare. Above all, improvements were made to the seating, which had been criticised on the earliest models, both by the trade press and operators.

Orders from the National Bus Company were running at approximately 500 per year, and nearly all subsidiaries had received at least some by 1975. In several cases, such as Ribble, Crosville and Midland Red, substantial numbers were in service.

In 1974 the Department of the Environment asked Leyland and the National Bus Company to convert a standard bus to battery-electric operation. The solitary 10.3 metre National in the Ribble fleet was chosen for the exercise and converted with a 360 volt traction motor, which had a continuous rating of 120hp.

Battery technology was not so advanced as it is nowadays, therefore Dyson built a two axle trailer, capable of carrying seven tons of batteries. They had sufficient range for fifty miles on a full eight hour charge. Because the vehicle and trailer exceeded maximum length limits, it was put into service on Crosville's Runcorn Busway, which was a dedicated roadway, exclusively for buses. It was a worthwhile experimental exercise, but the severely limited range ruled out further progress at that stage.

The GM RTS2 was a direct result of the Urban Mass Transit Administration's efforts to modernise American public transport systems. GM later sold the design and manufacturing rights to Motor Coach industries who transferred production to a plant in Roswell, New Mexico. Late in 1993, MCI confessed that it could make no money out of bus production and that the RTS2 facility would be sold or closed. Within weeks, DINA, the major Mexican bus manufacturer offered to buy the whole of MCI, not just the RTS2, but also the profitable coach range.

The battery electric National was eventually dismantled to provide body components to repair a badly damaged fellow vehicle in the Crosville fleet.

Above – A locally-bodied Bristol-built B21 seen in New South Wales Australia in 1978.

Upper right – Eastern Coach Works constructed the solitary C27 body on a powered underframe here seen in the Workington factory.

Right – The intake of Nationals into the larger NBC fleets became considerable and provided the opportunity for comparisons such as this. Note the short and long pods on the National 1s and the B series with no pod.

It was proving difficult to hold the important Australian market because the bodybuilding trade unions were objecting to the very high imported content, even in CKD Nationals. As a result, towards the end of 1974, C27 was added to the range. This had a National underframe and running units, also standard National front and rear end assemblies, including glass. The rest of the body was completed by ECW, using its customary aluminium framed body shell. The body was totally conventional, even to the extent of reverting to under-seat heaters instead of the modern overhead system used on the National.

The objective with C27 was to give Leyland a suitable product for those markets which were unwilling to accept completely built up Nationals. Because the underframe was not fully self-supporting, the bodywork had to be constructed carefully to ensure the structural strength of the total vehicle.

Unfortunately C27 turned out to be an orphan. It offered neither significant increases in local man hours which might have made it attractive in certain overseas markets, nor did it have quite the same reassurance of strength and repairability as the complete Workington National. The potential weight saving was only relevant in one or two countries like Australia and New Zealand, where the local bodybuilding industry was capable of building a competitive product.

In the latter half of 1974 the export effort was in full swing. A 10.3 metre two door model was sold for extended evaluation in Peking, now Beijing. It must have been used for several years in normal service, because there were regular orders for spare parts. Leyland worked with the Breda Group to secure an order for 200 Nationals from the Italian city of Genoa, at a time when deliveries from domestic manufacturers were taking well over a year. Fiat, however, applied enormous pressure to Genoa, and the contract was cancelled before any deliveries could commence.

Another illustration of the joys of export came from Cairo, where the Transport Authority went out to tender for 400 buses. Leyland offered to supply the National in CKD form, so that it could be assembled in Cairo, using local labour and some local content, for instance, the interior trim. All was going well until the Americans, probably by way of atonement for their stance in the 1973 Arab-Israeli war, offered Cairo a large fleet of modified Ward school buses on very long credit terms and at minimal interest. I cannot remember the exact figures, but they were something like 30 years at 3%! They turned out to be what the Americans called 'lemons', in other words, of very poor quality and reliability.

The Arab-Israeli conflict caused a dramatic surge in the price of oil, and for a period it looked as though public transport would have to play a much more important role.

One of the Nationals for the Venezuelan contract is hoisted aboard at Tyne Dock, Newcastle. Under the contract, only Venezuelan vessels were used. Sometimes they had cargo hold openings only inches longer than the buses.

It also meant that countries with oil resources had new found wealth, and one of those was Venezuela. The capital city, Caracas, is situated only 20 miles from the tropical Caribbean, but is about 1,000 metres above sea level, lying mainly in a long valley. Bus services were operated by many small companies, mainly using American school buses or truck derived chassis, with local bodywork.

The Caracas State Government was anxious to improve the image of public transport and set up an organisation called 'Inversionista del Transporte' for that purpose. It was intended that this company would buy modern buses and lease them to the operators. The company would also set routes, frequencies, fare scales, and so on. The Venezuelans were attracted to the Leyland National, not only because it was an advanced design, but also because it could be made available on relatively quick delivery. The Leyland sales machine swung into action.

An invitation was sent to every operator to attend an evening presentation on the Leyland National in a large room at the Caracas Hilton. Many operators came along with employees and families. The form of the presentation was a slide show, introducing the National, and showing many of its features. Eddie Brown and Louis Portman were to take the audience through the presentation, but, as neither spoke Spanish, each had an interpreter. It sounds rather dull and ordinary by to-day's standards of audio-visual presentations, but this was 1974, before the era of videos and other modern systems.

The hotel had trouble with the projection equipment but Leyland's Area Sales Manager, Mike Burt, kept the attention of the audience with copious supplies of Cacique, Venezuela's splendid light golden rum. After some delay, the presentation eventually got under way, but because of lost time, had to be made rather quickly. Eddie Brown jumped up and introduced the first slide by saying in English that it showed the new Leyland National. As he sat down, his interpreter shot up and translated into Spanish. Immediately, Louis Portman leapt to his feet to introduce the next slide,

Eddie Brown, the last of the old school of Leyland bus salesmen. He knew what made his customers tick and after hours, organised many a memorable golf competition for the industry.

68

Destination displays were supplemented with a whitewash brush when necessary in Venezuala as seen in this Caracas street scene. Note the 'Pay as you enter' sign, just behind the front entrance. This oversight in the detailed finishing instructions caused great amusement in Caracas.

explaining that the bus had two entrances. As he sat down, his interpreter jumped up, and so on, right through the presentation. After three or four slides, one could feel the rhythm in this show, held in a city famous for its carnivals.

Halfway through it was clear that the audience was greatly enjoying the performance, even if it was missing the finer points of the National in the uproar. It was for all the world like one of those animated demonstrations where four people are used to show the cycles of an engine, with the pistons popping up and down. By the end the Leyland team got a standing ovation. Operators weaved out of the hall into the warm tropical evening, asking if they could bring families and friends the following night! Weeks later, during the pressure of contract negotiations, the Venezuelan team would jokingly offer to concede a minor point if they could have the Leyland National cabaret again!

The Caracas contract was signed in January 1975, and deliveries commenced that summer. All 450 Nationals were 11.3 metre two door models, with the optional 200bhp engine, which was preferable for the city's altitude and operating conditions. Because of the tropical climate, a dual-ventilator unit was specified in place of the normal heater/ventilator. One detail of the specification was not covered quite so carefully. On many domestic market Nationals, there was a small illuminated sign, located beneath the first nearside window, with the words 'Pay As You Enter'. This was faithfully placed by the factory, in English, on the equivalent panel on the Caracas Nationals, much to the amusement of the local citizens, who referred to them as the 'Payazuenta' buses.

The Caracas contract was the largest export order ever received by the Workington factory. The negotiations had been hard, but sometimes hilarious. For instance, I recall sitting in the offices of lawyers in Caracas and asking about the Venezuelan law on a certain point. I will never forget the answer: "What do you want the law to be?" When it came to delivery, all the buses had to be shipped by the state owned Venezuelan carrier. They sent vessels into Tyne Dock at Newcastle, with cargo hold openings which were sometimes only marginally longer than the complete bus. Even so, they were all boarded safely.

When Harold Wilson had inaugurated the factory site in February 1970, he referred to 'convoys of buses going ...to Britain's principal exporting ports'. This was true of the Caracas contract, when up to eighty buses went on a single ship, after weaving through the cities of Carlisle and Newcastle-upon-Tyne. The Caracas contract was the high point of Workington's production. Home market orders were running at a good level and volumes got up to just over 30 per week. At that stage, the factory was very profitable. The highly automated manufacturing system proved to be much more capable of handling the extra business than a conventional labour intensive bodyworks.

The National was picking up other good export orders. Hobart, Tasmania, took sixty-three 10.3 metre models. The availability of the interim 10.9 metre model also enabled Leyland to satisfy the Dutch market, where the longer 11.3 metre version was fractionally excluded by regulations. Netherlands Railways ordered twenty five 10.9 metre Nationals which had a number of modifications to meet Dutch regulations. Most had the characteristic Dutch lantern style windscreen to reduce internal reflections. In addition, they all had roof escape hatches, which were mandatory in the Netherlands, in case a bus crashed into a canal. In the highly standardised Workington factory it was quite difficult to incorporate that feature.

It was hard to sell the National in continental Europe, partly because of the strength of local bodybuilders. Several already worked with Leyland on other chassis like the Worldmaster and Leopard, and they saw the complete National as a threat to their business. Nevertheless, three or four batches were sold to CCFE, a company which had the franchise to run tramways and bus services in the French city of St Etienne. The National also broke into the Norwegian market. A heavier duty floor had to be fitted to combat the effect of snow melting on footwear. Oslo Sporveier ordered three, and twelve were taken by Skoyens Bilcentraler, a large independent operator which had the franchise to run a number of routes in the suburbs of Oslo. The most loyal customer in Norway became a small independent, Vaagsbygdruta, based in the southern port of Kristiansand.

By this time Leyland Truck and Bus Division was running short of rear-engined single-deck chassis. The Panther had been taken out of production at Leyland, because of unacceptably high warranty costs and the Daimler Roadliner had proved disastrous. The AEC Swift was selling principally in Portugal, where UTIC cut the middle out of the chassis and incorporated the remainder into an integral coach structure. Apart from some small orders from British municipalities the Swift was no longer being sold as a low floor bus.

The bulk of chassis output at Bristol had been switched to the double-deck VRT, but the popular single-deck RE soldiered on, selling mainly in Northern Ireland and New Zealand. Both countries had local bodybuilders whom they wanted to protect. In New Zealand's case there was also an eight ton gross limit on the rear axle, which ruled out the National. High frame versions of the RE were also bought by some NBC companies and fitted with luxury coachwork.

By the beginning of 1975 Leyland had developed a separate rear-engined single-deck chassis, known as B21 and incorporating all the National running units. The radiator was relocated from the rear to the front, but otherwise it was pure National. Although stronger than the National sub-frame, B21 still relied on the bodybuilder for total structural strength.

Three very strange Nationals were delivered to British Airways in 1975 for air-side use at Heathrow. The airline had previously bought a number of AECs, specially constructed to be driven end-on to the mobile staircases which were used when aircraft were parked away from the terminal piers.

Wadham Stringer Sparshatt adapted three standard 11.3 metre Nationals which had an additional centre exit door on each side. They converted the driver's compartment to a half cab and rotated the normal front entrance doors through 90º, so that they sat at the top of an entry ramp, located alongside the cab.

In practice the arrangement was not ideal, because the buses had to reverse away from arriving aircraft with passengers on board. British Airways subsequently took many more Nationals, but all were standard models except for the addition of an offside centre doorway. The normal forward-facing seating arrangement was retained at the rear, but full length bench seating was provided on each side of the lower front section, so that a greater number of standing passengers could be carried.

Following the acquisition by the Government of 99% of the share capital of British Leyland at the end of 1974, Lord Ryder was asked by the Government to carry out a thorough review of all aspects of the Corporation's business.

Lord Stokes had resigned. Martin Adeney, in his excellent history of British car makers **(see Bibliography)** hit the nail on the head when he wrote that Stokes was

Below:
Six Bristol-built B21s were bodied by Alexander in Northern Ireland and operated by Ulsterbus. By 1991 they had been withdrawn as non-standard and sold to operators on the mainland.

Bottom:
One of the unusual Nationals for British Airways, modified by Wadham Stringer Sparshatt and designed to drive nose-on to aircraft steps. These were later reconverted to standard configuration.

All the Nationals for the Netherlands were shipped with standard screens, but were subsequently modified to the standard Dutch lantern style, to reduce internal reflections. The first of a batch of twenty-five is seen here before and after modification.

A typical British Airways National showing bench seats and doors on both sides, but without the front end modification seen opposite.

Rennies of Dunfermline took the only 10.9m National to operate in the UK and used it on oil rig contract work.

probably too kind a man to carry out the drastic surgery which the car side needed. John Barber also went immediately, and some Ryder appointees came in.

There was an awful lot of political in-fighting at a senior level. Within months George Turnbull, a popular and respected director, resigned. He took a lucrative contract to set up a car manufacturing plant for the Korean conglomerate, Hyundai, and then came back to very senior positions with Peugeot and the Inchcape Group before his recent retirement and untimely death.

A few months later Ron Ellis was ousted by people who knew little or nothing about the commercial vehicle business. He was seconded to the Ministry of Defence, as Head of Defence Sales, and was knighted on his appointment. He was an even greater loss to the Truck & Bus Division at this time than Lord Stokes, because the latter had been remote from the day to day running of Truck & Bus for ten years. Ron Ellis was the last head of the Division who had grown up with the business and knew every aspect of it.

From shortly after its formation, most of the export business of British Leyland had been conducted through British Leyland International (BLI). Largely through the influence of Stokes and Ellis, however, Truck & Bus Division had retained considerable responsibility for overseas licensees and major sales contracts. As part of the Ryder Review BLI was re-organised, and became almost exclusively responsible for all export activities. Henceforth salesmen were expected to go into a territory and deal with everything from a Mini to a heavy truck or bus. Fortunately the International organisation retained some good people with commercial vehicle experience, but the vital links between customers and factories got entangled in red tape. This was just the kind of fiasco where the Personnel people were in their element, oblivious to the fact that, at the end of the day, customers paid the salaries.

Although jointly owned by National Bus Company Workington was affected by the turmoil. The two years around 1975/76 were both the busiest and the most profitable for the plant, and it never saw the same standardised level of activity again. By way of emphasizing the point, about 35% of the plant's output, in volume terms, was in the first five of its twenty years existence.

A large organisation like Leyland (Truck & Bus) has a certain momentum which carries it through troubled times. Indeed, some of the first indications of nationalisation and the Ryder Report were encouraging, to the extent that the company had solid financial backing and that the Truck & Bus Division would be master of its own destiny. There were promises that profits would be ploughed back into the business and there would be investment in new models and facilities. They were a long time coming!

Smiles of satisfaction from the Transport Minister, John Peyton, and Ron Ellis as they pose for the photographer – the National project was clearly something to be proud of. Only a few months later, however, Ellis was moved to make way for others who knew little or nothing of the business. Leyland's competitors were the main beneficiaries of such internal bungling.

Containerisation brought revolutionary changes to shipping. Three Nationals for Trinidad are seen on flat beds which were designed to lock into a stack of containers – hopefully at the top!

CHAPTER SEVEN

Lost Opportunity

One of the Leyland exhibits at the 1973 Crowthorne Symposium had been a set of sketches of a new generation of double-deck bus. This was intended to replace the Atlantean, Fleetline and VRT, which had been in production for fifteen, thirteen and six years respectively.

Leyland coded the new double-deck project 'B15' and said that it would be offered with one overall length, width, and height, namely 9.56 m (31ft. $4^5/_8$ in.) by 2.5m (8ft. $2^1/_2$in.) by 4.4 m (14ft. 5in.). Following on the successful experience with the National it was decided to make the vehicle fully integral, with particular emphasis on the interior headroom in both saloons being greater than required under legislation. The complete bus concept was a significant potential threat to the traditional bodybuilders, some of whom had previously lost market share to the National.

By this time rear-engined double-deckers had become widely accepted, a situation reinforced by the Bus Grant Scheme, which stipulated that all buses, including double-deckers, must be capable of one man operation. Unlike the National, full size wheels and tyres were to be used, because of the greater gross weight capability. Passenger access and comfort, however, were still very high priorities.

In order to gain the maximum internal headroom, independent front suspension and a drop centre rear axle were specified. Many operators had been apprehensive about full air suspension on the Leyland National, but it had proved extremely reliable and easy to maintain. Air suspension was fitted as standard on B15.

Power was to be provided by a lightly turbocharged version of the 500 series engine, mounted vertically and transversely at the rear. The engine compartment was carefully designed to minimise noise and thus the engine was carried partly by flexible mountings on the frame and partly by tie-bars suspended from the upper deck floor structure. Access for maintenance was through sound-deadened side and rear panels. The radiator was mounted separately in another compartment, above the engine, driven by an electric fan.

Another innovation was the use of a hydraulically operated version of the popular Pneumocyclic gearbox, known as the 'Hydracyclic'. Although the National had full air brakes, B15 was designed with power hydraulic brakes, developed by Lockheed from the system in London Transport's Routemasters. At the time the reasons given were saving in weight and space, especially around the independent front suspension. In fact many B15s were later converted to full air braking.

The B15 underframe was built in a similar manner to that of the National, using Avdelok rivets. The main body shell was a coachbuilt aluminium structure. Leyland had initially thought about building a totally integral product, to the exclusion of other bodybuilders, but had second thoughts during 1974. The National had driven MCW towards Scania, and they were known to be working on a joint double-decker.

The artist's impression of the B15 with its exaggerated perspective.

The first Titan prototype, B15.01, seen on test, carrying bottles of sand to simulate a full load.

The front end of the Volvo Ailsa B55 chassis, showing how it was possible to accommodate a front entrance alongside the compact 6.7 litre turbocharged Volvo engine. The SCG gearbox was mounted remotely in mid wheelbase.

Another and more ominous threat came from a company called Ailsa Trucks Ltd. It had been formed in 1967 by Jim McKelvie, a prominent Scottish haulier who had sold his haulage business, and his partner, Jim Keyden. Their company was the Volvo truck importer and had grown very quickly, because of the great success of the F86 articulated tractor. The partners wanted to offer additional models which would meet the special requirements of the British market, but which could not be built economically on the Volvo production lines in Sweden. With Volvo's approval, they decided to establish an assembly plant at a former ordnance depot at Irvine, on the Ayrshire coast. In addition to trucks they announced plans for a front engined double-deck chassis, using the same small 6.7 litre turbocharged diesel as the F86, mounted alongside the driver on the front platform. It took up little space and complied with Bus Grant requirements.

Known as the Ailsa B55, it had an SCG gearbox mounted remotely in mid-wheelbase. The Scottish Bus Group had been involved in the project, partly because it avoided the complicated engineering inherent in rear-engined layouts. Volvo acquired 75% of the equity in Ailsa Trucks before production commenced and later increased its shareholding to 100%.

It was also known that Dennis was planning to re-enter the full size bus market. The fact that Volvo and Dennis chassis could be supplied to any bodybuilder made Leyland think again about an exclusive in-house product, even though the Atlantean, Fleetline and VRT were available as chassis to any external bodybuilder.

Leyland decided that B15 would be built at the Park Royal factory in north west London, but sought to secure other important customers by entering into licence agreements. Consequently, several meetings were held with Alexander, which had a tight grip on the Scottish market and had expanded into some important fleets in England. There was a similar proposal to enter into an agreement with Northern Counties, in order to secure business from Greater Manchester. Neither agreement was concluded, and efforts were concentrated on the production of five prototypes at Park Royal in 1975/76.

In June 1977 Leyland announced production plans for B15 and confirmed that it would be sold under the model name 'Titan'. By this time it had been decided not to proceed with the 500 engine. The standard production options were the Gardner 6LXB, or the Leyland L11, which was a development of the O.680. At the time the Titan had little connection with the National, although it was later to play an important part in the Workington story.

The phasing out of the Fleetline and Atlantean gave cause for concern with many operators who did not wish to be involved with the more sophisticated, and more expensive, Titan. Dennis stepped in and produced a straightforward rear-engined chassis, the Dominator, which they hoped would be attractive to such customers. They had recruited Bob Crouch, ex Daimler, from BL for just this purpose. One of Greater Manchester's prototypes is seen parked outside Leyland's test centre where it would be given the 'once-over' by Leyland engineers.

A number of detailed improvements was introduced on the National in April 1976, in what was known as the phase II version. There had been complaints from drivers and operators that the front end was too light, causing unladen Nationals to skid in wet and icy weather. Ease of driving and lively performance were probably contributory factors. Several operators had made their own small favoured modifications and some of these were built into phase II.

On a larger scale, Northern General had previously modified an accident damaged National by moving the batteries forward and reducing weight at the rear. In the phase II National weight distribution was improved by relocating the batteries from the rear

The last two Fleetline chassis were bodied by Eastern Coach Works. By that time the rectangular Leyland badge had been introduced as seen in the view above, and should have been complemented by the matching Fleetline badge. Old loyalties die hard and whilst the Leyland badge was dutifully attached the Daimler scroll was also fixed in its normal place. Just to complete the confusion the BL badge was also attached! They entered service in 1981.

Both Tehran and Baghdad were important markets for double-deckers. A typical Park Royal bodied Atlantean is seen in the Iraqi capital. The double-decker offered high passenger capacity without the greater capital cost and mechanical complexity of the articulated single-decker.

to a pull-out tray under the driver's compartment. This removal enabled the fitment of more sound-deadening material in the engine compartment, to comply with impending European legislation.

For the same reason the already excellent braking system was modified. EC Directive 71/320 required separate air reservoirs for the front, rear and parking brakes. A number of internal improvements was made, including modifications to the handrails and the adoption of anti-reflective interior trim. The prototype Phase II National entered service with the Bristol Omnibus Co, and an important order came from London Transport for fifty-one 10.3 metre models.

The British bus industry was still suffering a significant knock-on effect from the industrial strife of the winter of 1973/74. There were long delays in deliveries of conventional buses, particularly double-deckers. At first, the problem was principally due to shortage of chassis, and part of that was caused by the transfer of Daimler Fleetline production from Coventry to Leyland.

It has been suggested in the past that Leyland made a shambles of transferring Fleetline. In fact Lofty England, then Managing Director at Jaguar, had told Stokes that he needed the space occupied by Fleetline assembly to produce more cars. Daimler landed Leyland in a real mess. Many of the jigs and tools which came up from Coventry were in a dreadful state and it quickly became necessary to re-tool for Fleetline production at Leyland. Once that was done, production rose significantly.

Leyland had largely succeeded in reducing the shortfall by 1976, despite having won major export orders for double-deckers from Iran, Iraq and Hong Kong. Ironically, the bodybuilders were unable to handle the increased flow. Large numbers of chassis started to accumulate outside their premises, waiting to enter their assembly lines.

The Workington factory benefited from this imbalance and gained a number of small but nevertheless important orders from customers who could not wait for double-deck deliveries. Because the National was such a highly standardised product, it was quite easy to juggle with the programme and accommodate urgent orders. It also helped that National Bus Company was the partner in the plant and would accept occasional arrangements of this kind!

NBC continued to be the biggest customer, placing orders for 593 Nationals for delivery in 1977. Over 85% were longer 11.3 metre models and a high percentage had single doorways. London Transport ordered a further 160 10.3 metre models and, at the end of the year, the first order was taken from the Scottish Bus Group. Around this time some work which had previously been done externally was brought into Workington in order to retain added value. Mostly, it was fabrication.

A Series B National operating in the Ribble fleet. The model was immediately distinguishable by the absence of the rear roof pod.

The relatively simple and straightforward Bristol Eastern Coach Works models, like this LH, were phased out to be replaced by the National Series B although the latter was clearly a more sophisticated and expensive vehicle. Low volume manufacture was, and still is, expensive in the bus industry. There were compelling reasons for maximising production at Workington.

The National range was extended in March 1978 by the addition of the Series B. This was a lighter and simpler version of the National and was intended to fulfil two main functions. It was seen as a suitable replacement for the Bristol LH, which was being phased out of production, NBC finding that light buses were less economic over their whole life.

The Series B was offered only at 10.3 metres and was powered by a derated version of the 510 engine, producing only 150bhp. The sophisticated heating and ventilation system of the standard National, which was thereafter known as the Series A, was replaced by under-seat heaters and a separate heating/demisting unit for the driver. The interior trim was simplified and weight was reduced wherever possible. The price was set about 10% below that of a Series A National and production commenced in the summer of 1978.

The series B was intended principally for rural routes and could be distinguished from the series A by several features. Apart from the obvious absence of the roof pod, the series B had external access apertures instead of flaps, and a simpler and less comprehensive interior lighting system. Ribble took the prototype, and Crosville the first production models. The largest customer for the Series B, however, became London Country Bus Services, which eventually accumulated 166.

The export side was now starting to fall victim to inter-divisional bureaucracy. Frequently, Truck & Bus Division executives, who knew the bus business, could not get access to potential customers, because of the policies of British Leyland International. The finance department had grown enormously, but that was a mixed blessing. Certainly Truck & Bus now knew its costs much more accurately, but equally, youngsters were crawling over every proposed deal, and that was a decade before Nigel Lawson's derisory remark about "teenage scribblers". International competitors were starting to secure business before Leyland had a man into the territory.

Many of the finance people had been recruited from the Ford Motor Company which was more rigidly disciplined and less entrepreneurial than Leyland. They had been trained in cost accountancy on specific components on cars, like the Ford Cortina, and could not relate to the international commercial vehicle business. In many cases prices in international tenders had to be very competitive, but buses always provided a good long term pay-back in sales of spare parts.

There had been some use of lightweight Bedford and Ford models for bus work, and although this was fading by 1978, the series B National was intended to appeal to this section as well as users of the Bristol LH. These Willowbrook bodied Fords were operating for Trent in 1976. Ford ceased production of bus and coach chassis in 1981, Bedford finally withdrew from the market in 1986.

NBC's intake of the National 2 model was quite low, largely because the Market Analysis Project revisions of bus routes had put more emphasis on intensive use of double-deckers. It was also partly because most subsidiaries had modern single-deck fleets and the rate of replacement would have slowed, even without the withdrawal of Bus Grant. Sales elsewhere were insufficient to keep the factory busy but some notable orders included this former SBG model, seen here operating in Carlisle in 1990 after transfer.

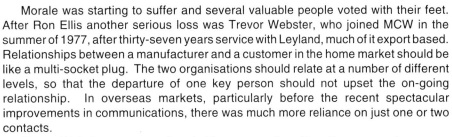

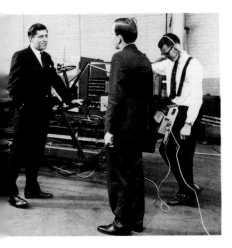

Trevor Webster, seen here in a BBC2 interview, was popular with colleagues and customers alike. His departure was a serious loss to Leyland Vehicles.

Morale was starting to suffer and several valuable people voted with their feet. After Ron Ellis another serious loss was Trevor Webster, who joined MCW in the summer of 1977, after thirty-seven years service with Leyland, much of it export based. Relationships between a manufacturer and a customer in the home market should be like a multi-socket plug. The two organisations should relate at a number of different levels, so that the departure of one key person should not upset the on-going relationship. In overseas markets, particularly before the recent spectacular improvements in communications, there was much more reliance on just one or two contacts.

Trevor Webster was exceptional. He was popular with colleagues and was very well known to many important customers, both at home and abroad. On the way to the UITP Conference and Exhibition in Montreal he found himself in the company of Harold Sansom, Chairman of MCW, who persuaded him to leave Leyland. His move was widely interpreted by customers as a strong sign that there were problems at Leyland, but he was frustrated by ever-increasing levels of bureaucracy.

Despite his sadness at leaving Leyland after 37 years service, he fought fairly for his new employers. Marcus Smith had moved from Workington to take responsibility for all the bus factories, and his place in Cumberland was taken by John Battersby, who had previously been at DAB in Denmark. When the SMMT formed a PSV Sub-Committee around 1977 it was Smith and Webster who joined forces in an attempt to persuade the operating industry to forecast future requirements for new buses.

Workington gained further small export orders from Vaagsbygdruta in Norway and from CCFE of St Etienne. The Caribbean area continued to produce substantial orders when fifty Nationals were sold to Trinidad. Despite the high humidity in this part of the world the National's anti-corrosion system proved superb. Demonstrations were made to several other countries.

Following the Portuguese revolution in 1975 many of the country's bus operators were nationalised, becoming part of an organisation known as Rodoviaria Nacional. Several of those operators were shareholders in UTIC, which for many years had been AEC's importer, and which was one of the few AEC agencies to take on a full Leyland commercial vehicle franchise after the merger. In this way, 60% of UTIC came to be state owned.

The new socialist government wanted to modernise the country's bus fleets and a National demonstrator spent several months in Lisbon. The plan was to build CKD Nationals, but that would have meant a considerable reduction in work through the UTIC factory. Because of that, and a lack of funds, the project was dropped.

From Lisbon that National demonstrator moved across the Straits of Gibraltar to Morocco. There, the largest vehicle manufacturer was Berliet Maroc. Although that company had been set up as a subsidiary of Berliet, the French manufacturer, Leyland had very strong connections with the Moroccans. Berliet could only supply trucks over 16 tonnes gross. In the 'sixties, when the Moroccans wanted a lighter truck, they entered into an agreement with the Bathgate factory for a bonnetted model which was shipped CKD and assembled in Casablanca with a locally built Berliet style cab.

By the mid 1970s sales of the Bathgate derived models were far outstripping those of the heavier trucks sourced from France. Although Berliet had by then become part of the Renault Group, which had a range of light trucks, Berliet Maroc resisted all attempts to make them switch. Indeed, the Moroccans, proud and competent people, enjoyed being in the position where they were courted by two powerful international manufacturers.

Leyland was more keen than Renault to increase the levels of local manufacture in Morocco and therefore became involved in two projects, one for agricultural tractors and the other for buses. The National demonstrator worked well, both in Casablanca and Rabat, but there was strong pressure from local bodybuilders who saw a threat to their traditional business. Once again the National failed to be acceptable because it was impossible to reach sufficient local content.

Government and transport officials examine a National demonstrator at Rabat, Morocco. Although it performed well, it was too much of a threat to domestic bodybuilders.

Another interesting approach came from the former USSR in 1978. The country was gearing up to host the 1980 Olympic Games and was considering how to update the Moscow transport system. I had to conduct negotiations with the Russian Trade Delegation in Highgate, London, and an 11.3 metre two door National was built for them late in 1978. It had the heavier duty flooring of the Norwegian specification and additional heating and insulation.

There was talk about setting up an assembly operation, but that would have been impossible within the time constraints for the opening of the Games. In the end additional buses were supplied by Ikarus of Hungary, which was the largest bus manufacturer in the world, until the liberalisation of Eastern Europe and the loss of the huge Russian bus contracts, under which Hungary and Ikarus had to supply about 8,000 buses annually to pay for Soviet troops garrisoned on Hungarian soil!

Normally when any model was delivered to a market for the first time, Leyland sent a service engineer to give essential training and ensure that the vehicle was properly commissioned. The Russians politely refused this offer and made one or two technical enquiries through their company in Letchworth which imported Belaz dump trucks. After a few months nothing more was heard of the bus.

At home Leyland was making plans to abandon the 500 series engine. It had cost the company many thousands of sales in the heavy truck sector of the market and had enabled continental manufacturers like Volvo, Scania and Mercedes to become very firmly established.

The solitary Russian National stands below the Plant Director's office before leaving for Moscow.

The 510 engine was not quite so vulnerable at the lower power ratings in buses. Many units achieved reasonably high mileages, provided they were carefully maintained. It would have been totally impractical, however, to continue producing the horizontal 510 version only for buses. At best the 510 was tolerated by bus operators, but it was never a popular engine. Many would have preferred an alternative, Gardner being the most frequent request. Even among the sales staff there was no enthusiasm for selling the engine, because of its reputation. The solution was to update the venerable O.680 engine which, after all, formed the basis of very reliable power units for Scania, DAF, Mack, Pegaso and the Polish licensee! Some changes were necessary, to comply with forthcoming noise and emissions legislation, but the normally aspirated L11 was ready in 1977 and the turbocharged TL11 followed about two years later.

Ribble took the first Leyland National 2, fitted with the more popular and reliable 680 engine. It is seen here at the 1978 Motor Show alongside one of the few Titans to be delivered to a customer other than London Transport. The Titan's sluggish start to life was boosted by transfer to Workington. It was the introduction of that model to the Cumberland plant which ended, once and for all, the concept of a one-product factory.

David Burnicle, Leyland's Technical Director, 1977-1986. He still has the great gift of explaining technical complexities in everyday English.

This change in policy meant that the National had to be re-engineered. During 1977 Ribble had fitted an O.680 engine in a Phase II National and found it quite a complicated task. The 11.1 litre O.680 engine was considerably bulkier than the flat 510. Leyland then converted another National, with a turbocharged 680 engine, and launched it at the 1978 Motor Show as the National 2. This prototype retained a rear mounted radiator and was therefore externally indistinguishable from the standard Series A.

By the late 1970s Leyland had become more skilled at marketing, through a combination of internal staff and external consultants. They believed that there was potential to sell completely built-up buses in certain tropical markets, particularly in the Middle East. The 500 family engines had been unsatisfactory in high ambient temperatures.

The O.680 engine with the help of heavy duty radiators had proved capable of operating in several very hot markets, such as Iran and Iraq, although the fan drive shaft was prone to failure. In such countries many vehicles stopped running from around noon to 4pm while drivers and passengers rested in the hottest part of the day.

David Burnicle, at that time Engineering Director for buses, contributed the following paragraphs to the story: 'The move to front radiators was mostly my doing. When we started rationalising the very mixed bag of bus products to come up with a smaller but much more flexible range we found a lot of inadequacies in the cooling systems. Fleetlines suffered radiator fouling in Hong Kong. Nationals in Jamaica needed a high speed fan drive to cool effectively. This drive was mechanically unreliable and also overheated the posteriors of rear seat passengers!'

'All this and we had to cater for engines which were physically large like the Gardner 6LXB and prepare for the next round of drive-by noise legislation with its possible need for heavy enclosures (6LXBs and O.680s were also not the quietest engines around).'

'So we decided that the best position for the water-to-air heat exchanger was at the front where it met the fastest, coolest, cleanest air and hence used minimum fan power. It also helped weight distribution, nicely separated noise sources, gave more working space in the engine compartment and was easier for bodybuilders to accommodate than side mounted or high mounted radiators. We took care to use as many common parts as possible to help operators of mixed fleets.'

There was also Bristol's good experience of front mounted radiators on the VR. It had a thermostatically controlled fan which came on infrequently, even in intensive city operation, admittedly with the cool-running Gardner engine.

Moving the radiator to the front of the National necessitated a redesign of the front-end structure to a more bowed style, incorporating windscreens which were already used by DAB in Denmark. These were more curved than the almost flat screens of the National 1 and therefore helped to reduce internal reflections. As a result, the overall length was increased by 300 mm, taking the two standard models to 10.6 and 11.6 metres respectively.

At first there was some resistance to front mounted radiators from sales staff and customers who argued that international competitors managed perfectly well with rear mounted radiators. The front layout involved long pipe runs under the floor and the

occasional intrusive noise of the fan into the driving and passenger areas. Having said that, it has to be admitted that Leyland's cooling problems disappeared.

On the National 2 it was decided to use the same rack and pinion power steering system as the Titan. The front and rear axle capacities were increased from $4\frac{1}{2}$ and 10, to 6 and 11 tons, respectively.

The former Series A and B specifications gave way to 'Standard' and 'Heavy Duty'. The Standard specification was built around the normally aspirated 680/L11 engine, developing 170bhp at 2,000rpm. It also had the close ratio Pneumocyclic gearbox and a floor mounted heating system.

The heavy duty option had the more powerful TL11 engine, developing 214bhp at 2,000rpm, coupled to a fully automatic version of the Pneumocyclic gearbox. It retained the roof mounted heating and ventilation system, and the larger 100 amp alternator. In practice customers were able to pick and mix between the two specifications, and could take any which had Engineering approval.

The first true National 2 prototype was built in the spring of 1979 and was a left hand drive two door model. It was first demonstrated in June at the UITP Conference and Exhibition in Helsinki. All the vehicles were on open air stands, in glorious sunshine, outside the Finlandia Hall.

Immediately after that, it returned to Britain and was converted by Willowbrook, who added a third doorway, in the bay immediately behind the front axle. The bus was intended for demonstration in Saudi Arabia, where women and children, who travelled less frequently than men, were accommodated in a small front compartment consisting of the transverse seats over the front wheel arches. Behind that, there was a full width partition. Men entered and left the bus by the two rear doorways.

The first launch of a proper National 2 on the home market came at the Scottish Show in November 1979, when a 10.6 metre model was exhibited in a modified version of the red and grey livery of Highland Omnibuses. Registered FAO 927V, this bus returned to Leyland and was used by Engineering on development work.

In October 1977, after several more suitable candidates had turned down the post, Michael Edwardes was appointed Chairman of British Leyland. A voluble little man, fond of promoting himself on television, he spent the bulk of his time in badly needed confrontation with

Production Mark 2 versions of the National had the more rounded screens developed by DAB in Denmark and were therefore 300mm longer.

The first left-hand drive National 2 was exhibited at the UITP Conference and Exhibition in Helsinki in 1979, then hastily converted by Willowbrook with a third door, before demonstration to Saudi Arabia.

the trade unions in the car plants, culminating in the much publicised dismissal of 'Red Robbo' from Longbridge.

Edwardes visited Truck & Bus Division only rarely, but started to implement the Government's policy of making clearer distinctions between the businesses. The Division became a separate legal entity, under the much simpler name of Leyland Vehicles Ltd.

The new company was then divided into its principal businesses, resulting in the creation of a Passenger Vehicle Division in 1978. This became responsible for the Workington factory, Bristol, ECW, Park Royal and Roe.

Marcus Smith was appointed Managing Director and surprised many people when he decided to move the headquarters of the operation to a suite of offices which had been refurbished hastily on the front of the AEC site at Southall. I became his Export Director, working with a semi-redundant British Leyland International. The choice of Southall was quite logical. It was closer to Bristol, Park Royal and ECW, and also much easier for international customers who were more likely to visit London than Leyland. Some of the antagonism to the move was simply the old rivalry between Leyland and AEC!

Passenger Vehicle Division was given responsibility for selling bus and coach chassis produced by Leyland and AEC, but there were still internal problems with BLI, particularly with truck derived chassis, like the popular Clydesdale and Viking range from the Albion factory in Glasgow. Even so, as recently as 1979, Leyland was the largest producer of buses and coaches, including chassis, in Western Europe!!

Leyland's Danish subsidiary was leader in its home market. Bodywork was built with Alusuisse sections. This articulated city bus for the major operator in Copenhagen shows the screens which were adopted for the National 2.

The Albion built Clydesdale and Viking models were major export earners. This special Clydesdale was bodied in Singapore by Chua Heng Industries for operation on services between Hong Kong and southern China. The short front and rear overhangs were to suit ferries on tidal rivers.

Among the grand schemes devised in Edwardes' early months was the possibility of a full scale merger between British Leyland and Renault. Both companies were nationalised and both had enormous problems, but it was thought that some savings could be gained by rationalising product ranges and factories. Marcus Smith, Brian Heath, one of the senior engineers, and I were deputed to look at Renault's bus and coach facilities.

They were based in the former Saviem factory at Annonay, and in part of the sprawling factory which Berliet had built at Venissieux, in the eastern suburbs of Lyon. We noted that the French had a well protected home market. Renault's range of buses was so distinctive that it was difficult to sell into France against them but, equally, it meant that their export markets were very limited. They suffered the same problem of resistance to fully built-up imports.

Both Renault and Leyland had over-capacity for bus and coach production. As far as I know, discussions never reached the stage, but, if there had been a merger, at least one important bus factory in France or Britain would surely have been closed. Knowing the French propensity for making the rules and the British tendency to obey them, Workington might well have been at risk.

Edwardes also courted Fiat. In 1973/74, Ron Ellis had met his counterpart at Fiat on several occasions, when there was talk about Leyland becoming one of the founder members of Iveco, along with Fiat, which included OM in Italy, Unic in France, and Magirus Deutz, based at Ulm in Germany. Those talks broke down, because of failure to agree on respective shareholdings.

The long running Saviem SC10, with its engine mounted horizontally under the driver, would have been under threat if Leyland and Renault had merged.

That was unfortunate, because the plan was to turn Iveco into a truly pan-European commercial vehicle manufacturer. This has been achieved. At the time of writing Iveco has factories in France, Germany, Italy, Spain and the United Kingdom and is a major force in Europe.

Edwardes revived the talks with Fiat and Iveco in 1978, and they came so near to fruition that Des Pitcher, who had succeeded Ron Ellis, was halted at Milan airport when on his way to sign an agreement. Leyland would have become a member of Iveco and Workington would almost certainly have been developed as the main bus factory.

At that time Iveco had only a comparatively small bus plant in Milan and relied heavily on external bodybuilders. Magirus had a modest bus factory at Mainz. The Workington plant could have had access to Iveco engines and other running units, and to the Italian and German markets. It would have been able to reach its capacity of 2,000 units per annum and would have been very profitable. That was a really serious lost opportunity, because it would have put Workington in a very strong position.

Within a couple of years of the deal falling through, Iveco built a large bus factory at Valle Ufita, in the south of Italy, inland from Naples. Although not as highly automated as Workington it was similar in size and also relied heavily on labour saving tooling and methods.

The reason for the failure to reach a deal with either Renault or Iveco was said at the time to be Edwardes' concern about loss of sovereignty, but maybe he was told to take that line by the almost exclusive shareholder, the British Government!

CHAPTER EIGHT

Diversification

When Margaret Thatcher and the Conservative party won the election in June 1979, the United Kingdom was in a mess. Inflation was rampant. It was not easy to go to the likes of London Transport five or six times to tell them that the contract price had risen, even before the first bus had been delivered! Another serious problem was the strength of the trade unions. They, and poor management, had turned the car side of British Leyland into a variety show joke.

It can be very wearing to work for a company which is the constant butt of press criticism. In the late 'seventies the *Daily Mail* was one of the worst offenders. They sniped constantly at the company, often reporting what they wanted to print, and not the fully balanced facts. Eventually the *Daily Mail* went too far and had to pay substantial libel damages to two senior executives.

Fortunately, the unions remained comparatively reasonable in the commercial vehicle factories, with one or two notable exceptions. The worst problems occurred at Park Royal. At one time it had been a very profitable factory, but there were many industries in the area, all competing for skilled labour.

The Titan was re-launched in June 1977, when it was ready to go into production. Leyland said that the first 100 units would be built at Park Royal, but thereafter production would be transferred to a facility at AEC, Southall. The Chairman of the Greater London Council's Transport Committee announced that Leyland and a consortium of major operators, including London Transport and the National Bus Company, planned to build the Titan at Southall in a joint venture.

The news caused considerable unrest at Park Royal and production of an initial order for 250 Titans from London Transport got under way extremely slowly. At that time Park Royal was building not only Titans, but also conventional bodywork on Atlantean chassis for Greater Manchester and on Fleetlines for West Midlands, having just completed the last of an order for 400 Atlanteans for Baghdad.

The AEC factory was itself under the microscope. Following the commitment under the Ryder Report to re-invest in the commercial vehicle business, it was decided to build a major vehicle assembly plant at Leyland, where land and skilled labour were readily available. Nobody actually said so at the time, but it was large enough to replace most other truck assembly lines in the company.

Production of Titans under way at Park Royal. The riveted construction was a carry over from the National, but the assembly methods were much more conventional and less highly tooled.

At Southall there was severe competition for skilled labour, particularly as Heathrow Airport was only five miles away. Much of the centre of the site was an open sports ground, protected by 'Green Belt' legislation and surrounded mainly by quite old buildings. There was no room on the site for expansion. By October 1978, it was announced that the AEC factory would be closed down, once orders on hand had been fulfilled. That announcement did nothing to improve the industrial relations atmosphere at Park Royal. Titan production was painfully slow, to the extent that other customers were cancelling orders. They included Greater Manchester which eventually took only fifteen out of an order for 190, and West Midlands which received five out of an order for 80.

Part of the problem was that management wanted the right to have some parts of the Titan assembled by semi-skilled, or dilutee, labour, which had proved perfectly capable of building the Leyland National. The trade unions at Park Royal refused to accept dilutees, therefore it was ultimately agreed that the factory would be closed. A redundancy and productivity deal was then negotiated with the workforce, following which production increased amazingly. The balance of London Transport's order for 250 was completed in May 1980.

This was a very difficult time at Leyland. Des Pitcher had resigned as Managing Director of Leyland Vehicles Ltd and his place was taken by David Abell, who dealt in numbers, rather than people. He was responsible, *inter alia*, for the resignation of Marcus Smith in the summer of 1979. That was another very serious signal to Leyland's bus customers, because they lost a man of great integrity who knew their business inside out. Soon afterwards he took up a senior position with London Transport. His successor as head of the Passenger Vehicle Division was Ken McIver, who had risen through the financial side of the company, but lacked the operating industry experience which had made Marcus Smith so acceptable. McIver came in at a very difficult time and was promoted by people above him who had little feeling for the truck industry, and even less for buses. Ten to fifteen years before Leyland had built its reputation on buses. Now they were rapidly becoming a sideline.

Once the decision to close Park Royal had been announced, Leyland looked at various alternatives for continuing production of the Titan. After all, apart from engineering costs, over £700,000 had been invested in jigs and tools. In December 1979 it looked as though agreement had been reached to extend the Eastern Coach Works factory at Lowestoft. News of these talks reached Workington where Ken Hargreaves held discreet talks with the unions. They knew that the ECW union committee was difficult and would almost certainly be demanding cash and other concessions. The Workington men said that they would be willing to build Titan without any change to existing conditions.

Help had also come from Leyland. Towards the end of the Park Royal days a Titan underframe was assembled at Leyland in the old bodyshop. With carefully designed bracing it was taken to Workington on a flat-bed truck, where it was studied very carefully. The Workington plant staff soon decided that they could do the underframe and mechanicals, as well as the bodywork. Their willingness was conveyed to McIver who terminated the faltering discussions with ECW by telling them that Titan would go to Workington!

Ken McIver , Managing Director of Leyland Bus 1979 - 1985.

The first production Titan for London Transport, built at Park Royal, together with one of the prototype models from the same factory showing the distinctive asymmetric rear.

The Titan became a key model in Leyland's fortunes. Union intransigence saw it leave Park Royal, only to be rejected by ECW, resulting eventually in the closure of both factories. It then caused a fundamental change in the thinking at Workington, bringing to an end the one-product plant. While the Titan assembly shop was being added to the original factory, the first production models were built in a small advance unit across the road. Part of the cladding had to be removed to let them out!

Leyland, DAB and Saurer combined to build this articulated bus which was demonstrated in Sheffield on its way home from the UITP Conference in Montreal in 1977. Saurer contributed a higher powered engine, heavy duty rear axle and turntable technology. Note the continental Trilex wheels.

That decision marked a major turning point in Workington's history. It had been built as a highly automated plant, to manufacture one product, using the most advanced techniques available. The introduction of Titan was not only a second product, but one built in more traditional ways, with a much lower capital investment.

A new factory of nearly 9,000sq m was built alongside the existing National plant, at a cost of £4 million. It was built at the rear of one end of the oblong main factory, making an 'L' shaped structure. The space between the test centre and the boiler house was also filled in to create an area for assembling Titan's underframe. Nearby a vacant factory was leased for the storage of parts, jigs and equipment, which were transferred from Park Royal when Titan production ceased. Some further engineering work was done, to enable Titan to be assembled by semi-skilled labour, thus introducing working practices compatible with those on the National. Pilot production commenced in the temporary facility while the new factory was being erected.

The term 'semi-skilled' when applied to a workforce is somewhat misleading and should not imply lower levels of skill. In most of the Leyland Vehicles factories the majority of the workforce had served apprenticeships in their skills and were therefore known as 'skilled ' or 'time-served'. Although this should have enabled them to turn their hands to a wide variety of work,in practice many carried out the same function, day in, day out.

When it became more difficult to recruit skilled workers, especially in areas which might not have had a tradition in the required crafts, people were given short intensive training courses in a very limited range of skills, hence the description 'semi-skilled', or the somewhat derogatory term, 'dilutee'. At Workington they proved to be very competent, and their range of abilities could be increased by further training courses.

The specification of the Titan was tailored to the needs of London Transport. With its aluminium alloy structure and power hydraulic brakes, there was obvious continuity with the very popular Routemaster. On the other hand, it was very different from the all-steel integral National.

The people at Workington were very proud of their achievement on Titan. It took almost exactly one year from the date of the decision until the first Titan came off the line in the new extension. In that time, short by motor industry standards, the new extension was built and equipped, including the transfer of many jigs and tools from Park Royal. Additional workers were recruited and trained in the temporary facility.

In addition to the hydraulic braking, there were two other features which tended to restrict Titan's popularity. The fixed overall height of 4.39 m (14ft. 5in.) was not acceptable to many NBC and SBG fleets, where 4.16 m (13ft. 8in.) was the standard. Secondly, many customers still had loyalty to traditional bodybuilders, including many of the NBC fleets which preferred Eastern Coach Works, and Scottish and other operators with Alexander. Throughout 1979, while the future of Titan was being decided, Workington continued to produce the National 1. Towards the end of the year, part of the factory was closed for two weeks so that it could be re-tooled for volume production of the National 2.

Workington also became involved in another fascinating project, an articulated single-decker. They were popular in continental cities, where they were advocated as

the best way of moving large numbers of passengers. Very few cities on the continent are suitable for double-decked vehicles, because the infrastructure had developed over the years to a general maximum height around four metres. Leyland had access to articulated technology through its DAB subsidiary in Denmark and had exhibited a left-hand drive DAB artic at the UITP Conference in Montreal in 1977.

That bus visited Britain on its return journey and was demonstrated to a number of cities. At the time articulated buses were not legal on public roads in Britain, but it was expected that they would become so, because of impending harmonisation with European legislation. The city which showed most interest was Sheffield, where one busy route offered a variety of operational challenges.

South Yorkshire PTE gained Government dispensation to carry out a two year programme to assess the potential for articulated buses. The order for ten buses was split equally between MAN and Leyland. MAN supplied right hand drive versions of its standard West German city bus. Leyland took five mid-engined articulated chassis from DAB. They had horizontal turbocharged O.680 engines and ZF fully automatic gearboxes.

They were then delivered to Workington, where the bodywork was assembled, using a very high proportion of standard National components. Because the DAB chassis was about 170 mm higher than the National underframe a three step entrance was necessary. In order to compensate for this difference in height, spacers were added above each of the doors and deeper skirt panels were fitted all round.

The first of these buses was exhibited at Helsinki at the 1979 UITP exhibition and all five entered service with South Yorkshire PTE shortly thereafter. The Department of Transport eventually accepted articulated buses, and they were certified for fare paying service. Unfortunately an industrial dispute at South Yorkshire meant that they could not be further used there. They were subsequently resold and turned up in various parts of the country with a succession of operators during the 1980s.

British Airways took seven very similar vehicles in 1980 for airside use. They had three doors on the nearside and two on the offside and were assembled at the Roe factory, using National components.

A Leyland DAB artic with National bodyshell in service in Sheffield. After successful trials, carrying passengers without charge under the terms of the dispensation, Department of Transport permission was given for normal operation. The vehicles were sent to Roe for fitment of electronic ticket issuing and cancelling equipment. This was a complicated and extremely expensive exercise, because machines were fitted at each door and had interlocks with the chassis systems. SYPTE crews then demanded very high premium rates to operate the vehicles, making the whole exercise non-viable and all ten artics were sold. Here one is seen later in its life operating with McGill of Barrhead.

British Airways also bought the Leyland DAB National artic, with doors on either side of the bus to facilitate loading from aircraft.

Assembly of one of the first articulated Nationals taking place at Workington in 1979. Note the higher than normal body line and the provision for an emergency door in each half of the bus. Articulated single-deckers are considerably more expensive and much heavier than double-deckers, yet they carry only a few more passengers.

The British Airways articulated Nationals were assembled at the CH Roe factory in Leeds, using components from Workington. Roe was no stranger to the National – the plant had successfully tilt tested the prototype in 1972, as seen above.

The articulated single-decker has always been an expensive bus to build, because it requires a turntable, bellows, and a third axle, which is usually steerable through a linkage with the front part of the vehicle. The cost has traditionally been about 70% higher than a two axle version of the same model. A double-decker has normally been around 15% more expensive than the equivalent single-decker. On that basis, the articulated bus only makes sense when there is restricted overall height or where easy and fast loading and unloading is important.

By 1979 problems were starting to gather for Britain's bus industry. Under the impetus of Bus Grant the average age of bus fleets had fallen sharply. Operators were getting to the point where they were starting to replace buses before the end of their economic lives. The reduction was all the more noticeable in the single-deck sector, because Workington usually had an excellent delivery record. During 1979 some operators switched to Nationals because they were readily available, rather than wait months for double-deckers.

Production at Workington fell from 917 units in 1978 to 849 in 1979. The export business for fully built-up buses had slowed to a trickle, although there were still some good enquiries around. For instance, the Greek authorities were interested in modernising public transport in Athens.

I became involved in a project to supply 400 Nationals CKD, to be assembled locally with some Greek content. Once established there was every prospect of further orders. The Greeks were not willing to pay a penny more than £32,000, because of stiff competition, including the offer of much cheaper buses from Hungary and Romania.

The Leyland finance men stuck at £34,000 minimum, despite a small amount of local content and even though the extra business would not only have contributed substantially to the overheads at Workington, but would also have generated highly profitable sales of spare parts for at least fifteen years.

Three or four years later, in an attempt to promote the National in Singapore, at that time a market for front engined buses, one of the main perpetrators of that impasse was willing to go as low as £26,000 per bus, despite intervening inflation! With internal politics like those, who needed competitors?

While the Titan had been going through its trauma, Leyland was also working on a model to replace the Atlantean, Fleetline, and Bristol VRT. All were quite elderly designs, lacking features which had become acceptable almost to the point of being obligatory, such as air suspension.

Forthcoming European legislation on noise would have required extensive re-design if the old models were to continue. The logical answer was to develop a new generation of double-deck chassis, incorporating some of the more desirable features of the Titan. The project was code-named 'B45'.

Marcus Smith had started this as almost a pet project, taking up an internal challenge to have the prototype chassis built and running outside Lancaster House, the headquarters building in Leyland, within twelve months. He recalls it as a straight forward piece of design, done with the minimum of paperwork, and built almost entirely on the factory floor at Bristol. It had to be built largely with existing components, although the front suspension was completely new.

The new chassis was to be available for home and export markets, in right and left-hand drive. After all, Tehran and Baghdad between them had bought well over one thousand Atlanteans in the 1970s. Leyland's 1979 Corporate Plan envisaged an order in 1980 from Baghdad for 400 Titans, but this forecast was then changed to 400 B45s, with bodywork to be assembled locally. In fact the order eventually materialised for 200 Atlanteans, bodied in Britain by Willowbrook to Park Royal designs because the Iraqis distrusted air suspension.

In order to comply with various regulations in different parts of the world, B45's chassis was designed in three modules. The first contained the front axle, steering gear and front end assembly. The second carried the rear axle, which was the same drop centre unit as used in the Titan. The third consisted of the engine compartment, with gearbox and angle drive. The sections between the axles, and between the rear axle and the engine sub-assembly, could be varied, depending on desired wheelbase and overall length.

This proved to be a very clever piece of engineering. At the outset, it was forecast that there would be demand for 30ft. and 33ft. long versions on the home market. Within a few years, there were requirements for 36ft. long double-deck coaches on two axles, and three axle high capacity double-deckers in various lengths up to 40ft. (The maximum length actually became 39ft. 4in., the imperial equivalent of 12 metres.) The B45 concept was able to accommodate all the variations relatively easily.

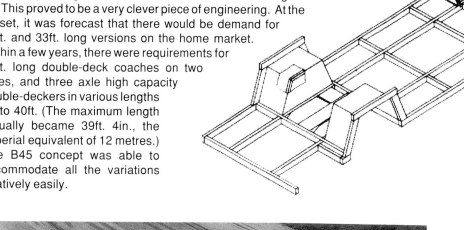

This was an early proposal sketch for the B45 underframe. It was clever in its simplicity and the model did much to allay the fears of those customers who had considered the Titan to be too sophisticated for their fleets. Production models of B45 had rectangular frame members over the wheelarches, unlike the sketch.

A three-axle Olympian chassis fitted with a temporary structure which could carry test weights and simulate the ride and handling of a laden double-decker.

A left-hand drive Olympian chassis, showing the front mounted radiator and the perimeter frame, including sections up and over the axles. Compare the squared-off frame over the wheelarches with the angled design of the concept on the previous page. The production version was obviously more acceptable to bodybuilders.

Amongst the very first production Olympian bodies built at Eastern Coach Works was a batch for Merseyside PTE. The specification included laminate trim between the external window pillars and specially printed laminated ceiling coving incorporating the Merseyside skyline. The production management might have wished for a more straightforward initial contract!

B45 was launched at the 1980 Motor Show and given another old but little used Leyland name, 'Olympian', a curious choice, given that it had previously been on a low volume single-deck integral bus built by MCW with Leyland running units. It had the Leyland TL11 engine as standard, with the Gardner 6LXB as an option, although sales of the latter far outnumbered the former for several years.

By this time the Hydracyclic gearbox had been developed to incorporate an integral retarder and was offered with either semi- or fully automatic control. While the rear axle and sub-frame were the same as the Titan, the front axle was a normal beam, compared with the Titan's independent front suspension. This enabled a lower floor height downstairs and an overall height within 13ft. 8in., or greater headroom in each deck if overall height was not critical.

While independent front suspension should have facilitated a very low floor height on the Titan, there was a deep beam under the frame, connecting the two main parts of the suspension. A lower gangway height had not been considered important when London was the main customer.

Full air suspension was fitted on the Olympian as standard, with the bellows mounted as far outboard as practicable, in order to minimise roll. The radiator was located at the front, which was preferable in hot climates.

The Olympian was produced at the Bristol factory with output building up while orders for the VRT ran down. NBC had ordered 498 Bristol VRTs for delivery in 1980, but reduced that to under 300 in 1981. That was balanced by orders for over 200 Olympians, shortly after it was launched. At this time the Olympian was not relevant to the Workington story, but that was to change later.

The Conservative Party announced its plans for public transport early in 1980. The Prime Minister was very keen on the idea that competition was good for business and that there should be free market forces. This soon became apparent in the Transport Act of 1980, which, amongst other things, deregulated all express bus and coach services over a distance of thirty miles. That was to have more impact on Workington than one might think, as we shall see shortly.

There were also two other very important factors. The country started to enter a recession, caused by the need to curb inflation and become more competitive internationally. The bus industry was also hit hard by the Government's decision to progressively phase out Bus Grant. The idea had been proposed, because of pressure on spending, by Jim Callaghan's departing Labour Government but was accelerated by the Conservatives. Bus Grant fell to 40% with effect from 1 April 1980 and was reduced by a further 10% each year, until finally phasing out at the end of March 1984.

The decision was taken on the very narrow premise that Bus Grant had achieved what the previous Labour and Conservative administrations had wanted. It is often forgotten that the Labour Government introduced Bus Grant at 25%, but the Conservative Government of Edward Heath used the powers of section 32 of the Transport Act 1968 to increase the Grant to 50%. It had been effective in greatly reducing the average age of the nation's bus population.

The removal of Bus Grant totally failed to recognise that buses would still need to be replaced, though not in quite the same volume, in order to keep the age of the fleets down to sensible and economic levels. The effect on Workington was serious. The average age of the nation's single-deckers was even younger than the double-deckers, partly because the factory had an excellent delivery record, but also because some operators had bought Nationals when double-deckers were unavailable.

Deregulation of express coach services came at a bad time for Leyland. Production of the AEC Reliance had ceased and the Leyland Leopard was coming to the end of a long and illustrious life. Volvo had been selling the B58 since 1972, but it was more expensive than the Leopard and the sales operation had been a low key adjunct to the successful truck business. In the seven years from 1972 to 1978, Volvo had registered 397 B58s, or an average of sixty a year. Then they advertised for a General Manager to run their bus and coach operation. A couple of applicants from Leyland, amongst others, were beaten by an economics graduate who had trained with Ford and then successfully introduced DAF trucks to Scotland.

Sandy Glennie, who was later to have a significant part in the Workington story, arrived at Irvine. He promoted B58 aggressively, talking intensely to operators about running costs, reliability, service, residual values and other business terms, which were not really part of Leyland's more fluid selling technique. He pushed B58 registrations to 216 in 1979, followed by a staggering 393 in 1980, capturing many previously loyal Leyland and AEC customers.

Leyland had a new coach chassis in development, coded 'B43', but it was not due into production, as the 'Tiger', until mid-1981. Almost at the same time, Volvo changed from the B58 to the B10M and stepped up another gear. Despite the success of the Tiger, from then on Leyland's sales and commercial people followed Volvo in the domestic coach market, even to the extent that Leyland models were priced below what they perceived to be the price that the market would pay for the B10M!

Prior to deregulation National Bus Company and the Scottish Bus Group had enjoyed a near monopoly of express services. With the notable exception of vehicles used on the overnight services between Scotland and London, they had tended to buy fairly standard coaches which could be cascaded in later life onto local services.

A small number of independent operators took advantage of deregulation to set up a competitive network on the busiest express routes. Some used high specification coaches, including continental bodywork on Volvo chassis. They introduced features like reclining seats, double glazing, on-board toilets, and hostess facilities.

The Scottish Bus Group woke up to the competition more quickly than NBC, by buying much more comfortable coaches. They responded rapidly with high specification Duple bodies on Volvo B10M and Leyland Tiger chassis. It took NBC several months longer to react, but they also introduced much more luxurious coaches. As far as Workington was concerned money which might normally have gone to the replacement of service buses was diverted to an urgent upgrading of coach fleets.

A J M (Sandy) Glennie, now Managing Director of Volvo Bus Ltd, who played a major part in the second half of this story.

A group of Leyland Bus managers photographed at a hotel near the Workington plant after a Leyland Bus board meeting in 1983. They are from left to right:

Geoff Trippas (Accounts),
Roy Shubert (Plant Director, Roe)
John Kinnear (Service Director)
Keith Lloyd (Commerceial Director)
Charles Fairfoot (Personnel Director)
John Battersby (Plant Director, Bristol)
David Bower (Personnel Manager)
Ken McIver (Managing Director)
Steve Worsley (Plant Director, Farington)
David Burnicle (Engineering Director)
David Quainton (Plant Director, Workington)
Peter Mitchell (Plant Director, ECW).

By 1980, the Volvo B58 was taking a significant share of the British market. This example had a short lived version of the Plaxton Supreme body, with shallow side windows.

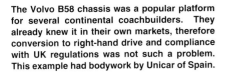

The Volvo B58 chassis was a popular platform for several continental coachbuilders. They already knew it in their own markets, therefore conversion to right-hand drive and compliance with UK regulations was not such a problem. This example had bodywork by Unicar of Spain.

Production of Nationals fell in 1980 to 647 for the domestic market and 51 for export. Of the latter, 50 were supplied to Trinidad and the remaining one was a demonstrator, which was initially sent to Kuwait. Apart from the earlier Saudi demonstrator, they were to be the only export versions of the National 2.

This was despite the fact that Leyland's Corporate Plan projected sales of 170 National 2s to Kuwait and 700 to Saudi Arabia in the period from 1980 to 1984. Export market forecasting had improved in the latter half of the 1970s, then fell away badly and became hopelessly unreliable.

Orders from National Bus Company subsidiaries fell to 383 National 2s in 1980, along with the last seven of the previous model with the 510 engine. These were delivered to Hants and Dorset, bringing to an end a production run of 6,550 National 1s, a British record for a standardised bus.

The fall in orders from NBC can be attributed to the Market Analysis Project (MAP) service revisions, which indicated more need for double-deckers and resulted in a surplus of single-deckers in some fleets. To a small extent the NBC shortfall was made up by an increased level of deliveries from Workington to the Scottish Bus Group, with most subsidiaries receiving small batches of Nationals.

Availability on relatively quick delivery continued to be an advantage, particularly as Bus Grant was being progressively phased out. Merseyside PTE bought 59 National 2s, followed by a further 25 in 1981. West Midlands, West Yorkshire and South Yorkshire all acquired National 2s, some of them at quite short notice.

The combined effects of the reduction in Bus Grant and the recession started to hit Workington hard during 1981. Production of Nationals fell to 294 and that included an order for 69 from London Transport, for operation on the Red Arrow routes between some of the capital's main railway stations. On the other hand Titan production was quite labour intensive and it was during 1981 that the Workington headcount reached a peak of 516 people.

National Bus Company, which was itself under financial and political pressure, had written off the Workington factory as a £1 million loss in its 1981 accounts, then sold its 50% shareholding in Bus Manufacturers Holdings Ltd to Leyland Vehicles Ltd in 1982, so that the latter company then owned 100% of the share capital of each of Leyland National, Bristol, Eastern Coach Works and Charles Roe.

It was a logical decision, bearing in mind how the Government was thinking about the manufacturing and operating sides of the industry. NBC was concerned about the prospect of falling sales of new buses, and could not afford the further losses which were likely to be incurred. It was a crucial break in the close and beneficial relationship between operator and manufacturer, however, and another turning point in the Workington story.

Merseyside Transport bought a substantial number of National 2 single-deckers in the three years from 1980 to 1982, partly to modernise the fleet while Bus Grant was still available.

The Volvo B10M was as big an improvement on the B58 as the Leyland Tiger on the Leopard. The B10M became a runaway success in Britain, including examples like this with bodywork by Jonckheere.

CHAPTER NINE

The Formation of Leyland Bus

There was further re-organisation in March 1981 when the Passenger Vehicle Division became known as 'Leyland Bus'. Although the organisation was still legally part of Leyland Vehicles Ltd, it was given complete autonomy for design, development, manufacturing and sales, including export markets.

At the time there was considerable euphoria about the apparent independence, but it had a very significant downside. Leyland Bus relied on Leyland Trucks for a number of components, including engines which now had to be bought at commercial rather than internal prices. As total engine production was low in international terms, the cost per unit was very high. Within two to three years Leyland Bus found that it could buy engines more competitively from Cummins, which was keen to break into the British bus market!

There was a similar problem with spare parts, which were the responsibility of the third arm, Leyland Parts. Because of the high level of commonality, and the inability to distinguish whether the end user was a truck or bus operator, Leyland Bus was deprived of a proper share in this profitable trade. The average bus has a life at least twice as long as the average truck, therefore consumes about four times as many parts in its lifetime.

Much of the older Farington site at Leyland was transferred to Leyland Bus, including the old assembly plant which was still known by its wartime code name, BX. Thereafter the new assembly plant which had been opened at Spurrier Works about two years previously, and which initially built some bus chassis, only built trucks.

Even BX was quite a large facility, having been capable of assembling up to 200 truck and bus chassis per week. At first it concentrated on producing the Leopard, Atlantean and newly introduced Tiger coach chassis. In 1982 the former Guy factory at Wolverhampton was closed and production of the rugged front-engined export only Victory was transferred to BX. The main markets for this model were Singapore and southern Africa.

When the Passenger Division headquarters at Southall were closed staff moved to an unpretentious office block at Bow Lane, Leyland, on the opposite side of the main London to Glasgow railway line from the factories. To the surprise of many Ken McIver

The Ryder report recommended substantial investment in Leyland's truck and bus activities. The assembly plant (LAP) was one manifestation of this investment whilst the Technical Centre, below, was another.

then moved the headquarters to Thurston Road, Leyland, a large pre-war ferro-concrete framed building which had previously housed offices and canteen/kitchen facilities in addition to Leyland's photographic department but which was now almost empty. Admittedly, he had to find a home for engineering and other staff who had been based on the Spurrier site, but it was an expensive exercise.

In January 1982 David Quainton became Plant Director at Workington. An energetic character, with a knack of getting things done, he was to oversee tremendous diversification. Later in the year Leyland Bus expanded the Workington site by buying a neighbouring factory unit from Millson Engineering Ltd. The 1,700sq m building was refurbished and surrounded by a perimeter fence in preparation for its use as a small prototype facility for the main plant.

There was still pent-up demand for double-deckers, particularly from London Transport and some of the PTE fleets. Orders for double-deckers held up quite well from NBC and SBG subsidiaries, partly as a result of the Market Analysis Projects, which had found that double-deckers, when properly used, were more economical than large single-deckers. Although Bus Grant was falling operators were still keen to stock up with double-deckers, before Bus Grant was withdrawn altogether.

Leyland had caught up with the backlog in orders for double-deck chassis about two years earlier. The last Fleetline chassis had been built in the summer of 1980 but, for several reasons including congestion at bodybuilders, some did not enter service until as late as 1982. Bristol and Eastern Coach Works had co-operated very closely over the years, so the problem was not quite so marked in the case of the VRT. The last deliveries of that model were made in October 1981.

The Atlantean carried on longer, boosted in part by substantial export orders from Iran, Iraq, Singapore and Indonesia. It was known, however, that it would not meet new European legislation on engine noise, to take effect on vehicles first registered on or after 1 April 1983. A twelve month dispensation was granted, partly to help bodybuilders with their production backlog. Future double-deck policy had to rely on the Titan and Olympian.

Titan production resumed at Workington before the end of 1980, with pilot build of the first of an order for 175 from London Transport. The Workington Titan was only slightly different from that built at Park Royal, but some savings in weight were achieved. Production built up steadily, achieving 145 by the end 1981.

A Titan demonstrator was built to encourage orders from other customers. It spent several weeks at the end of 1982 with Tyne & Wear PTE, where it was favourably received by drivers, passengers and engineers but, under the impetus of Bus Grant,

David Quainton, Plant Director Workington 1982-1986.

Top left:
The Technical Centre (seen on page 93) included a section of pavé in its test track facilities. An early Tiger is seen on test, whilst a completed model for Merseyside, carrying Duple coachwork can be seen top right.

Centre left:
One of a batch of five Leyland Titans with Workington bodywork, bought by Reading Transport in 1983 for operation on express services into London. The specification included 66 comfortable high backed coach seats.

Centre right:
Five further Titans delivered to Reading in the same year carried 70 seat dual-doorway bodywork for local services.

Bottom:
Ipswich was the only British mainland customer to take B21 chassis, which were assembled at Bristol. Alexander (Belfast) built the 47 seat dual-doorway bodywork.

that fleet had been modernised to such an extent that no new double-deckers were bought until 1986. Looking back, this demonstrator was superfluous. Before it was built it was clear that the lion's share of the market would go to the Olympian, which was less expensive and could be fitted with a variety of bodies.

Apart from London only Reading took Workington Titans, adding ten in 1983 to the two earlier Park Royal built examples. Five of them were fitted with high ratio rear axles and Lazzerini coach seats for services into London.

Fortunately London placed further orders for 250, 210 and 240 Titans, to be delivered in 1982, 1983 and 1984 respectively. Production at Workington ran smoothly, free from the industrial problems which had plagued Park Royal. Output reached a peak of approximately seven a week in 1982/83, and included the incorporation of several mechanical modifications, principally in the braking system. David Quainton remembers that, because they were almost all built to one specification, a very high level of routine was achieved. "You could literally set your watch to when they came off the line and went across to the test centre."

Orders for the National 2 fell drastically in 1982. National Bus Company required only 50, which went principally to Southdown, Cumberland and Ribble. Total production for the year was only 71.

Two or three operators had experimented with the installation of Gardner engines in the earlier National 1, including Crosville, Eastern Counties and Eastern Scottish. Dennis could offer the same engine in the full size Falcon chassis and was nibbling at three or four municipal operators. Leyland then quietly introduced the option of the Gardner 6HLXB engine in the National, at the end of 1982.

Even that did nothing to boost production. The National Bus Company ordered 57 National 2s for 1983 delivery, with locally based Cumberland Motor Services taking the first Gardner engined Nationals. It took only six weeks to achieve the first model off the track, despite changes to around 250 parts. After sign-off, regular production of the Gardner option commenced in January 1983 and one of the first orders came from Brighton Borough Council for seven, its first Nationals.

Partly to protect Workington further rationalisation became inevitable and the next victim was the old established Bristol chassis plant. Production of the long running RE single-decker had finally ceased in 1980, with the last orders going to Ulsterbus and Christchurch, New Zealand. Once again, there was a backlog at a bodybuilder, in this case Alexander (Belfast), and many of the Ulsterbus RE's were not registered until 1981.

Leyland had tried to promote the B21 as a National underframe and successor to the Bristol RE. Small numbers were supplied to Belgium with locally built Jonckheere bodywork, and to Australia. Six were bodied by Alexander (Belfast) and supplied to Ulsterbus for appraisal, but all were withdrawn as non-standard and sold to Ipswich at the end of 1991. The only other domestic order for B21 had also come from Ipswich, for four diverted from an export order and delivered in 1984, also with bodywork by Alexander (Belfast).

Since 1981 Bristol had concentrated almost exclusively on Olympians, but the plant was running well below its designed capacity. David Quainton thought that Bristol was doomed from the moment it switched from the VRT to the Olympian. Two thirds of the Bristol plant was occupied by machine shops, making the VRT front and rear axles, and some parts of the SCG gearbox.

The Olympian front and rear axles, and the Hydracyclic gearbox, were produced at Leyland, therefore there was a collapse in work at the machine shop in Bristol, despite substantial recent investment in new equipment. By that time John Battersby had moved from Workington to Bristol. He tried to persuade McIver to centralise machining at Bristol, rather than Leyland, but it was a forlorn effort. It was very rare for Leyland to give up work to one of the satellite plants.

Production of Olympian chassis was transferred to Workington and Bristol was closed in September 1983. The decision was spurred by an announcement from London Transport during 1983 that it intended to stop

Upper – The Workington Titan assembly line with LTE vehicles in build. Centre – This Guy Victory J, with Alexander bodywork, was one of the last to be supplied to Kowloon Motor Bus Company, Hong Kong. Foot – London Transport also bought a fleet of National 2 models with dual-doorway bodywork for Red Arrow services, principally between mainline stations.

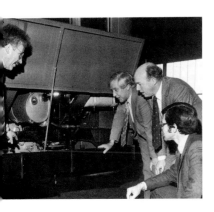

Ken Hargreaves, left, Factory Manager Workington, shows the first factory built National 2 with a Gardner engine to Jim Weeks, Chief Engineer and Peter Townley, General Manager of Cumberland Motor Services while David Quainton, Plant Director, crouching, looks on.

demanding buses to its own specification and would in future buy standard vehicles. Several trial buses were bought, including three Olympians with ECW bodywork.

Production of Olympian chassis built up rapidly at Workington. The first chassis was completed right on time and several were delivered to bodybuilders before the last of the Bristol built models. Within twelve weeks of start-up Workington was up to thirteen units a week. The rate of build out of the two plants can be checked by looking at chassis numbers.

Bristol had built up to chassis number ON995 in little under two years. Workington started a new sequence at ON1001 and had produced 514 chassis by the end of 1983. It was significantly different from the transfer of Titan to Workington. When the latter was moved from Park Royal there was a break of nearly a year before production recommenced. With Olympian there was complete continuity of output.

Ever since the announcement that Bus Grant was going to be phased out progressively, Leyland had foreseen that the home market could no longer sustain the sales volumes enjoyed in the 1970s. Consequently, there was a major export drive to obtain orders for the Olympian. Much of the early impact fell on Bristol and ECW.

The Brislington factory built a three axle 12 m long chassis late in 1981. It had the addition of a self steering axle, located slightly ahead of the standard driven rear axle. ECW built a body with 104 seats, 73 of them upstairs. On the lower deck, there was space for three doorways, 31 seats and 53 standing passengers.

This bus was demonstrated to Kowloon Motor Bus Company, which subsequently ordered a production batch of twenty chassis. They had to be assembled at Workington, then sent to Hong Kong, where they received Alexander bodies, which were shipped CKD for local assembly.

Another variation, produced both at Bristol and Workington, was a 11 m two axle chassis. Several were fitted with ECW double-deck coach bodies for longer distance commuter services into London, but they have since become widely dispersed.

When Park Royal had closed there was almost no sympathy, except for some loyal staff who became redundant. The closure was seen as inevitable, because of rampant abuse of trade union power on the shop floor. The country as a whole was becoming sick and tired of the unions and Park Royal had been the black spot in Leyland Vehicles. The decision to close the plant appeared fully vindicated, especially when the unions agreed to step up the production rate to clear outstanding orders in return for a closure package.

With Bristol, it was quite different. There was genuine sadness about the closure. The products had generally enjoyed a good reputation. The workforce was loyal and reliable. The declining market meant that Leyland Bus had to cut costs by closing factories and concentrating production in a smaller number of units. At the same time, substantial cuts were made in the headcount at Eastern Coach Works.

By 1983, knowing that London was not going to buy any more bespoke buses, it was obvious that Titan production would soon come to an end. It would have made sense to close Workington and retain Bristol, because the National was also nearing the end of its production span. That was not done for a number of reasons. Firstly, Bristol was an old factory, whereas Workington had been open just over ten years. Secondly, development work was proceeding on a replacement for the National. It was planned to be an integral, again built exclusively within Leyland Bus.

Thirdly, the closure of Workington would have meant relying on Charles Roe and Eastern Coach Works for in-house bodywork. The unions at the latter had refused to agree terms for building the Titan after the announcement about closing Park Royal. That snub was not forgotten!

Fourthly, and probably most significant to the decision to keep Workington open, Leyland had been working closely with British Rail Research Derby to investigate the production and use of lightweight diesel railcars (or railbuses as they are more usually known). That avenue was starting to look promising, although David Quainton described the waiting time as "one of the longest gestation periods for any product".

British Rail was working, concurrently, on a prototype diesel-electric multiple-unit (DEMU) four-car train for its future needs. Known as its class 210, the train was to be produced to a high specification and had a projected cost, even in the early 1980s, of around £1 million per set. This was causing alarm within the PTEs, for they were expected to be among customers for this new class of bogie vehicles, to be operated on their suburban services as replacements for some of the 3,000 worn out 'first generation' early BR diesel units. Under pressure, BR was forced to think again and came back to the idea of lightweight railbuses on which Leyland had been working.

The Workington factory had produced three single-unit four-wheeled vehicles, to its design code R1. Work on R1 had begun in 1976 and Marcus Smith recalls that it

was built in a fair degree of secrecy, largely over one weekend. This was possible because the main sections had been pre-assembled. At first the bodyshell was placed onto a non-powered long-wheelbase underframe to allow test running to take place in order to monitor riding characteristics.

The 12.4 metre long body was assembled from eight standard short National bay modules, six glazed and, as first built, one doorway and one front end module at each end. In order that the vehicle could serve platforms on either side of the track it had doors on each side, and, as stated, initially at both ends. Standard National four leaf doors were used. These were later changed when it was found that the air pressure from a passing high speed train could force them open.

The four wheel underframe, BR's portion of the project, had been tested and proven as part of the development work on the infamous Advanced Passenger Train (APT) remembered for its tilting carriages and its expensive failure to meet requirements. The trials with the vehicle included trips hauled by a locomotive at speeds up to 80mph and were sufficiently encouraging to allow the next phase to be initiated.

This involved converting the non-powered unit into a self-contained self-propelled single unit by the addition of a 510 engine, SCG gearbox and mechanical transmission, together with braking systems and the fitment of driving cabs at either end. In this mode, and now known as LEV1, Leyland Experimental Vehicle 1, it carried out extensive trials in Britain and America. By chance, many of its passenger trial journeys took place between Ipswich and ECW's local railway station in Lowestoft. Unfortunately, the trials failed to reveal a serious design limitation. The long wheelbase was totally unsuited to track with short radius curves which abound on most branch lines as became apparent when the production Pacers started to cut away the rail head with a shrill squealing noise. Perhaps too much emphasis was being placed on riding at speed. Nevertheless, sufficient interest was aroused in America for a second unit to be commissioned by the Boston and Maine Railroad.

Among the many trials were those involving testing to ensure that the unit could stand up to railway end loading collision requirements, in addition to the stress testing of the bodyframe. Recognising the need for additional experience, Leyland went to Wickhams of Ware for the construction of LEV2 and an altogether more sophisticated vehicle was produced. It was 15.3 metres long with eight standard long National bays in addition to doorway bays and full width cab modules at each end. The vehicle weighed 19.8 tonnes and could carry 64 seated and up to 40 standing passengers. The driving controls could be mounted either side of the centre line in the half width cabs.

LEV2 was shipped to the Boston and Maine Railroad in 1980 and a third unit, to similar specification, but with the doors and driving cabs diagonally at the opposite ends to suit UK running, made its public debut at the 1981 UITP conference in Dublin. This unit was constructed by Leyland and BREL and after working on BR tracks went to Northern Ireland Railways who later purchased it.

Leyland was looking to an on-going relationship with British Rail Engineering Ltd (BREL), the privatised railway workshops formerly owned by BR, and a consortium which became known as ART (Associated Rail Technologies) was formed to develop the railbus business.

British Rail was now beginning to clarify its railbus policy, partly following the outcome of the Railbus Conference held in November 1981, and partly as the result of the Railway Inspectorate's report after a collision at Chivers Crossing in December 1976. It saw little need for single-unit railcars since very few of its services could be handled by such small vehicles. It is significant that out of several thousand 'first generation' units from the 1950s and 1960s, less than 40 were single units, and none of these had the 4 wheel configuration which Leyland was building. Many of these had already become surplus after Dr Beeching closed their branch lines. What BR needed were replacements for its multiple unit fleet.

Leyland accordingly started to design a two-car unit in collaboration with its partner in ART. The National structure had been shown to be less expensive than the traditional railway coach but there was a snag. The 150 tonne compressive loading at the couplers could be met but the 30 tonne compressive loading at the cantrail could not, partly due to the large curved glass windscreen.

BR, still undecided as to what to do with its very expensive prototype class 210 unit, stepped in, and in a move which put the whole project back many months, required the new Workington two-car unit which become the class 140 to be fitted with the cab ends from the 210, since these were already in build for another of its units, class 317. The fact that the Workington body was

Second top and left:
The National 2 prototypes, R2 and R3, were 'handed', as shown. Note the longer construction, using 8 long bays, plus door bays and cab modules.

Below:
The mock up end and one half of a virtually completed 141 twin car set. The finished bodies were sent by road to Derby to be mounted on the underframe

10in narrower can have done little to facilitate such an amalgamation, but in BR's eyes the cab ends were available, and also they had union approval. The result was to produce the ugliest of BR's ugly duckling railcars! The project dragged on and on and Leyland began to despair of ever seeing the solitary class 140 set leaving the factory.

Eventually it was completed and entered trial service. It was supposed to be lightweight and assembled from standard National components, but in fact it was not fully either. BR finally recognised that it had required Leyland to build a vehicle which had lost most of the attributes which had made it attractive in the first place!

A sense of reality returned to the project and the ART team continued with their original concept, now to be class 141 in the BR series. Using standard National 2 components but with a re-designed end to meet the compressive requirements, they secured an opening order from West Yorkshire PTE in 1982 for 20 two-car sets to be operated on contract to BR in the PTE's area. Production extended to 1986/7.

Whilst these represented the opening order which had so long been awaited, they were far from ideal as a universal replacement for the existing DMUs. The National bus body, at 2,500mm wide, was appreciably narrower than the standard BR coach which measured 2,816mm. This reduction in width not only affected seating capacity but also meant that passengers were at risk on stations, particularly those with curved platforms, where the entrance step could be some distance away from the platform edge. Stations with curved platforms are often found on branch lines . . . !

On the positive side, there was a conscious effort to incorporate more standard bus parts in the 141 class, compared with the 140, therefore they had normal National doors and stepwells. Other fitments included a toilet and a secondary heating system which supplemented the waste engine heat, fed in the normal National manner through the roof-mounted heat exchanger.

The additional heating system was necessary because there was a larger interior volume, and, in rail operation, engines spend a considerable time idling, with a correspondingly low heat output. Each car had a horizontal Leyland TL11 engine and an SCG gearbox which could provide four speeds and reverse in either direction. It also had a free-wheeling facility, for increased fuel economy. A double battery system was provided on each car, with one battery being used solely for starting the engine. The inadequacy of the SCG gearbox became apparent in squadron service, leading to massive rework costs when Leyland Bus was obliged to fit Voith transmissions to many of the vehicles.

The completed bodies were transported by road from Workington to Derby, for final assembly by British Rail Engineering Ltd. The total price of a class 141 two-car unit was around £340,000.

In 1982 Workington became involved in another rail exercise. British Rail Research and Leyland Bus set up a project to replace the existing body of a Mk I railway coach with a National derived body. The underframe, which had been completely refurbished at BR Derby, sat on a pair of B4 bogies. Workington constructed a body consisting of twelve standard long bays plus vestibules at each end.

The interior was fitted out with a toilet compartment, and various types of seats were installed for sampling, including coach and aircraft type recliners. The body was transferred from the factory to the railway track at Workington, where it was mounted on the renovated bogies. It was put into trial service early in 1983, but the rebodying exercise was not pursued, despite a second underframe, M4872 – RDB977171 – having been prepared in 1984. It is said that passengers likened the finished product to rejuvenated *3rd* class coaches.

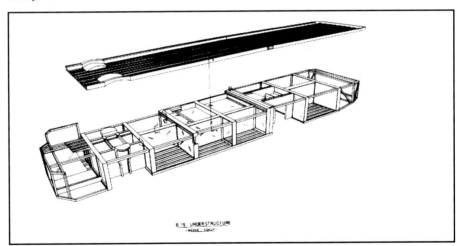

The Royal Tiger underframe (right) was unlike anything previously produced by Leyland. It had space frame construction and relied heavily on the bodywork for the integrity of the complete vehicle.

The partially completed prototype Doyen is seen below with a Van Hool bodied Tiger from the demonstration fleet whilst the completed vehicle with Leyland's own dramatic body style is seen on the test track at the then fairly recently opened Technical Centre at Leyland.

Shortly after that the factory built three single car demonstrators which were sent to Greece, Indonesia and the United States. The Greek railbus seated 64 passengers and had a conventional bus type driver's cab and passenger door arrangement.

The second prototype seated 70 passengers in a 3+2 arrangement, with a central area for standees. The American demonstrator had a central driver's cab, with narrow doors, either side, in the front bays. There were additional passenger doors in the middle, with access for wheelchair passengers. This railbus had full Sutrak air conditioning and bullet proof double glazed windows!

Returning now to road transport matters, one of the almost immediate effects of the Transport Act 1980, which liberalised coach services, was the growing continental competition in the heavy duty coach sector of the market. This sector was dominated by models with horizontal mid-underfloor engines, like the newly launched Leyland Tiger and the Volvo B10M.

Rear-engined coaches had only been sold in Britain in comparatively small numbers. By far the most popular model had been the Bristol RE, available from around 1963 to 1975, often with a Gardner engine although also for coach application with a special version of the O.680 engine rated at 208bhp. These were supplied, in both versions, almost exclusively to NBC and SBG operators.

The German manufacturer, MAN, offered a fully integral rear-engined single-decker in Britain from 1979. It was technically advanced and much more powerful than any contemporary British model, and picked up some small but significant orders. Mercedes, Setra and Neoplan all had suitable well established models in production and were known to be looking at the British market. DAF and Bova, the Dutch integral coachbuilder, started to offer medium weight rear-engined coaches, including a Bova underframe with Duple coachwork.

Several Leyland operators were impressed by the rear-engined layout of this new model, principally because it offered more readily accessible luggage accommodation. Whereas the Leopard or Reliance had been limited to a maximum of around five cubic metres, some of the rear-engined layouts offered nearly twice that capacity, without any significant increase in height.

Deregulation of journeys over 50 km helped to open up a major new market for continental tours and excursions. Coach operators all across Britain were able to organise domestic and continental tours without the previous need for licences. Higher luggage capacity was becoming essential on longer trips and on certain types of traffic, for instance, to winter ski resorts. Hard on the heels of the Tiger, Leyland decided to hedge its bets by planning a rear-engined underframe, suitable for semi-integral coachwork, and known as the B50 project. Shortly after that the complementary B54 project commenced, for the construction of the bodywork part of the vehicle.

B50 and B54 were launched together at Brighton in November 1982. The B50 underframe was given the famous old Leyland name 'Royal Tiger'. It consisted of a space frame, made from square section steel tubes which were welded to form a rigid box structure. In contemporary fashion the gangway was set in a channel approximately six inches below the main floor level. The weight reducing space frame was used to maximise luggage capacity. However a fully laden vehicle could still exceed the maximum permitted gross vehicle weight when utilised to the full!

Mechanically the Royal Tiger used a number of components which were already familiar in the Leyland range. Power was provided by a TL11 engine, mounted horizontally in-line at the rear, producing 245bhp at 2,100rpm. The Leyland Hydracyclic gearbox with integral retarder was offered as standard, although the Cummins L10 engine, ZF S6-80 manual gearbox, ZF automatic gearbox and Telma retarder were available as options. The rear axle was an Eaton 23120 unit, rated at 11,000 kg gross, and already used by DAB and UTIC in Leyland designed coaches. The front axle, rated at 7,000 kg gross, and the steering layout were taken from the Olympian, with the air bellows being located close to the edge of the frame. The combined axle capacities of 18,000 kg gross gave B50 considerable leeway over contemporary British gross vehicle weights. The braking system was the same as the Tiger and the radiator, once again, was mounted at the extreme front.

The Doyen badge

The complete integral B54 was in many ways a dramatic coach. It was called the 'Royal Tiger Doyen' and was very distinctively styled, in a futuristic way. It was certainly not inspired by any continental design, but it looked dramatic. Typical of Leyland's ability to coin new phrases, the Doyen was said to be designed 'outside in'. The launch and the early publicity were very confident. The Doyen was marketed under the slogan: 'Who else but Leyland.' Literature went on to describe 'the coach everyone's been waiting for..' and '...in short all the power, performance, economy, reliability and comfort you've come to expect from Britain's premier builder of coaches – Leyland.'

The overall design was the work of an external specialist, John Heffernan. The style transferred remarkably easily from conception to production. The large one piece windscreen was set into a matt black surround, making the Doyen look even taller than it actually was.

Many of the other features reflected the best of contemporary continental practice, such as the use of bonded glazing, and thermostatically controlled ducted heating and ventilation. The top few inches of the side windows were silk screen printed with black bands which prevented the interior racks from being visible outside. It was a fussy detail which detracted from many other good points in the overall design.

Reclining seats, sun blinds and many other features were fitted as standard. Aircraft style lockers were offered as an option to open luggage racks. Some of the interior trim was very fashionable, but not sufficiently durable for coach operation over several years. As one would expect from Leyland, the layout of the driver's compartment was excellent, with a large semi-circular instrument panel.

All controls were well placed and within easy reach, yet the driving area was compact, releasing valuable space for passenger legroom. The front grille carried an enormous badge, depicting a tiger's head and crown. One or two wags said that the size of the badge helped to transfer more weight to the front axle!

The Doyen structure was designed to meet not only British legislation, but also all contemporary and anticipated European legislation. The corner pillars were of double thickness and the roof members were reinforced to provide a very strong 'roll cage'. There were serious plans to sell the Doyen into selected continental markets.

The initial design failed to cater for the diversity of options which customers were starting to demand, and which other coachbuilders could provide. Despite the claim that there had been extensive market research, incredibly, there was no provision for a driver's bunk, centre offside continental exit, or toilet.

Continental coachbuilders like Caetano, Jonckheere and Van Hool were very innovative and could adapt their basic coach structures amazingly quickly to meet the needs of individual customers. Leyland was still suffering from fairly rigid Engineering disciplines, much more relevant to models like the National, but within a couple of years the underframe had to be modified quite substantially to accommodate those features, with a consequent loss of luggage space.

Eddie Brown of Helperby was a regular Leyland customer and one of the first to take the Royal Tiger Doyen.

Leyland tried to promote the Royal Tiger underframe with Duple, being unaware that the Blackpool coachbuilder was developing its own integral product (right). The Cummins L10 engine gave excellent fuel economy in this rather underrated model.

The development cost of the Doyen was around £2 million, a very substantial amount at a time when top specification coaches were selling for around £50,000.

Leyland took the surprising decision to build both the underframe and the complete coach at the Charles Roe factory in Leeds. Until that time, Roe had been a traditional builder of bodywork on chassis, principally double-deckers, for which demand was forecast to fall. Roe was probably seen as an experienced plant with capacity becoming available.

Roe relied largely on skilled workers who were used to building bespoke vehicles for a variety of customers. If a detail was missing from a drawing, they could manage. Their experience meant that they should have been able to cope with the demands of individual coach operators. A considerable investment was made at Roe, including the provision of paint spray ovens. Everyone tried very hard to introduce the new models on time, but there were considerable difficulties, particularly with the Doyen.

The root cause appears to have been that every part of B50 and B54 was strictly defined in Leyland engineering drawings. On numerous occasions the drawings were not quite accurate. Although the workforce was developing the skill to rectify deficiencies it was not allowed by Engineering to do so. At the risk of being accused of hindsight, it was wrong to try to build luxury coaches in such a strictly controlled manner without effective Resident Engineering. The blame cannot be put on Roe.

As a result, production of B50 and B54 slipped badly and delivery promises were broken. Build quality was also suspect, and the original difficult cable gear linkage had to be replaced by an air-assisted system. Leyland might have ridden these problems with NBC, but the Doyen was aimed mainly at the independent sector, where Volvo and others were able to pounce on any slippage. There was little alternative but to add more Tigers to the demonstration fleet, then loan them to customers who were waiting for late Doyens.

Leyland then announced that production of the Royal Tiger underframe would be transferred to Workington during the latter half of 1983. By this time, Plaxton and Van Hool had indicated that they would body the Royal Tiger for the 1984 season. More sophisticated jigs were installed, so that higher production volumes could be achieved. Leyland also talked to Duple about bodying the Royal Tiger, unaware that Duple was developing its own integral coach! Duple had been bought by Hestair which also owned Dennis and therefore had the necessary engineering expertise.

Soon after, it was decided that Workington should also take on responsibility for building more standard versions of the Doyen body, leaving Roe to concentrate on very high specification models. For the second time in little over a year a Leyland Bus factory was equipped with high bake paint spray ovens, necessary for the application of the new acrylic or isocyanate based, paints, which rapidly became the standard finish for luxury coaches.

This plant was installed in the autumn of 1983, at a cost of £600,000. It was located as a line of seven booths across the middle of the factory, integrated with existing conveyor systems, although primarily intended for the Doyen. The plant was capable of handling bodies up to 12 metres long by 4.5 metres high, so it could be used for double-deckers. It could carry out the complete process, from priming through to the application of top colour coats.

David Burnicle recounted an amusing story about the commissioning trials for this plant. In order to demonstrate the process, the contractors used the next National coming down the line. All went well with the robot paint spray guns until they came to what they thought was the back of the bus. Their photocell system told them that they had reached the end of the bus so they moved inwards to paint the rear. There was a crash because the chosen bus was one of the airport types with centre door apertures on both sides. The photocell light had shone through the doors and not across the back of the bus! No harm was done but a lesson was learned.

This was only part of a very substantial investment programme at Workington, some of which was necessary because of the factory's increasing role in product development. The computer was upgraded to meet the new demands and Computer Aided Design equipment acquired, at a cost of £180,000. A second paint facility was installed, for smaller parts, doors, valances, and to spray engines and axles. Other expensive installations included a dynamometer.

A considerable amount of engineering work had to be done, in order to adapt the Doyen for assembly by semi-skilled workers. This proved to be an expensive exercise, but the general opinion in the industry was that Workington Doyens were of a higher standard than those built by Roe. Also, full use was made of skills previously acquired by some of the workforce. For instance, a man who had been a carpet fitter became the soft trim specialist.

It would probably not be fair to attribute the differences solely to the two workforces because of the on-going engineering work which continued while production of the earliest models was in progress at Roe. The bulk of production at Roe had long been double-deck bodywork, but the weekly average output had declined from three in 1981 to just under two by 1984, as demand for double-deckers fell. A total of 19 Royal Tiger underframes and 42 complete Doyens had been built in the three year period from 1982. With a forecast decline in the market and high costs being incurred on the Royal Tiger, it was decided to close Roe before the end of 1984. Quite a lot of plant and equipment was then transferred to Eastern Coach Works.

Once again, an old established factory fell victim to the need to keep Workington running, only, in this case, rescue was at hand. Russell Richardson, a former Roe plant director, and the West Yorkshire Enterprise Board, along with many of the employees, bought the factory from Leyland Bus. Many workers invested the redundancy money which they had received from Leyland Bus in the new company, called 'Optare', from the Greek 'to choose'. Optare adapted quickly to the changing market conditions and became one of the industry's survivors in a dreadfully tight market.

Meanwhile, Workington was rapidly becoming a multi-product factory.

National bus and railcar bodies being assembled on adjacent lines at Workington.

CHAPTER TEN

'Thatchered'

Margaret Thatcher's Conservative Government was re-elected in 1983 and promised to push ahead with its programme to open up competition still further. A major part of the policy was to sell off state owned companies, in the belief that they would fare better in the private sector. For Leyland and the bus operating industry it was an ominous manifesto.

The late Nicholas (later Lord) Ridley, whose views on the virtues of privatisation and deregulation were very close to those of Mrs Thatcher, became Secretary of State for Transport and proceeded to draft the White Paper which eventually led to the Transport Act 1985. A man of very dogmatic political opinion, he ignored all the advice from the industry and proceeded, with the advantage of a large Parliamentary majority, to prepare the ground for an Act which was to do very serious damage to Britain's bus manufacturing industry. The lady had to be obeyed!

It is worth reflecting how Ridley became Secretary of State. Cecil Parkinson had a well publicised affair with his secretary and resigned from the Cabinet. Tom King had been in the transport post for only a few weeks, but had shown that he was prepared to accept the industry's views on at least some of the problems which it faced. In the ensuing Cabinet reshuffle, Margaret Thatcher moved him to the Northern Ireland Office, bringing Ridley from the Treasury to Transport. Just reflect for a moment. If Parkinson had not been a naughty boy, the rest of this story might well have been totally different!!

By the middle of 1984 Workington, which had been set up as a one product plant, was producing Nationals, Titans, Olympian chassis, Royal Tiger underframes and complete coaches, and various railbuses. On top of that, the factory had become involved in another new model. The B60 single-deck bus project had been started in 1982, with the premise that it would have to be available both as an underframe and a complete vehicle. This would widen its appeal and enable it to be sold in overseas markets, where local bodybuilders were frequently protected.

A Workington built Royal Tiger Doyen in Leyland's impressive demonstration livery. The reintroduction of the Leyland scroll name was widely appreciated in the industry.

The word 'underframe' started to appear in bus industry terminology around this time. The concept was not new, having been used in models like the Bristol LS single-decker in the 1950s, but the word came into general usage and was used to describe a chassis which was not sufficiently strong to be fully independent. Underframes were introduced in an effort to keep down unladen weight. They carried all the mechanical units and auxiliaries necessary for the motion of the bus but relied quite heavily on the bodywork for the structural integrity of the complete vehicle.

The plan was to produce B60 initially for export, to be followed by a bodied version which would eventually replace the National 2. Because B60 had a welded underframe, some major facility changes were necessary at Workington.

Leyland Bus Marketing wanted the underframe to be available to domestic bodybuilders and a frame was exhibited at an Earl's Court Show, but Ken McIver was willing to make only one exception, namely Alexander (Belfast) for Ulsterbus. Otherwise, all production for the home market would be built at Workington. McIver's intention was to maximise Leyland Bus revenue at the risk of losing some orders to rival chassis builders who could offer a choice of bodies. The first prototype was completed before the end of 1983.

While sales in the home market were shrinking rapidly, because of reducing Bus Grant and the uncertain future created by the politicians, export sales were also falling. Leyland Bus put inadequate resources into the export effort, and tended to concentrate on traditional markets. The only exports out of Workington were Olympian chassis, at a rate of just under two a week in 1984.

The last level of Bus Grant was phased out in March 1984, and the domestic market really started to slow down. Much worse was to come. Ridley's plans for the future of the bus industry, fully supported by Margaret Thatcher, were set out in a White Paper and Bill which duly became the Transport Act 1985. One of the two most important proposals was the deregulation of all bus services, outside London. That set off alarm bells throughout the industry.

NBC perceived that the main threat to its traditional bus services might well come from taxi operators, and therefore experimented with minibuses, on the grounds that they would be more frequent, more friendly, and more accessible to parts of towns which had narrow streets. After successful experiments in Exeter, NBC ordered large numbers of minibuses, initially conversions of popular panel vans, and within a year or two, also coachbuilt bodywork on light truck chassis. It is deeply ironic that Ridley had to resign from mainstream politics because of some characteristically blunt and offensive remarks

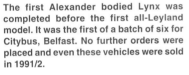

The first Alexander bodied Lynx was completed before the first all-Leyland model. It was the first of a batch of six for Citybus, Belfast. No further orders were placed and even these vehicles were sold in 1991/2.

about what he saw as German domination of European politics and trade, yet by far the biggest beneficiary of his Act and the move to minibuses was Mercedes-Benz!! That is a prime example of the incompetence of our politicians.

The Bill which became the Transport Act 1985 also proposed that the National Bus Company would be sold out of state ownership. Ridley accelerated the process whereby some of the larger companies were to be split into two or more portions, to prevent them dominating a significant part of the country. A slight preference was to be given to management teams, who wanted to buy their companies.

Many of those managers quickly realised that, if they wanted to bid for their companies, they did not want to be burdened with large quantities of new buses, which would not have had the advantage of being written down in their accounts. Even though they might not get the opportunity to Buy Out for two or three years, many fleets took the decision to buy next to nothing in 1985 and 1986. As a result, registrations of Leyland Nationals were only 44 in 1984, with a slight improvement to 57 in 1985.

There was another threat to the B60 project. Whereas National Bus Company had been Leyland's partner until 1982, it had set up a bus development unit in 1983 in Carlyle Works, Birmingham, under the leadership of Barry Fox, a bright young engineer. This unit was responsible for the development of existing buses and coaches in the NBC fleet, but was also working on new vehicle specifications.

On more than one occasion Fox went so far as to say that manufacturers might be invited to tender for the construction of buses designed by NBC. He must have had authority from a very high level to make that statement. It was amazing that NBC was so out of step with the times, when the costs of research, development and production were affordable only by the larger international companies. It was harking back to the old principles of operator-led design, which London Transport had just renounced!

While the NBC unit made some progress with plans for a National replacement, it soon had to spend the bulk of its time on minibus development and the monitoring of manufacturers who were supplying NBC. Following the decision to break up NBC, the unit was disbanded in the autumn of 1986.

Leyland Bus lost approximately £80 million in the three years from 1982 to 1984. There were many problems, both internal and external. Leyland Bus had retrenched under McIver, with the closures of Park Royal, Bristol and Charles Roe. It is probably fair to say that each of these plants was closed one year too late. The problem was caused by the board of Leyland Vehicles, which tended to procrastinate. If a new truck had to be launched, the announcement of a plant closure would be held back.

The Bristol factory was in the parliamentary constituency of Tony Benn. Dennis Healey was the local MP at Roe, and Jim Prior, another political heavyweight, held Lowestoft, the base of ECW, another, though later, candidate for closure. The Leyland Vehicles board knew that these were political hot potatoes and therefore did not grasp them soon enough.

Internally there was the apparent refusal of Ken McIver to recognise how steeply the domestic market was falling, and to take action accordingly. His staff were preparing accurate marketing projections, which showed a deepening downward trend. It is said, however, that no-one at board level was willing to put such pessimistic figures before him, so they were boosted to a level which was quite unrealistic!

McIver was a finance man, driven by numbers. When it came to the crunch, as the market declined, he changed policy and competed with traditional allies like Alexander, because Leyland Bus had neither the products nor the expertise to attack the real competition among the international chassis builders.

He undercut Alexander in order to sell ECW bodies on Olympian chassis into Lothian Region Transport, where Alexander and Leyland had previously sold in harmony for over twenty years. That apparent naivety brought a sharp response when Alexander, well established in the Leyland stronghold of Singapore, introduced Mercedes to the Far East market, selling 200 double-deck bodies on the 0305 chassis.

Leyland Bus could not handle that kind of scenario and the directors seemed to flap. They even visited Gothenburg to see if there was any way of working with Volvo, or even if Volvo would acquire Leyland Bus. They

It is ironic that Mercedes-Benz became the main beneficiary of the large scale introduction of minibuses. This is a typical early conversion of an L608D panel van. National Bus started the design of the next generation of such vehicles with BAMBI (Build A Minibus Investigation) and the concurrent 'Big Bus' was known as BABS (Build A Bus Scheme)!!

Leyland's main competitor in the rapidly shrinking double-deck market was the MCW Metrobus, an example of which is seen below in West Midlands Timesaver livery. London Transport was taking equal quantities at the rate of 250 of each model per year although in the early 'eighties both manufacturers had production problems. Relationships between the two companies were not improved when Leyland presented LT with an all-or-nothing situation whereby it would only build any vehicles if it obtained the whole order in one particular year.

had become obsessed with the success of Volvo in the British market. Courteous as ever, the Swedes received them, but having looked at the accounts and forecasts, declined any kind of alliance.

Talks were also held with MCW to see if there was any way in which the two companies could collaborate. There was a suggestion that MCW would give up the complete Mark II Metrobus and concentrate on building bodywork on Olympian chassis, but those talks broke down.

It would be unfair to blame Ken McIver for the sad decline in the standing of Leyland Bus. He had the misfortune to be Managing Director at a time when the change in political direction had undermined the foundations of the British market in a way which would never have occurred in the home markets of Mercedes, Iveco or Renault. His superiors within the BL hierarchy were of little or no help to him. As one of his directors later said in his defence: "None of them had much feel or caring for bus products, the bus market or its customers."

In January 1985, having forecast further substantial losses, he suddenly left the company, being replaced by another Scot, Ian McKinnon, who had risen through the ranks at Bathgate and Leyland Trucks. He brought two or three other directors with him, effectively forming a new top management team, soon to be known, somewhat disparagingly, as the 'Scottish Mafia'.

Addressing employees in the summer of 1985, McKinnon said: "A reduction in costs, better quality and improved financial performance are the key objectives to securing a return to viability for Leyland Bus". He went on to say that nothing had happened to stem the substantial losses incurred in 1984. He warned that the company had to cut its costs substantially and quickly, if it was to get the business back on an even keel.

Recognising the responsibility of Leyland Bus to its Government shareholders, McKinnon said: "It is fundamental to our future that we re-establish confidence in us within BL and the Department of Trade and Industry. They are our bankers and provide the funding for the business."

He went on to bemoan the very low order levels and said that those few orders could not generate profit at the levels needed to re-invest in new products and manufacturing facilities which were vital if the company was to remain internationally competitive.

He must also have been aware of the possibility of a significant swing to minibuses,

The decision to undercut Alexander for Lothian's business was ill-considered. An ECW bodied Olympian heads an Alexander bodied Atlantean along Princes Street, Edinburgh.

though probably no-one forecast that annual registrations would go from around 50 to nearly 3,000 in just four years. Unfortunately, Leyland Bus had no suitable product. Development of one would have been very sensitive, partly because the Freight Rover Sherpa was available from another part of BL.

McKinnon spoke with the knowledge that the political climate was totally against Leyland Bus. The United Kingdom was in a deep political schism, of a kind unprecedented in an industrial nation. The Labour Party was trying to distance itself from its traditional allies in the trade unions. The Conservative Party was far too chummy with the fast-buck merchants of the City, totally unable or unwilling to understand the longer pay-back periods required in major industrial investments.

Margaret Thatcher wanted rid of state owned industries, whatever the price, regardless of people and the consequences for the country which she so fervently supported in those matters which appealed to her personally. She was fed up with the whole of British Leyland and considered it a serious drain on the public purse. On more than one occasion she reminded Parliament that BL had cost every taxpayer in the country £200. She wanted rid of it, and did not mind whether it went as one company or a number of parts. Leyland Bus was to be 'Thatchered'.

Production of the Titan had ceased in 1984, with delivery of the last order to London Transport. Between them, Van Hool and Plaxton took 65 Royal Tiger underframes, the bulk of which had been built in 1984.

Both bodybuilders complained that they could not compete with the Doyen on price. Indeed, there were accusations that Leyland Bus had deliberately raised the underframe price in order to make the complete Doyen more competitive. As a result neither Van Hool nor Plaxton placed further orders for Royal Tiger underframes, and production of that model was effectively foreshortened.

One of the last Workington built Titans, seen in the livery of Westlink. This low cost subsidiary of London Buses is expected to be the second subsidiary to be privatised, probably by the time this book goes to press.

A Van Hool bodied Royal Tiger.

The completed bodyshell for an export demonstrator leaves Workington on a low loader, prior to being married up with the underframe.

One of the original narrower class 141 railbuses nearing completion in the Workington factory. It had the same overall width as a standard National bus, as evidenced by the cove panels.

In contrast, the class 142 railbuses were built to a greater overall width, immediately identifiable by the splayed cove structure between the pillars and the roof sticks.

The competitors of Leyland Bus seized on the incursion into the body building market – Leyland's sales staff were naturally trying to promote the complete Doyen first, followed by a choice of Tiger or Royal Tiger chassis.

The consequent alienation of coachbuilders led to their promotion of sales of their bodies on other makes of chassis where there was the slightest risk of Leyland promoting the Doyen. As the other chassis builders did not have in-house coachwork, with the exception of a brief period when Volvo was able to offer the integral C10M alongside the B10M, they were not seen as competitors. Dealers saw Leyland Bus promoting direct sales to operators at this time. Later a number sold out to manufacturers as the market contracted!

Considering the enormous investment sales of the Royal Tiger Doyen were particularly disappointing. Only twenty were built in the whole of 1985. The high unladen weight was a disadvantage, with the ever present risk of exceeding the legal weight limit on the rear axle when carrying a full load of passengers and luggage. Another factor was the very poor Leyland parts and service support on the continent. Volvo had efficient coverage throughout Europe for the high volume B10M.

DAF could offer both mid and rear-engined coaches and had excellent support on the continent. DAF vigorously promoted its emergency aid and insurance schemes, including extended warranties. Coach operators did not appear to interpret this as indicating any weakness in the DAF product which was likely to cause it to break down! It was always seen as reassurance that if a DAF coach suffered a failure then help would soon be at hand.

At Workington it wasn't all gloom and doom. The railbus business was at long last starting to bear fruit. British Rail had ordered 50 two-car class 142 trains in 1984 and deliveries commenced in the summer of 1985. These were an improved wider-bodied version of the Class 141, but outwardly looked very similar. The bodies were built on a special line at Workington and delivered by road to BREL's works at Derby, painted, glazed and fully trimmed.

The previous Class 141 rail vehicles had been criticised because they were the same width, 2,500 mm, as the National and therefore failed to take advantage of the greater width available to standard gauge trains. British Rail normally works to a width of 2,815 mm (9ft. 3in.) which can comfortably accept 3+2 seating. The problem was that the highly tooled roofsticks could not be cut and lengthened.

An ingenious solution was found by incorporating cove pieces which effectively added half the desired extra width into each side. Thus the Class 142 railbuses achieved a nominal overall width of 2,800 mm. At the same time the opportunity was taken to include in these cove brackets the necessary reinforcing members to meet the railway vehicle end-loading requirements.

It had been intended to offer this increased width as an option for customers who required it. In the event Alexander cut the ground from under Leyland's feet with its class 143, built jointly with Andrew Barclay & Sons of Kilmarnock, which met BR's existing width specification and Leyland was left with no choice but to offer the wider version at no extra cost for the whole of the class 142 contract – the so-called wide bodied vehicles. This decision had severe financial implications but was indicative of the area into which Leyland, with BR's assistance perhaps, had propelled itself.

Metro Cammell, based in Birmingham, was also fighting for a share of this market. It had many decades of railway building experience and knew what its customers' requirements would be. Indeed Met Cam had supplied BR with its first DMUs when the former went to outside suppliers in the 1950s modernisation scheme and these same units, class 101, can still be seen at the time of writing in every day service in many parts of the country. Leyland, on the other hand, was paying dearly for acquiring its expertise and knowledge – and worse was yet to come. It should be recorded that Leyland escaped one problem – the Alexander/Barclay units were blacked by the unions until a High-Court ruling sought by BR forced the union to back down!

ruling sought by BR forced the union to back down!

Mechanically the class 142 trains had a Leyland TL11H engine rated at 200bhp, driving through a bi-directional gearbox, made by Self Changing Gears. Both Leyland and BREL were actively pursuing export business and had demonstrated the class 142 in Denmark, Thailand, Indonesia, Malaysia and the United States. The low operating costs were strongly emphasised.

There were high hopes of securing a major contract from Bangkok for the modernisation of the city's suburban rail and bus network. It was said to be worth up to £385 million at 1985 prices but despite thousands of hours of effort and very considerable expense nothing materialised. Meanwhile the financial position of Leyland Bus became even worse, recording a loss of £33.2 million in 1985.

The Transport Act 1985 duly received the Royal Assent and set out the timetable for radical changes to the operating industry. National Bus Company was to be denationalised as soon as practical. The PTE and municipal fleets were to become arms-length companies, to facilitate privatisation. Scottish Bus Group was to be privatised at a later date, and plans for London were deferred. All services outside London were to be deregulated.

Those operators who wanted to run commercial services under the new Act were given until the end of February 1986 to register the routes which they thought they could run without any subsidy. From then until October local authorities had to work out where there were gaps in the network and where they wanted to provide a subsidy for uneconomic routes which were nevertheless socially desirable. Having awarded contracts, deregulation took effect from 26 October 1986.

Leyland Bus recognised that demand would switch to light van derived vehicles and old second-hand buses in order to reduce operating costs. The funds available to local authorities were being severely constrained by central Government. Leyland feared that the local authorities would have insufficient funds to support the correct levels of bus services, particularly in rural areas.

Adrian Wickens, Business Development Manager of Leyland Bus, addressed a BCC Conference in Manchester in 1985 and said that there was a fundamental difference between providing bus services in urban areas, compared with rural areas. He took the view that it was impossible to legislate for the two sectors under the one Act. He concluded by saying that: "The cost factors advocated by the deregulation enthusiasts are flawed and will result in lasting damage to the industry."

Leyland's concern about rural areas led to the rapid development of the 'Swift', as a low cost 35-40 seat bus for services in a deregulated environment. The Swift used high volume components like a mid-mounted Cummins 'B' series engine and Allison fully automatic gearbox. It replaced the Cub, which, with its front mounted engine and poor entrance arrangement, was more directly derived from the Terrier truck range.

During 1985 the last of a long line of Nationals left the factory, being delivered to Halton Borough Council, a very loyal customer over the years. This was a very significant stage in the Workington's history, because it was the end of the highest volume standard bus ever built in the United Kingdom.

Leyland Bus was running into even more severe problems. Sales were continuing to fall. The Transport Act 1985 was blamed for the drop in domestic orders, but there was also an admission of failure to win substantial orders in export markets.

Before the end of 1985 it was announced that 505 jobs would be cut in Leyland Bus, including 97 at Workington. Ian McKinnon said that a reduced range of core products would form the basis of the product plan and that the selling effort would focus on those markets offering the best sales opportunities.

Halton took the very last National 2 which is seen here with an early National 1 from the same fleet.

It was the Olympian which was largely responsible for keeping Workington going, with 578 and 563 units produced in 1984 and 1985 respectively. Among the few bright spots was an order from London Transport for 250 Olympians, to be bodied by ECW and delivered in 1986.

The Olympian was starting to do particularly well in Hong Kong. One new operator was Citybus, which bought three double deck Olympian coaches to operate regular services between Hong Kong and the Shenzen special economic zone in Guandong province, China. The ECW bodies had 77 coach seats, soft trim and full air-conditioning. They were to be the first of many similar buses, but with Alexander bodywork.

Leyland Bus had also entered into a marketing agreement with the American bus manufacturer, Gillig, to promote sales of the Olympian in both public and private sectors. A left-hand drive two door demonstrator was shown to public operators in several American cities during 1985.

American operators were impressed by the quality of build, ride and handling, and the fuel consumption. When the public authorities ordered buses, however, it was a condition of public funding that they should have the maximum American content, hence the association with Gillig.

That restriction did not prevent Gray Line, the San Francisco based tour operator, from buying ten three axle Olympians in 1986. They had Cummins L10 engines and Voith fully automatic transmission. ECW built the luxurious bodywork, which had 78 reclining seats, full air conditioning, public address facilities and a toilet. They were used on

Top to bottom:

As the domestic market started to decline steeply, Leyland and ECW turned their attention to export. This was a prototype built for Kowloon Motor Bus, Hong Kong, with that operator's typical single width entry door and full depth sliding windows.

The effort to secure export orders even resulted in left-hand engineering, shown here on the prototype which toured North America, and below on the solitary order gained in that market. Despite considerable interest in the concept, and collaboration with Gillig, with the exception of Gray Line the Olympian failed to break the 'buy American' policies of public owned bus companies in the United States.

One of Gray Line's magnificent three-axle Olympians loads passengers for a sight-seeing tour to Muir Woods, California.

sight-seeing tours in the San Francisco area and the neighbouring Californian wine regions.

Leyland Bus claimed that the demonstrations in America were a two way exercise. American authorities were made aware of the advantages of double-deck buses, and many of their staff gained practical experience of them. In return, Leyland learned a great deal about the expectations of American operators, passengers and drivers.

There were plans to step up the sales drive by preparing detailed specifications to suit the different operating requirements, after which Leyland would be in a position to respond to tenders. Apart from the Gray Line order, however, no further business came from the United States.

As Leyland had found with the eight Atlanteans delivered to New York in 1976, the cost of product liability insurance premiums for the United States

After the management and workforce bought Charles H Roe from Leyland, the company was renamed Optare and built a small number of double-deck buses under contract to Leyland, including this example for Cambus.

A typical standard Leyland Olympian with ECW bodywork for the home market. This example started life with Crosville Motor Services, but subsequently passed to Midland Fox.

One of the batch of 20 Olympians which were delivered to Athens in 1982 and are still in service at the time of writing.

A high-capacity Workington-bodied three-axle Olympian in service with KMB in Hong Kong.

market is quite prohibitive, especially when only small numbers of vehicles are supplied. Compliance with the relevant sections of the Federal Motor Vehicle Safety Standards and the emissions regulations was costly and time consuming. America may be the most glamorous market in the world. It is also one of the most difficult to penetrate successfully and profitably.

Meanwhile, there had been progress with the B60 project, including the development of a complete integral body structure. The model was given a long standing Leyland truck name, 'Lynx'. Although it was offered at one standard length, 11.18 metres, early plans had envisaged two lengths, one with a shorter rear overhang which would not have been able to accommodate the option of the longer Gardner engine.

The Workington built body incorporated many features which had been requested as a result of customer experience, including the total absence of curved glass. The driver's screen was recessed and angled back, to reduce glare, and all the side windows were bonded, giving a smooth external appearance.

Whereas the National's structure was riveted, the Lynx underframe was welded from open steel sections and the body from steel tube. Because of welding, the metal could not be pre-treated against corrosion, although epoxy powder coating was used on interior panels, ironically, the decorative purpose for which it had originally been developed.

All the major sub-assemblies such as the sides and roof were built on separate jigs, then brought together in a marry-up jig. The Lynx was then mounted on the same bogies as the National for the remainder of its build. The next stage was the corrosion protection plant. All bare metal was cleaned with an alkaline solution, then, a zinc phosphate base, an epoxy primer, and a polyurethane top coat were applied in succession. Nonetheless corrosion problems arose, creating large warranty costs.

Next, the exterior panels and glass were added. They were bonded to give a smooth appearance, which was in sharp contrast to the rivets all over the National. The one piece roof panel was added, then the Lynx moved into the paint plant which had been installed for the Royal Tiger.

Two pack acrylic paint was applied as standard, with no restrictions on colours or paint layout. After that the Lynx moved like the National to the final line stations for completion. Once again the engine, gearbox and axles, which represented about half the material costs, were added almost at the end of the process.

The first order came from West Midlands PTE for six models with Gardner engines

The 'X' suffixes on the registration date these early design concepts for proprietary bodywork on the B60, or Lynx, underframe to 1981/82. They were prepared as seen, above left by Bova of the Netherlands, above right by the INBUS consortium of Italy, and right by Wadham Stringer. It is interesting to note that the Bova scheme appears to have a much lower driving position than either of the other two concepts, or of any production Lynx. No vehicles were built to any of these designs.

Below: Not quite what it seems. The Lancashire registration number gives away the fact that this Lynx was a demonstrator, painted in West Midlands colours at the time of the handover of the first of that large order.

and four speed Hydracyclic gearboxes. They were to be evaluated in a competitive trial alongside six Volvo B10Ms with Alexander bus bodywork.

A badly needed boost came in January 1986, when Leyland Bus won further orders from British Rail to a total value of £36 million. The first part of the order was for a further 92 class 142 cars, which would make up 46 twin-car sets, principally for services on rural lines. As before, Workington built the bodies, which were then transported to Derby for mounting on rail bogies. Production of the Class 142 units followed straight on from the previous order and was completed by the end of 1986.

The second part of the order was for 70 larger and heavier multiple units, of a new type known by BR as class 155, or 'Super Sprinter'. They were to be built completely at Workington for service on cross-country routes, carrying passengers in greater comfort and over longer distances than the class 142 railcars. They were designed to operate as twin-car units, carrying up to 160 passengers at speeds up to 75 mph, on inter-regional services.

Leyland Bus had previously assessed its engineering and manufacturing resources and had decided to bid for the Sprinter. It was the first time that a complete project was developed on the Computer Aided Design facility at Workington. The system proved its worth in September 1985 when the vehicle length was increased by 3 metres, and the new underframe drawings were released within ten days!

Super Sprinter represented a major change in the position of Leyland Bus as a rail supplier. In a reverse of the previous arrangements, running units were to be delivered from BREL, and Workington was to take responsibility for production of the complete trains. Thus Workington moved from being a supplier of components, albeit very substantial, to a supplier of complete trains. At the time there were high hopes that this would pave the way for supplying future orders for diesel and electric multiple units.

Jim McKnight, Product Development Director, described the Super Sprinter project in his Chairman's Address to the Institution of Mechanical Engineers Automobile Division in April 1992. Each of the two cars was 22.64 m long, 3.75 m high and 2.69 m wide. They were not quite as wide as the Class 142 railbuses but had similar modified cove pieces.

Power was provided by a Cummins NT855-R5 14 litre engine, producing 285bhp and driving through a Voith T211r automatic gearbox. The unladen weight was 76.59 tonnes. These dimensions indicate that the Super Sprinters were a different business from buses.

The order necessitated a major revision of the factory. It was an expensive and disruptive exercise, because Super Sprinter production needed a lot of space. Each car consisted of a welded steel underframe, which, together with the sides and roof, formed an integral structure. The front and rear crash structures were of welded steel.

The National body jigs had to be extensively retuned to make Super Sprinter side sections. The passenger doors were of the sliding plug type which were used extensively on European railways, but representing new technology on a BR train. Plug doors were chosen because the air pulse from passing High Speed Trains had blown open the standard National bus door. The original design proved to be unsatisfactory leading to expensive rectification shortly after they were placed in service. The rectification costs in this area together with transmission problems on the class 141 and 142 units would very probably have put Leyland Bus out of business had the Directors not previously sold the company to Volvo.

Another factory unit had to be acquired, at Derwent Howe in Workington. It was connected by a siding to the main Cumbrian coast railway line. The bodies were carried by road from the main factory to this unit, where they received their rail bogies.

The design work commenced in July 1985 at the risk of Leyland Bus, until the contract was signed in January 1986. The first body shell was delivered to BR's research and development unit at Derby in June 1986 for structural testing, which was completed by September. The pre-production two-car set was ready by April 1987 and the first production trains followed in July.

The first Sprinters entered service between Cardiff and Birmingham in October 1987 and the contract was completed by May 1988. They were not considered to be wholly satisfactory and were later separated into single units. This involved a rebuild of one end and they then had the rather restricted driving cabs at both ends, forming a new class, 153. During 1987, 90 per cent of Workington's output was rail based, and the workforce reached its second highest peak in the plant's history, at just on 500 people. The Lynx was being built at the rate of one a week and Royal Tiger production was down to a trickle.

A symbolic picture both in production and operational context, taken in Wolverhampton. The National takes second place to the Lynx and an Olympian overtakes the pair of them! The Lynx is owned by a former PTE company now in employee ownership, the former NBC Olympian has passed to a British Bus subsidiary and the much-travelled though smart second-hand National belongs to a new-generation 'Independent' fleet.

This was a model of a proposed double-deck suburban train, to be built largely from standard National sections. The concept was feasible in terms of overall height, but the narrow doorways would have restricted passenger entry and exit, increasing station dwell time. This problem had previously been found on two trains of double-deck coaches operated by the Southern Region and withdrawn in the late 1960s.

The class 155 'Super Sprinter' trains required a major rearrangement of the Workington factory. This shows the first of the trains in original two car form. Within four years the vehicles from the first order were converted to separate single car units, becoming British Rail's class 153 in the process.

A Lynx 2 in the Nottingham fleet. After the brave attempt to keep the factory buoyant with railcar business it was soon obvious that the Lynx and Olympian were to be the only models with any future.

Leyland Bus was clearly delighted to win these two large orders, and was working closely with British Rail Engineering. Both companies were very hopeful of orders from overseas railways, claiming that the advanced design and production technology of the National, allied to recent developments in rail vehicle engineering, had resulted in a light, cost effective train, offering high levels of passenger comfort and significant fuel and maintenance savings over traditionally built trains.

Notwithstanding extensive demonstrations, not one single export order was received. Maybe the lack of any local content was a decisive factor. Only one more domestic order was received for railbuses, from West Yorkshire PTE for seven two-car Super Sprinter sets, valued at £4.7 million. They were a variant known as Class 155/1 and production followed the last of the BR vehicles.

The collapse of the domestic bus market because of the Transport Act 1985 had forced Leyland Bus to diversify. Great effort went into the rail business, but with too little experience. It was not the solution to the company's problems and probably only served to add to them.

CHAPTER ELEVEN
The Management Buy Out

An international bus and coach exhibition was held at Earls Court in September 1985. Leyland Bus used that opportunity to display a Royal Tiger Doyen with the newly available 260bhp version of the TL11 engine. It was built for Charles Cook (Biggleswade) Ltd and had 49 Vogel reclining seats, toilet, driver's bunk area and TV/video equipment.

Quite significant revisions were made to the interior trim for the 1986 season. Even so, within weeks of Earls Court, the Royal Tiger project was put under intensive review and was very nearly taken out of production.

Sales and Marketing argued that its withdrawal would not only alienate dealers who had unsold stock and customers who would suffer loss on resale values, but it would also do severe damage to Leyland's credibility in the whole coach sector, which was mainly in the hands of private operators and therefore not greatly affected by the Transport Act 1985. The termination of production would have hit Tiger sales and led to redundancies at Workington.

David Quainton recalled that the Workington management "..fought a rearguard action for several weeks and really against all logic, even though we felt it had a future."

Marketing was asked to look at the total domestic market for coaches, which was running around 1,100 units per annum, and predict the share for integral coaches.

They came up with an estimate of 100, to be shared by the Royal Tiger with the Duple 425 and several continental models. Even so, after great deliberation, it was decided to keep the Doyen in production and hope that the new and improved model could win an increased share of the market!

Other exhibits on the Earls Court stand included a Lynx. It was announced that it could be supplied with different levels of superstructure to meet bodybuilding needs overseas. Leyland Bus was willing to follow the same practice as Mercedes, which offered its O405 city bus, first introduced in 1984, with a standard front end structure, ready to marry up to locally built bodywork.

A Royal Tiger coach in production at Workington.

The first Workington bodied Leyland Royal Tiger Doyen. It was generally agreed that Workington Doyens were better finished than the earlier models out of the Roe plant.

An intriguing artist's impression of what is described in Leyland records as a 'Bury trolleybus' but what seems to have been a forerunner of the Greater Manchester Metro, a contract eventually placed in Italy.

One month later, at the European Bus and Coach Fair at Kortrijk, Leyland announced that Belgium would be the first Lynx export launch market. It would initially be aimed at private sector bus operators, but longer term plans included competing for public sector business. Versions of the Lynx, developed to meet Belgian requirements, were scheduled to enter production at Workington before the end of the year, and demonstrators with Belgian bodywork were due to become available during 1986.

Although Belgium traditionally had been a good market for Leyland Van Hool had developed its own complete range of integral buses and was therefore a powerful local competitor. Jonckheere was developing its own underframe to meet the very low floor height requirements of the major Belgian operators.

It was therefore an astonishing announcement, because Van Hool and Jonckheere had a very strong grip on the Belgian bus market and both wanted to promote their own products. Van Hool's ability to build its own integral buses was by this time well known, but perhaps Leyland failed to realise how near Jonckheere was to launching its model. Not surprisingly the announcement of a European bridge-head into Belgium came to nothing. Only one Lynx underframe was exported around this time, and that was to Australia.

Ian McKinnon and George Newburn, the Manufacturing Operations Director, spent a lot of time looking at manufacturing models between Workington and Farington. McKinnon wanted an ideal world, building core products in volume for core markets, with the minimum amount of manufacturing facilities. His intention was to whittle the range down to a small number of profitable products.

He must have envied the ability of Volvo to fulfil British market demand for bus, coach and double-deck applications from one model, the B10M. That was not possible with Leyland's history and the fragmentation of the product range, including the few remaining export markets.

At first the spotlight centred on Workington as a centre for manufacturing, even to the extent of moving machining operations from Farington. Much time and effort was also spent on examining the feasibility of moving all assembly operations to Workington, which would have been quite a crush. There were even thoughts about building a separate dedicated railbus facility at Workington, linked to the British Rail track.

Within a few months there was an obvious change in direction when it was probably realised that, even if all the range was to be built at Workington, the plant was still too dependent on rail, and that if the rail business did not materialise in sufficient volume, then Workington would not be viable. Anticipated lower order levels from bus customers also influenced the management's thinking.

National Bus orders in 1986 called for only 133 Tigers and 41 Olympians, because the group was about to be dismantled. Once again, Olympian production was moved, this time to Farington. The declared reason was to create space for Sprinter production at Workington. The undeclared reason was to secure work for the BX assembly plant at Farington, because order levels for Tiger were fairly low. The other half of Farington was producing some components, but its main business was spare parts. In other words, the transfer of Olympian was a security move for Farington, but it was a serious threat to Workington, because the future of the factory was now clearly dependent on rail orders.

As with the previous transfer of Olympian from Bristol to Workington, there was a phased period of several months, during which chassis were produced at both factories. Farington built 16 Olympians in 1985, followed by 345 in 1986. Workington ran out of Olympian production with 293 units in 1986, having built a total of 1,948 in the four years from 1983. Fortunately, 286 Olympians were exported in 1986, almost all to Hong Kong.

The Government was trying to sell British Leyland, in whole or in part, and events reached a climax in the first quarter of 1986. Both Ford and Volkswagen had already looked at the car companies, then a number of parties expressed interest in parts of Leyland Vehicles and Land Rover. General Motors came on the scene and made an offer to buy Leyland Trucks, on condition that Land Rover was included, for a price rumoured to be £230 million. The GM plan would have involved rationalisation of its elderly

The Lynx underframe, seen alongside an early completed model.

The radiator grille badge which was designed for the Lynx, but only fitted on a small number of orders.

Bedford truck range with the much more modern and comprehensive Leyland line-up.

That caused a short-sighted but very noisy protest, led by certain West Midlands Members of Parliament, who thumped their chests and said that they did not want to see a British institution like Land Rover pass into foreign control. They failed to pass any comment on the Leyland commercial vehicle operations, which were more valuable than Land Rover, but they were backed by Land Rover enthusiasts, who organised rallies to London, and so on.

The Cabinet was still suffering from the Westland affair, which had caused the resignations of Leon Brittan and Michael Heseltine. Nicholas Ridley was said to be willing to get rid of BL at any price, and backed the GM offer. At least initially, the Prime Minister took the same line. Norman Tebbit, Chairman of the Conservative Party, thought that the sale of Land Rover to GM would be politically damaging before the local elections to be held in May. At least Tebbit was honest!

Sir Austin Bide had become the Chairman of BL, succeeding Sir Michael Edwardes. Executive responsibility at main board level was held by Ray Horrocks for cars and David Andrews for commercial vehicles, including Land Rover. Andrews was a great survivor, a grey finance man who had come from Ford in 1969. He was described in the broadsheet press at the time as 'a man who could effortlessly disappear into a crowd of three!'

The *Financial Times* of 10 March 1986 wrote: 'The Leyland Trucks management feels very strongly that it has been left in the lurch by Mr David Andrews, the BL executive director responsible for commercial vehicle operations, who has taken leave of absence to head the consortium hoping for a management buy out of Land Rover.' He was never popular in Leyland, but that left a very sour taste.

Throughout March the arguments raged in the press, with rumours of various cabinet ministers for or against the GM deal. Back-benchers joined in. For instance, Michael Grylls, Chairman of the Conservative Backbench Trade and Industry Committee, wrote to *The Times* on 11 March: 'There is no doubt that almost any owner would be better than Government. Government is no longer a good owner. For Governments are made up of politicians and civil servants, generally with a lack of understanding of industry's needs, but with an insatiable appetite for day-to-day interference in the firms they control.' How perceptive!

The Cabinet tried to find a compromise which would keep Land Rover in British control. Even 51% was said to be acceptable! General Motors stuck to its guns and said that it was only prepared to buy Land Rover and Leyland Trucks, together and outright, and that no other deal would be considered. Other parties entered the fray, including Aveling-Barford, which had been sold out of BL in 1983 to an American entrepreneur, Adrian Eschallier. He wanted to buy Land Rover and Leyland Bus.

For three to four weeks the Cabinet dithered. There were suggestions that other prospective bidders, including the Lancashire Enterprise Board, had been excluded. There were angry scenes in the House of Commons when a Labour Member of Parliament asked whether any of the Cabinet had relatives who might be associated with the prospective purchasers. That struck straight at the Prime Minister whose son was then employed by Lotus Cars, which had been bought by General Motors a few months earlier.

Although all the public and political debate was about the car and truck subsidiaries, the Government had also made it clear that it wanted to sell Leyland Bus. Early in February, Ian McKinnon and David Quainton were told to expect important visitors at Workington. They turned out to be Peter Steadman and Ron Jones, two directors of MCW. McKinnon and Quainton had the unenviable task of showing them around the factory, which was not too busy at that time.

The MCW men were pretty blunt about Leyland Bus, and Workington in particular. Steadman told his hosts that he had been at a meeting at number 10 Downing Street and, according to him, the Prime Minister had promised that the Laird Group, MCW's parent, would get Leyland Bus. That was why he was so brash during his visit. He behaved as though the deal was already done.

The MCW Metrobus Mk II was a competitor to the Olympian. If MCW had bought Leyland, the most likely outcome would have been MCW bodywork on an Olympian chassis.

MCW thought it would be logical to amalgamate two manufacturers who were involved in buses and trains, especially in a declining market. MCW's bus sales were almost all to a small number of major operators, especially London and some of the PTE's, but they were usually sold in large batches.

The Metroliner double-deck coach had been sold mainly to NBC and SBG subsidiaries, but had almost saturated that limited market. The new 25 seat integral Metrorider was coming on stream. It was an imaginative venture, intended to appeal to operators who wanted something better than van-derived minibuses, but, as events turned out, unfortunately it was rather hastily developed. Even so, at the time of MCW's approach, there was the basis of a more comprehensive bus and coach range.

MCW was much stronger than Leyland Bus on the rail side. The Birmingham factories had supplied British Rail and London Underground for many years, and had won prestigious orders for the Hong Kong Metro. John Gardiner, Chief Executive of the Laird Group, said that his company was not interested in Workington or ECW and that they would be closed. The Leyland team understood that operations would have been centred on Birmingham for trains and bus bodywork, and on Farington for general machining and certain bus chassis.

There was some support in the Government for MCW's plans, which valued Leyland Bus around £12 million, but Leyland Bus was apprehensive about what it perceived as the arrogance of MCW. The intervention of MCW stung McKinnon into action. He quickly realised that there would have been no place for him and some of his colleagues in an MCW owned Leyland Bus.

Within days of the MCW visit, McKinnon approached the BL Board and asked if he could investigate the possibility of a management buy out of Leyland Bus. Permission was granted, and it is perhaps a measure of the minor role of Leyland Bus in Corporate affairs that he was allowed to retain his executive duties, whereas Andrews was given leave of absence to mount his bid for Land Rover.

The Board of Leyland Bus mounted a defensive action. The directors enlisted the help of several people including the local Member of Parliament for Workington, Dale Campbell-Savours. He made an approach to Volvo to see if they would be interested. At that time, Volvo was cash rich, sitting on funds equivalent to more than £1 billion.

Having looked at the Leyland Bus accounts and forecasts, Sandy Glennie advised his parent company not to become involved. Leyland Bus was expected to lose around £46 million in 1986, and there was no certainty that the Government would have made any concession to a foreign purchaser.

Campbell-Savours then helped the management with its buy-out plan. He said that he lobbied every member of the Rover board and Government ministers, especially Peter Morrison, the Industry Minister. He told the *Times and Star* in Workington: "I am leaving no stone unturned and I am giving a considerable amount of my time to the issue of Leyland." He went on to say: "This whole affair only arises because of the Government's desire to privatise and follows on the Government's disastrous policy of deregulation of buses."

Meanwhile, on the car side, Ray Horrocks spoke out boldly and said that the Government's dithering was damaging car sales. A figure of £240 million worth of lost sales was quoted. He was soon dealt a bad hand. Sir Austin Bide retired and his place as Chairman of BL was taken by Graham Day, a Canadian lawyer who had impressed the Government during his tenure at British Shipbuilders. Horrocks told the press that he had been punished for his criticism of the Government and he left BL after declining another post under Day.

In April, the Government changed its mind and decided not to accept any offer for Leyland Trucks or Land Rover. The General Motors team returned to Detroit in disgust, having refused to accept any compromise deal. Having failed in his bid for Land Rover, Andrews disappeared from the industry almost immediately. Day announced in June that BL would henceforth be known as the Rover Group.

There are few things more dangerous than politicians interfering in industry. The management of Leyland Trucks had supported the GM proposal, but the opportunity to secure the future was lost. Shortly after that, GM announced its decision to cease manufacture of Bedford trucks and buses at Dunstable. GM had argued that it needed the combined size of the two businesses to make a viable commercial vehicle operation, and they would surely have concentrated on the much more modern facilities at Leyland.

It is a prospect which could be debated at length. There are those who argue that Bedford was bureaucratic and had a tired model range. On the other hand GM sorted out the Vauxhall car range, raising its image greatly, and turning it into the most profitable volume car manufacturer in Britain. By taking the best of the Bedford and

If the Government had agreed to sell Leyland's commercial vehicle operations and Land Rover to GM, the Bedford Venturer, seen here with Willowbrook bodywork, might have become a complementary member of an expanded bus and coach range. Its most obvious shortcoming, an engine barely powerful enough for the weight of the more luxurious bodywork offered, might have been met by use of a Leyland unit.

Ian McKinnon (left) handing over a Duple bodied Tiger to Bob MacLeod, Deputy Chairman of Scottish Bus Group, at Stirling Castle.

Leyland dealers GM could have built a very strong organisation.

Leyland Trucks, however, had not been idle during the GM negotiations. Within days of that deal collapsing there was the announcement of a contract with DAF Trucks, which had at one time been a Leyland licensee. The Dutch company would distribute Sherpa vans and lighter Leyland trucks, under 15 tonnes gross, through its continental dealer network. It was a logical deal, because the DAF truck range started at 17 tonnes gross, and the Leyland models would give DAF dealers a comprehensive range to sell and service.

Around the same time Cummins bought Self Changing Gears, principally to gain access to the latter's technology in railcar transmissions and be able to offer complete power packs.

Ian McKinnon and his co-directors were making progress with their buy-out plans. They were encouraged by the knowledge that the Rover Group would meet the cost of any factory closures and redundancies necessary before they took control. In July 1986 there was an announcement that the Government was prepared to sell Leyland Bus to the management team for a sum of £11.7 million, which included a 33% stake in Leyland Parts.

The deal was not concluded immediately. Within a month, Leyland Bus announced further grim news. The domestic market was forecast to fall even further and the company made 1,250 redundancies, out of a total workforce of 2,600. This included the closure of Eastern Coach Works at Lowestoft and the loss of a further 131 jobs at Workington. David Quainton became Sales & Marketing Director of Leyland Bus and Roy Nicholson succeeded him as Managing Director at Workington.

Nicholson's appointment caused alarm at Workington. He was a finance man, with little knowledge of buses or the wider industry. There were fears that his skills might be needed for closure of the factory.

There were 468 job losses at Farington and a further 158 disappeared with the closure of the head office in Thurston Road, Leyland. McKinnon seriously considered stopping chassis production at Farington and moving it to Workington, but Sprinter production occupied too much space to make that possible.

Total British registrations of all makes of double-deck buses fell very steeply, from 945 in 1985, down to 754 in 1986, and then an absolutely disastrous 177 in 1987. That alone was sufficient to make the closure of Eastern Coach Works inevitable. This time there was no rush to transfer production elsewhere, although the jigs and tools for the Olympian double-deck body, the only product which ECW had built since 1983, were in due course transferred to Workington.

There was no news of the management buy-out for several months, then the Government admitted to talks between the Rover Group and two prospective foreign purchasers for Leyland Trucks. It emerged that they were DAF, which had recently entered into the agreement to distribute certain Leyland trucks on the continent, and Paccar, an American group which built the famous Kenworth and Peterbilt trucks, and which had earlier bought Foden. DAF was also supplying its 8.25 litre engine for a version of Leyland's Constructor 6 truck chassis for Ready Mixed Concrete.

Although it was rumoured that Paccar outbid DAF, the Dutch were willing to take on the Freight Rover van plant in Birmingham and that is said to have tipped the

Government's decision in favour of the Dutch.

There was strong speculation that the buy-out of Leyland Bus had been held up in order to give DAF the opportunity to take it over, in addition to Trucks and Parts. DAF looked at Leyland Bus and dismissed the idea. It would have made little sense, because the two product ranges were largely competitive, with the notable exception of the Olympian double-decker.

McKinnon's team received a lot of help from prominent people in the operating industry who genuinely wanted to see the company survive. The late David Graham, Director General of Greater Manchester PTE, was particularly helpful, making introductions to banks and other advisors. It was intended that the PTE would provide some of the funds, but, at the very last minute, the Government prohibited the PTE from investing in a private company.

This happened when McKinnon was on his way to the continent on holiday. He was stopped at Dover and had to ditch his caravan, while he returned to find other sources of finance! He tried to persuade several companies to take a share in the buy-out. There were fruitless talks with Scania, which was looking for bodybuilding capacity. Alexander, at that time still controlled by the family shareholders, showed some interest, but eventually decided not to get involved.

According to popular rumour at the time McKinnon and Newburn kept chipping away at the price which the Department of Trade and Industry was prepared to accept, until they were finally given a 'take it or leave it' ultimatum of £4 million, when the company was capitalised at £17 million!

The price included £2.5 million of railcars about to be invoiced to British Rail, and the Government wrote off £55 million of debt! And, as if that was not enough, there were no restrictions on the future ownership or control of the company. All these factors showed how desperately the Government wanted to get rid of Leyland Bus!

The deal was finally concluded on 13 January 1987, when it was announced that Leyland Bus had been sold to a consortium of the management and banks. The consortium held 72% of the company; 12% was held for other potential shareholders, including Lancashire Enterprise, which figured prominently in the original plan; and the balance of 16% was due to be offered to the remaining 1,250 employees.

The Workington and Farington factories were included in the buy-out, along with the bus and coach service centres at Nottingham, Chorley, Bristol and Glasgow, also Leyland Bus Hong Kong and certain rights to the specific bus parts business. Leyland DAB remained part of the Rover Group until its own management buy-out, although it continued its commercial and technical relationship with Leyland Bus until later deciding to join the United Bus consortium.

The decision not to take a stake in Leyland Parts was surprising, because that was the main profit generator. It was also an important means of keeping in contact with prospective purchasers. Probably the management team felt that they could not afford the estimated £7.7 million for a 33% stake. Instead, they came to an agreement where they had certain rights to parts which were intended exclusively for buses and coaches.

The management buy-out was a brave move in the midst of the ravages caused by deregulation and denationalisation. Certain customers supported the new arrangement very solidly, particularly Ulsterbus, which placed an order for 195 Tigers within one month of the buy-out. On the other hand, one or two of the former NBC companies, which had been largely dependent on Leyland products, moved elsewhere. In

Ulsterbus was a strong supporter of the Tiger, almost all of which received bodywork built by Alexander (Belfast).

Badgerline purchased 36 buses from Volvo at a time when Leyland might reasonably have expected to get the order. One of the Alexander bodied single-deckers is seen here.

one notable deal Badgerline placed an order with Volvo for 36 buses.

Several competitors thought that the new team at Leyland Bus was vulnerable. Quite a number of operators were concerned about the finances of Leyland Bus and the company's ability to survive as a long term player. Volvo was best placed to exploit this weakness, promoting the B10M very strongly against the Tiger.

When the registration statistics for the first quarter in 1987 were released, Volvo had taken the lead for the first time in the British bus and coach market. It was a position which Leyland had held for many years and which was officially confirmed from 1973, when SMMT began collating and publishing registration data.

Nevertheless, as Chairman and Chief Executive of the new company, McKinnon was sounding confident. He claimed that the deal was not highly geared and that the funds for the purchase would be paid back with interest at the end of three years. Bankers Trust of America, the seventh largest commercial bank in the United States, had considerable experience of management buy-outs and claimed that every one had so far been a success. Another early boost to the new owners came with an order from Hong Kong for 110 three axle Olympians.

When Leyland Trucks and Leyland Bus parted company, it caused a radical rethink on major mechanical parts, particularly engines and gearboxes. The new Truck company was quick to confirm the true cost of building very small volumes of TL11 engines, especially in horizontal form, and the Leyland Bus team was already aware of competitive terms from Cummins. They looked not only at Cummins, but also Iveco, both as solus suppliers and as alternatives, before opting for Cummins.

Another problem was the Hydracyclic gearbox, which was proving to be neither as simple nor as reliable as the previous Pneumocyclic unit. A number of customers preferred either Voith or ZF fully automatic gearboxes, particularly the ZF Ecomat, which was gaining an excellent reputation.

Leyland Bus therefore entered into an interesting agreement with ZF, whereby Farington made certain components for the German company. Leyland Bus also gained the right to assemble and manufacture ZF's automatic gearboxes, which became standard on the entire heavy duty bus range and optional on coaches. ZF, which was faced with ever increasing costs in Germany, gained access to a well equipped lower cost base in Britain and secured the lion's share of Leyland's gearbox requirements.

In June 1987 the Conservatives were re-elected with a very large majority. That meant that there would be no change in their policies towards the bus industry. About the same time Leyland Bus strengthened its board by the appointment of two non-executive directors. Irwin Dalton had been Executive Vice-Chairman and Chief Executive of Operations at National Bus. Malcolm Norgate had recently retired as Chairman and Chief Executive of Quinton Hazell.

In another move, later to become more significant, Sandy Glennie resigned as Director and General Manager of Volvo Bus UK to become Managing Director Marketing of the Plaxton Group. A few months before this old established coachbuilder had been taken over by the Kirkby Group, its largest dealer. The new Chairman, David Matthews, and his team revitalised Plaxton and had ambitious plans for its future.

Glennie's brief was not only to consolidate Plaxton's position in Britain but to take

Proposals to sell the Lynx into Belgium would have come up against stiff domestic competition from the likes of the Van Hool A600.

the company into export markets. His departure came at a critical time for Volvo, which had become the world's largest exporter and second largest manufacturer of buses and coaches over 12 tons gross.

Workington was still pre-occupied with Sprinter production. While the rail business was welcome, it was spasmodic. None of the export drives had produced results. The directors faced the dilemma of having to decide whether to push harder for more rail business because Workington could not survive on Lynx alone.

By then British Rail was planning the aluminium framed class 158 railbus, which represented a move away from the steel framed National structure. Workington seriously considered bidding for this business, even to the extent of looking at other factory sites, but eventually the contracts went to BREL.

In the second half of 1987 there were signs that the market was starting to pick up. Following the closure of Eastern Coach Works Leyland Bus no longer had any double-deck bodybuilding capacity.

In a curious twist of fate a short term licence agreement was made with Optare, so that the former Roe factory could build some batches of double-deck bodywork to ECW designs, using some ECW tooling which was temporarily loaned for the purpose. About thirty bodies were built to semi-coach specification for Yorkshire Rider, Maidstone, Cambus and Reading. This was purely a temporary measure.

Production of the Lynx commenced very slowly, because of denationalisation and deregulation. There were 25 registrations in 1986, rising to 62 in 1987. Early in 1988 Workington received an order from Caldaire Holdings for 50 Lynx.

Caldaire had been formed by the management team of West Riding, when they bought out their company and its subsidiaries from NBC. Subsequently, they acquired United Auto, based at Darlington. Caldaire had previously taken Lynx, but fitted with Gardner engines. They joined a growing number who were switching to the newly available horizontal version of the Cummins L10, which developed 210 bhp.

By the latter half of 1987 the directors were having serious doubts about the company's future. Jim McKnight recalled this period in his Chairman's Address to the Institution of Mechanical Engineers, when he said: ".... it was clear that while rationalisation plans had achieved avoidance of a loss, there was not enough cash being generated within the business to provide funds for new product development and in particular to combat the competitive threat anticipated from the European producers with 1992 in mind.'

There was a lot of talk about the creation of the Single Market, which would remove internal barriers in the European Community and permit totally free trade. The proposed and actual commencement date was 1 January 1993, but the British and certain other member Governments promoted the change as '1992', presumably in a sensible effort to make businesses plan ahead and be ready for the actual date.

The Single Market initiative concentrated the minds of commercial vehicle manufacturers located inside the Community. This was particularly true in the bus

Lynxes and an Olympian seen in the Vehicle Test
Centre at Workington, just before delivery.

Facing page top to bottom:

Some of the National tooling was adapted
for Lynx production. Once again, engines,
gearboxes and axles were fitted late in the
production process.

The Lynx underframe relied quite heavily on
the body for total structural integrity, but
could be moved under its own power with
the temporary bracing shown here. The very
low floor line is also clearly visible.

The West Riding livery of green and pale
cream was simple and yet effective when
applied to the Lynx.

DAF was not interested in buying Leyland
Bus at the same time as Leyland Trucks,
largely because it had its own competitive
bus and coach range. This shows a typical
rear-engined SB model, with Caetano
Algarve bodywork.

sector. It was very rare for German, French or Italian bus companies to buy other than domestic products. That was partly because many tender documents were written in a precise manner which made it difficult for other than the chosen manufacturer to succeed. The major manufacturers saw opportunities to increase sales in the home markets of their competitors, but also feared the invasion of their home ground.

The plans for the Single Market also caused great concern in the boardrooms of companies located outside the European Community. They had noted the very strong and fully justified resentment about the rising volume of Japanese car imports to the Community. Peugeot and Fiat were particularly strong in their complaints that the playing field was not level, because the Japanese used every means, fair or foul, to restrict car imports to Japan. There were similar complaints about other nations in many other industries.

That created an atmosphere where many companies believed that the European Community would set up stiff tariff barriers against imports. The popular conception was 'Fortress Europe'. In the motor industry, it stimulated companies like Nissan and Toyota to build factories inside the Community. It also worried manufacturers in countries like Sweden and the United States, because they could not afford to lose their share in the world's largest market.

At the same time the bureaucrats in Brussels were producing masses of proposed legislation on every topic under the sun. The motor industry was subjected to a barrage of Directives, many of which were desirable, such as reducing vehicle emissions. Only the largest manufacturers could cope with the volume of legislation and the cost of research and development necessary to ensure compliance. As Jim McKnight indicated, the directors of Leyland Bus realised that they could not handle this burden on their own.

Ian McKinnon started looking for partners or purchasers. His quest took him to Plaxton and David Matthews, who put the idea to his Board in October 1987. They included Sandy Glennie who had taken a long hard look at Leyland Bus only a few months before. Plaxton knew Leyland well, through its Kirkby dealership side, but the Board felt that it was too ambitious, even for an ambitious company!

McKinnon was not unduly upset. He had other irons in the fire. He was quietly in contact with some of the continental manufacturers to see if any of them might be interested in acquiring Leyland Bus. Once again, the travel agents arranged flights to Gothenburg.

CHAPTER TWELVE

Sell Out

One of Ian McKinnon's prospective buyers was Volvo Bus. There was some hypnotic quality in the Swedish giant which seemed to attract Leyland Bus like a moth to a light. Leyland had lost the initiative to Volvo, even in the home market, on vital matters like pricing policy and the franchising of coach dealers. From about 1981 onwards directors and senior executives of Leyland Bus had an obsessive interest in what Volvo was doing.

McKinnon probably sensed a change in climate. The parent AB Volvo had enjoyed a number of very successful years and had a substantial cash mountain. Yet the Volvo Board was concerned that costs were rising in Sweden and that the country was at that time unlikely to join the European Community. Probably because of concern about 'Fortress Europe' the parent board had decided not only that there would be no further expansion in Sweden, but that the subsidiaries should look for opportunities to expand within the European Community.

The President of Volvo Bus Corporation was Larserik Nilsson, a long-standing Volvo man who had been appointed in September 1985. Nilsson and his staff had drawn up a strategy to improve the position of Volvo in the bus and coach market into the 1990s. In 1986 he had told a press conference that: "We are in a unique position in today's bus and coach world – we can afford to work with a very long term view".

The negotiations with Volvo were kept very quiet, but senior executives came in and out of Britain, apparently unobserved. A top level team visited Workington, under the guise of prospective customers from Germany! At that time the plant was heavily involved with Sprinters and starting to build up production of the Lynx. There was also considerable activity at Farington, with the Leyland Bus board claiming buoyant order books. It looked as though the domestic market was picking up, with sales in the first quarter to March 1988 up 55% on the equivalent period in 1987.

McKinnon and his co-directors had got Volvo on the line, then picked up a rumour that the Government was planning to change the rules on Capital Gains Tax, with effect from the fiscal year commencing 6 April 1988. In an effort to conclude a deal before that date they applied pressure to Volvo. On 28 March 1988 it was announced that Volvo Bus had acquired Leyland Bus, just fifteen months after the company had been sold to its management team. No price was mentioned, but reliable estimates put it around £22-£24 million.

Larserik Nilsson became Chairman of Leyland Bus. Jürgen Bahr, Marketing Director of Volvo Bus Corporation, was temporarily appointed as Managing Director. McKinnon stayed on the board in a non-executive capacity. He turned up a few days later at the annual Scottish BCC Conference at Gleneagles.

On the first evening, before any of the formal sessions had begun, several senior figures from the operating side of the industry soon made it very clear that he was not welcome. They felt betrayed, because he had sought their help and their orders when buying out from the Government, but had presented the Volvo deal as *fait accompli*. Most of them only learned about the deal when they read it in the press. By the morning, McKinnon was gone from Gleneagles, and the bus industry!

The media emphasised Nilsson's unfortunate statement that there would be no redundancies at Farington and Workington, and that the factories would form a platform for a drive into continental European markets. To be fair, he was a very genuine person and was almost certainly not aware of the serious state of affairs which existed at Leyland Bus.

The Lynx was undoubtedly one of the factors which interested Volvo when it considered purchase of McKinnon's Leyland bus. Its potential in Europe, marketed through Volvo and with Volvo engines, appeared to offer considerable potential but it was not to be. When the photographer wanted a new angle at a handover, however, Sandy Glennie was happy to join Ken Hodgson and Mike Hunter both of Caldaire, when they got the polish out to a new Lynx 2.

Nilsson saw the Volvo and Leyland product ranges as largely complementary and said that Leyland's highly skilled design engineers were among the best in the world. Another attraction was the Lynx. Nilsson said that it would have taken Volvo three to four years to develop a similar model in order to compete in Europe.

Most employees at Farington and Workington greeted the announcement with relief. Many felt cheated that they had not received the promised share allotment but thought that Volvo would represent a much more secure long term future. There was considerable resentment towards McKinnon and his co-directors, of whom only Jim McKnight, and briefly Owen Quinn, stayed on. Only a few weeks earlier McKinnon had been questioned by senior managers about a rumoured sale and had replied that he was "...proud to be the owner of Leyland Bus!"

Critics claimed that the buy-out team had been production led and had little idea about sales and marketing. Others thought that they had been extremely lucky to find a buyer and make such a handsome profit on their investment. Reliable sources said that McKinnon made about £8 million!

At the time of the purchase it was announced that Volvo Bus (GB) Ltd would continue to run as a separate organisation, selling Swedish built products in the British market. Bill Russell had succeeded Sandy Glennie as General Manager of that company and was continuing to find new customers for the B10M. Shortly before the purchase of Leyland Bus he had appointed Arlington as a Volvo coach dealer, thereby eliminating the last coach dealer which was solely dependent on Leyland products, and had been very loyal to Leyland.

Volvo Bus Corporation had made a profit of £16.36 million in 1987. The price paid for Leyland Bus was tiny in comparison with Volvo's total wealth. It soon became apparent, however, that the order book was nothing like as healthy as it appeared.

The directors of Leyland Bus were particularly optimistic, if that is the right word, when talking about forward orders. Large numbers were in fact stock orders, built on speculation that customers would be found at some future date. A small amount of stock might have been justifiable in the unstable market created by deregulation and denationalisation, but not in the model mix and quantities which they had built, and continued to build for some months thereafter.

'Commercial Motor' had written a special feature on Leyland Bus in February 1988, unaware of the negotiations with Volvo. Brian Weatherley of CM interviewed Owen Quinn on sales performance and observed: 'Leyland Bus finds it is better to measure its performance in terms of vehicle output, even though in the public arena, it is registrations which are most frequently used as the yardstick.' He subtly emphasised his point by noting that Leyland's registrations in the UK market, according to SMMT, had fallen from 873 in 1986 to 441 in 1987!!

Volvo and Leyland had fundamentally different ways of conducting business. Because of the Swedish company's systematic approach to all liabilities they were not aware that individual Leyland directors and managers could make deals with customers on matters like deeper discounts and extended warranties. Leyland's approach to sales and marketing frequently resulted in spot deals and, inevitably, some important points were not disclosed.

Volvo's Bus Assembly Plant at Borås in Sweden developed a dock assembly system for putting chassis together. Instead of the traditional assembly line, with workers at each stage, a team is responsible for assembling a complete chassis from start to finish, largely at one station. The principle of making a small team responsible for individual chassis had been used much earlier in a simpler way by some of the British manufacturers including Thornycroft and Bristol.

Jürgen Bahr settled into the post of Acting Managing Director and held a press conference about six weeks later. He identified the four main priorities as strengthening aftermarket support, developing the export business, product development, and preparing for the production of B10M in Britain.

This last point was particularly interesting. The main Volvo Bus assembly plant at Borås in Sweden was working at full capacity. Parts came from a variety of suppliers, principally in Sweden and Germany, and some from Britain. It then made sense to use available capacity in Britain, not only to supply the domestic market, but also neighbouring continental countries.

It was also stressed that Leyland Bus would be run as a separate limited company, answering direct to the main Volvo Bus Board. In the short term that created some embarrassing managerial problems in the British market.

Volvo built up a very successful export business. This front engined truck derived coach chassis with local bodywork is typical of large numbers sold into south America.

Two models were abandoned almost immediately. The Royal Tiger Doyen had failed to live up to expectations. After the transfer from Roe, Workington had built a total of 46 underframes and 108 complete Doyens, and none was on order at the time of the announcement. Yet, in the interview with 'Commercial Motor' mentioned above, Owen Quinn had hinted that the Royal Tiger Doyen would be offered with the Cummins L10 engine, rated at 290bhp, for the 1989 season. He claimed that the use of this engine would broaden the model's appeal to long distance tour operators.

Total Doyen production from Roe and Workington was only 150 units. Spreading the development and facility costs of more than £6 million, at a conservative estimate, over this production, meant that the cost per unit was over £40,000. That did not allow for any material or labour or overhead costs for actual production, at a time when the selling price was around £60-65,000! No wonder Volvo abandoned it so quickly, even though it had no competing rear-engined model.

The other model which was dropped was the Leyland Lion, built by DAB in Denmark, but with a high percentage of British sourced components. Ironically this underfloor engined double-decker had been introduced by Leyland as a panic measure to combat the increasing level of orders for double-deck versions of the Volvo B10M.

Bahr also announced that domestic market models would continue to use proprietary engines, but that the Lynx would be sold abroad as a Leyland with a Volvo engine. Volvo Bus had already spoken to its European importers, who expressed their strong interest in the Leyland Bus franchise.

More ominously he had also looked at the arrangements for supplying spare parts through Leyland DAF. McKinnon and his team had felt unable to handle the distribution of Bus parts and struck a deal with the Truck company whereby they received a commission on sales of parts which were exclusive to bus and coach models. This was very difficult to monitor. Although there had been meetings, Bahr commented: "..in the long run it is not feasible'.

At the same time Bahr announced the appointment of a new Managing Director for Leyland Bus. John Arkell held the same position at Volvo BM (UK) Ltd, the plant and construction division, based at Duxford, near Cambridge. A big sociable man, he had trained as an agricultural engineer, working earlier in his career with the British Motor Corporation in America and subsequently with Leyland Tractors at Bathgate. He took up his new position on 1 August 1988.

The jigs and tools for the Eastern Coach Works double-deck body on the Olympian chassis had been transferred to Workington, but production did not commence immediately. A number of detail design improvements were incorporated into the structure to cure known weaknesses, with the aim of increasing durability.

The ECW designs were also modified so that the body could be assembled by semi-skilled workers in Workington. A new body line was installed. All the structural parts, numbering about 1,200, were to be built in the small unit opposite the main factory, by that time known as 'Unit 2'.

The method of construction of the Olympian body was totally different from the National or the Lynx. It was much more traditional, which put further skill demands on the diversifying but still quite standardised plant. It was intended that there would eventually be eight body variants, based on different heights, wheelbases and door configurations.

Chassis came up from Farington and were prepared for bodybuilding, then went through various stages. Wheelarches were fitted almost at the beginning, followed by the right body side, intermediate floor, left body side, front, rear and staircase. Piping,

wiring and panels were then added, before the vehicle passed into the railbus paint plant, which was separate from that used for the Lynx. From there, Olympians passed to the final trim lines, where seats, doors, destination equipment and trim were added.

When production restarted, initially at one per week, the first examples were built on Olympian chassis for Colchester Borough Transport. The body looked virtually identical to the ECW product, although a number of improvements were incorporated. Other early orders came from Isle of Man Transport, East Yorkshire Motor Services, Southern Vectis, and Metrobus of Orpington. The feeling in Workington was more optimistic than it had been for some time.

After the desperately low sales in the British market in 1986 and 1987, registrations in 1988 picked up quite dramatically. Leyland registrations rose from 441 in 1987 to 779 in 1988, an improvement of 76.6%. Volvo rose from 411 to 591, a gain of 43.8%. Together, that gave the Swedish owned company a share of well over 60% of the British market for large buses and coaches (over 7.5 tonnes gross).

During the early months of Volvo ownership some of the stiffest competition to Leyland Bus came from Volvo Bus at Warwick. In September 1988 it was announced that sales, marketing and service for the two marques would be brought together in a new company, to be headed by Sandy Glennie, who returned from Plaxton to Volvo.

This company received the rather unwieldy name of VL Bus and Coach (UK) Ltd, which prompted one senior executive in the operating industry to refer to them as the 'Very Lovely' people. VL immediately assumed responsibility for sales and service of Volvo Bus products in the UK and Eire.

The new company was due to take over responsibility for Leyland products from 1 January 1989 but, following protests from Leyland, a small number of key fleets remained under the control of Leyland Bus for a few months thereafter. The purpose was to effect a gentle gradual introduction to Volvo.

Top to bottom

An Olympian double-deck body under construction in the Workington Plant. The workforce quickly adapted to some of the more traditional skills required in the construction of this product.

Southern Vectis took three batches of Workington built Olympians from 1989 to 1991. This is one of the last batch, awaiting delivery.

Both the chassis and the bodywork of these Olympians were built entirely at Workington. Although in different liveries, both were seen when working for the former Colchester Borough Transport.

As the new sales and marketing team took over, the uncomfortable stock building situation was uncovered. Leyland had anticipated a continual rise in the market, following deregulation and the rise in sales in 1988. Volvo had an enviable reputation throughout the industry for more accurate market forecasting. There must have been some awful arguments, but eventually VL was confirmed as the credible force.

An interesting Lynx underframe was built to the maximum 12 metre length and received an Alexander body, with a Lynx front end grafted on to the aluminium framed structure. It was exhibited at a UITP exhibition in Singapore in 1988, in the livery of Singapore Bus Services, then went on extended trial.

Workington entered 1989 largely as a one product plant, having completed the last of the railbuses for British Rail and West Yorkshire PTE. The new year started well, with West Midlands Travel placing an order for 150 Lynx, strengthening its position as Britain's best selling single-deck bus.

Unfortunately there were two or three serious technical problems, particularly back pressure from the fuel supply system which could cause hot diesel to surge up the fuel filler pipe when a depot attendant refuelled the bus. There were also problems with some of the bonded glazing, but, excuse the pun, they were quickly cured.

Despite the optimistic words shortly after the take-over about exporting the Lynx, the plans never came to fruition. A left hand drive Lynx underframe was fitted with a Volvo THD100 engine, basically the same unit as the B10M, and displayed at the RAI Show in Amsterdam in the spring of 1989.

It next appeared on the stand of Volvo Concesionarios at the Barcelona Show in May 1989. Volvo's Spanish importer was reputed to be keen to order 100, partly on the strength of Leyland's reputation in the Spanish market. Apart from the fact that Leyland had supplied thousands of buses to Spain, the principal domestic manufacturer, Pegaso, was still building some products under Leyland licence.

Just hours before the Show opened there were frantic telephone calls from Gothenburg. The Lynx could not be removed from the stand. Therefore it was to be displayed as a concept vehicle, but no orders were to be taken.

Three reasons for this sudden change of mind eventually emerged. Firstly, Leyland Bus had frequently told the parent company that the Lynx was an underframe and that it needed careful co-operation with the bodybuilder to ensure the integrity of the complete product. It was not a simple chassis like the B10M. Some say that this advice caused second thoughts in Gothenburg.

Secondly, Volvo was by then starting to develop a new rear-engined bus chassis which would have a high percentage of parts in common with the B10M. It was eventually launched at the end of 1991 as the B10B. It made little sense to promote the Lynx in continental markets if it was only going to be a stop-gap model.

Thirdly, by this time, Volvo had found that the Lynx was very expensive to build, compared with the profitable B10M. Volvo builds almost all its main components in high volume, suitable for several applications, and benefits from a production system where one semi-skilled man can control several modern highly-automated machine tools. For instance, the 9.6 litre engine is used in trucks, buses, construction equipment, and other applications, including marine. The core engine is produced in large numbers. The unique accessories for each application are added later.

In contrast, many of the main components of the Lynx were being built in very small numbers, often by skilled people at Farington, using old machines which required constant attention. That was a legacy of the failure to re-invest in the 1970s. It also meant that Leyland Bus was unable to negotiate the most favourable terms with suppliers, because there was not the volume base. Volvo could not make these facts public at the time. It was three or four years later that the compelling arguments for B10B over Lynx became clear.

The B10B also replaced the B10R, which had been available for a decade, but never been offered on the British market. Although it had a lower frame height than the B10B, it had far fewer components in common with the B10M, and it did not quite enjoy the mid-engined model's reputation for reliability. The last B10Rs were forty delivered to Maastricht at the end of 1991.

Even so there had been considerable work on a programme to increase the Volvo content of Lynx, in place of proprietary units. That also came to an end, after completing the engineering work for installing a Volvo engine. One of the major costs of the Lynx was the hub reduction rear axle, which had been planned for the Lynx and subsequently extended to the Tiger to obtain more volume. If the standard high volume B10M rear axle and certain other units had been fitted, there would have been further substantial savings, estimated at 8% of the Lynx price.

The net effect of engineering work on the B10B and the Lynx was to abandon any

The first of the large Lynx order for West Midlands Travel was handed over in glorious weather at a hotel in the Lake District. This view shows the split step entrance arrangement.

The left-hand drive Lynx underframe, fitted with Volvo's 9.6 litre horizontal engine.

The Lynx had a wide two step entry onto a floor only 520mm above the ground. Note the traditional habit of laying brown paper on the gangway floor, immediately before delivery.

Compared with the National, a wide variety of interior seating and trim arrangements could be fitted in the Lynx. This view shows traditional leather-cloth seating for Fishwick of Leyland.

The Volvo B10R was in effect a rear-engined version of the B10M, but was never offered on the British market. A typical continental model, with bodywork by Hainje, now part of Berkhof, is seen in Maastricht.

prospect of selling the Lynx outside the British market. Indeed, it was not going to be part of any future development programme, although that decision was kept very quiet at the time.

The left hand drive Volvo-powered Lynx went from the Barcelona Show to Portugal, where there had been talk about using it as a demonstrator. It was bodied by Camo, in which Volvo had a shareholding, but then returned to Leyland as a test vehicle. At the time of going to press, it was still being used to evaluate sophisticated units which could well be incorporated in future products.

British companies often announce bad news around Christmas, and 1988 was no exception, only this time it was MCW's parent, the Laird Group. They put the MCW bus, taxi and railway subsidiaries up for sale. MCW had diversified into the manufacture of the integral Metrorider minibus which attracted many orders. That led to production problems which were so severe that the Managing Director and Finance Director had resigned during the summer. Although provisional plans for an 11 metre integral single-decker had been released in May 1988, it was never built.

It was widely believed that MCW's bus activities were losing money heavily, probably as much as £55 million from 1986 to 1988. Laird's Chairman, John Gardiner, said at the time that if his company had been permitted to buy Leyland Bus, it would have become a major force in the British bus industry. Probably MCW was turned down by the Government because its plans would have included the closure of Workington and ECW. Although parts of the MCW bus range were sold to Optare/United Bus, Workington outlived the MCW plant in Birmingham, for so long a major force in the British bus building industry.

When Volvo acquired Leyland Bus many operators and trade journalists assumed that the B10M would replace the Tiger. It would have been a logical decision, because the B10M was lower, lighter and more versatile. By this time, the Tiger relied on bought-in engines and gearboxes, and was considerably more expensive to build than the B10M.

Dealers reported a sharp drop in interest in the Tiger. Competitors like DAF and Dennis set their stalls out for Tiger operators, but Volvo had to continue selling the Tiger stocks which had been built up at Farington.

Meanwhile, plans were advancing for the assembly of the B10M in Britain. This very popular multi-purpose chassis had first been introduced in 1980. The B10M MkIII was launched in the summer of 1988, incorporating a number of improvements, including optional engines with more power but better fuel consumption and lower emissions. For the British market, Volvo offered either the THD102KD engine developing 340bhp or the THD102KA at 262bhp.

The top of the range GLE and the B10MT, with a third trailing axle for higher gross weights, were fitted as standard with Volvo's new seven speed synchromesh gearbox. It was controlled by a small car-size gear lever, mounted on the side of the driver's seat, and called EGS, for Easy Gear Shift. This system was optional on the standard GL version of the B10M.

Facing page top to bottom

MCW was quick to exploit the demand for small buses which came as a direct result of deregulation and denationalisation. In concept the Metrorider was a great improvement on van-based models. Unfortunately, inadequate development and production problems caused substantial losses, contributing significantly to MCW's decision to pull out of the bus market. There was much in favour of the Metrorider's concept and quality improved dramatically after Optare took it over.

Top of the Volvo B10M range was the three-axle B10MT, seen here with Jonckheere coachwork, which qualified as a double-decker for tilt purposes, because the main deck was above the small rear lower deck lounge.

One of the very few Leyland Lynx models in the various fleets of Stagecoach Holdings, this one is seen working with Cumberland Motor Services.

The Leyland Swift was quickly developed to meet a perceived demand for mid-size buses, in the 35-45 seat sector. Reeve Burgess, a subsidiary of Plaxton, built the attractive body on this example operated by Stevensons of Uttoxeter, a traditional independent operator which expanded rapidly after deregulation.

John Arkell (right) with Robert Atkins, Member of Parliament for Preston South, and Roads and Traffic Minister. The latter would have been better advised to recognise the damage his party did to the bus industry than indulge in shabby sniping at Volvo.

In Sweden Volvo had successfully introduced a dock assembly system, using a team of workers to build a vehicle in one place from start to finish. It had been found very successful in relieving the monotony of constantly carrying out the same task on car production lines. While it was not the most cost effective way to build cars, it was ideal for bus and coach chassis production. Apart from the fact that higher job satisfaction led to better quality workmanship, any warranty claims could be traced back to the team which built the chassis.

Although Farington had at one time looked the favourite, it was announced in July 1989 that the B10M would be built at Workington. The programme forecast the production of 80 B10M's in 1990, building up to 1,000 a year by 1994, including exports. Workington would be responsible for assembling the chassis, incorporating kits of units from Borås and suppliers. The intention was to source more parts in the United Kingdom, as production built up.

Volvo invested £6 million in Workington to assemble the B10M by the dock system to Volvo quality standards. Around the same time it was announced that production of the Olympian would be transferred from Farington back to Workington, where it would be built on the dock system. It was a logical decision, because some Olympian bodywork was already being built there.

Roy Nicholson had departed. Ken Hargreaves recalled that the Workington people received the new model developments very positively. He became General Manager of the Chassis Division, responsible for introducing chassis production to Borås methods. In effect, he was project leader for the introduction of team working and what he described as 'Volvo's excellent quality and auditing systems.'

Towards the end of 1989 there were signs that the growth in bus industry registrations was starting to fall. Within months the country entered the longest recession since the Second World War. By January 1990 it was inevitable that there would have to be further reductions in headcount.

It was announced that all chassis production would cease at Farington, following the transfer of the Olympian to Workington. That made 380 people redundant at Farington, leaving only the technical and engineering staff, the component manufacturing operation, and the company's administrative headquarters. The announcement raised an outcry from Robert Atkins, the local Conservative Member of Parliament, who accused Volvo of behaving in "a false and shabby manner.' As Roads and Traffic Minister at the time it would have been better for him to have examined the reasons for the decline in the industry, which his party had caused, and then try to find a remedy. It was Atkins who behaved in a false and shabby manner.

On 1 March 1990, John Arkell wrote to all Leyland Bus employees advising that much of his time had been taken up with the transfer of responsibility for sales, service and parts to the marketing company. Having almost completed that task, he and two other directors were resigning and Ivan Wheatley, the Manufacturing Director, would take his place as Managing Director, because his "skills are in the manufacturing and product development areas that are so important to the future.'

With that announcement Sandy Glennie was appointed Managing Director of all Volvo Bus activities in the United Kingdom, with the clear task of re-shaping the Leyland manufacturing activities into the normal organisational framework of Volvo.

He inherited a very difficult situation. Not only was the market starting to decline because of the recession, but there were considerable stocks of unsold chassis, many of which could be traced back to the period just before and after the acquisition of Leyland Bus by Volvo. Difficult times lay ahead.

The decision to cease manufacture of buses in the town of Leyland was both momentous and inevitable. Farington was a large plant, yet it turned out just 364 Olympians and 98 Tigers in 1990, equivalent to less than three weeks production in the heyday of BX. Output in 1991 fell to 95 Tigers and 20 of the mid-sized Swift chassis.

The first of literally thousands of buses, delivered all over the world, had left the Lancashire town in 1900. The last left in 1991. That was a measure of the severity of the recession. It was also recognition that Volvo had faced up to the sheer size of the Workington plant and had concluded that all vehicle production would have to be transferred there to minimise costs and overheads.

The Laird Group was having no success in finding a buyer for MCW as a going concern. Duple, once the country's leading maker of coach bodywork, until overtaken by Plaxton in the 1970s, was on its last legs, closing early in 1991. Even one or two of the builders in the minibus boom of 1986 to 1988 had gone bankrupt.

The Workington plant had actually outlived them – and MCW, Park Royal, Roe, Eastern Coach Works, Willowbrook and several others – and even mother Leyland! That was beyond reality.

CHAPTER THIRTEEN

Into the Recession

There is an old saying in the commercial vehicle industry that half the manufacturers disappear every decade, whether by acquisition, merger or closure.

The major European manufacturers were becoming more and more vertically integrated, that is to say that they were building an ever increasing proportion of their vehicles in house. The United States had a different philosophy, where customers could select their preferred choice of engine, gearbox and axles from different makers, then find a vehicle manufacturer prepared to build a truck or bus around that driveline.

American component manufacturers, like Cummins, Allison, Eaton and Rockwell, had come to Europe in strength, mainly in the 1960s, and mainly to Britain. The pendulum started to swing in the other direction when Volvo, Mercedes and Renault bought into American heavy vehicle manufacturers in the 1980s. The major vertically integrated manufacturers were starting to build a volume base which would enable them to supply world markets from within their own manufacturing facilities.

In February 1990 it was announced that Volvo and Renault intended to take cross-shareholdings in order to build another world scale manufacturer. In addition to share transfers in their respective car divisions, it was agreed that each would acquire 45% of the shares in the other's bus and truck subsidiaries.

Volvo built considerably more bus and coach chassis than Renault and therefore had a higher level of registrations which, at first glance, made it appear the dominant partner. This was deceptive because the bulk of Renault's production consisted of complete integral buses and coaches.

Early press announcements said that the two companies would co-operate on industrial and technical matters, but each would retain its own product range and distribution networks. Those intentions failed to recognise that demand for buses and coaches in France was relatively constant, free from the political dogmatism which had caused havoc in the British market. Yet Renault had considerable capacity for the manufacture of complete buses and coaches, a point which was surely not lost on the Volvo Bus management when looking at forward planning.

Although there were no immediate repercussions in Leyland Bus, the Renault factor must inevitably have figured in medium to long term planning from that date onwards. The combination of Volvo Bus and Renault Bus et Car put them in first place in western European bus production at the critical time when the UK market was starting to decline sharply. It suddenly put Volvo into the centre of the European stage, alongside giants like Mercedes and Iveco. Companies like DAF, Scania and MAN formed a second division.

Volvo and Renault first started to collaborate in February 1990. The fully integral Renault R312 citybus was a modern design and might well have figured in medium to longer term planning. This example was borrowed to demonstrate on a park and ride scheme in Nottingham in 1992.

By May 1990 it was becoming clear that the British bus market was sliding further into recession, and that new registrations were falling even lower. Higher interest rates were holding back investment. The community charge, or poll tax, meant that many bus passengers could no longer afford non-essential journeys and operators were suffering from a general downturn in revenue.

A further 120 jobs were cut at Farington and plans to recruit 70 people at Workington were abandoned. Jobs were reallocated in preparation for production of the first Volvo B10M chassis, which was ready for handover by the middle of June. In a bold show of confidence Sandy Glennie received it from Ivan Wheatley on behalf of Douglas Park, proprietor of Park's of Hamilton, and long renowned as the toughest purchaser in the operating industry, but nonetheless a man of his word.

The plan was to construct 80 B10Ms in 1990, building up to 200 in 1991, with a forward projection as high as 1,000 units by 1994. At first, Workington concentrated on the standard B10M coach chassis with manual gearboxes but had the capability of building other versions, including those with automatic gearboxes, and the double-deck model.

The dock assembly system was working very well, producing B10Ms at very acceptable cost levels. The Volvo quality system was a major factor. This success prompted Volvo to begin pilot dock assembly of Olympian chassis, turning out 51 in 1990. There had been a lull in export orders for the Olympian in 1988, but 182 were shipped to Hong Kong in 1990 as that market started to recover confidence, following the agreement between the British and Chinese Governments to hand back the colony in 1997.

In the domestic market there was a partial break with the custom that buses were sold direct by manufacturers to operators, unlike coaches which were traditionally sold through dealers because of the more fragmented nature of the coach industry. Following the decision to put certain London bus routes out to tender, on a basis which made the provision of new or nearly new buses a requirement, Kirkby and Arlington each ordered small batches of stock double-deckers. One of the first deals saw the sale of 12 Olympians with Alexander bodywork to Armchair Coaches of Brentford for operation on LRT's route 260.

May 1990 saw the announcement that the Lynx would be made available as an underframe to independent bodybuilders in the United Kingdom, principally to satisfy customers who wanted aluminium framed bodywork. At the same time the Volvo THD102KF engine would become a regular production option. This was promoted as a 'green' engine, developing 245bhp at 2200rpm. In the same month, the 800th Lynx came off the production lines at Workington.

Around this time a number of internal improvements was made to the Lynx. The Department of Transport had produced a list of features to help disabled and handicapped passengers, known collectively as the Disabled Passengers Transport Advisory Committee (DiPTAC) specification. They included brightly coloured handrails which had a crinkly non-slip material, bell pushes on the handrails

Top to bottom

A group of workers line up to see the first Workington built B10M handed over to Sandy Glennie (standing on the left of the picture).

The large Scottish coach operator, Park's of Hamilton, was the first customer for Workington built B10M's, one of which is seen here with Plaxton Paramount bodywork carrying tourists.

Large orders for the three axle Olympian came from Hong Kong. Most had bodywork assembled from kits in the colony, but some were fully built up by Alexander at Falkirk. This air conditioned example is being reversed on board ship for the long voyage.

which could be operated by a palm, and chequered nosings to the main steps and any interior step.

Many operators called for these features on the Lynx, including the Badgerline subsidiary, Bristol City Line, which took 29 to full DiPTAC specification. Other improvements around the same time included better engine soundproofing and an uprated ducted heating system.

All these improvements were carried through to the Lynx II which was launched in December 1990. The most noticeable difference was a new full width front grille which protruded below the windscreen. At the time it was designed Leyland and Volvo engineers thought that engines might need to be intercooled to meet forthcoming levels of European noise and emissions legislation. The new front was designed to conceal a much larger radiator, but the effect was hardly flattering.

Softer front air suspension with new shock absorbers gave an improved ride for passengers. The original four 6 volt batteries gave way to twin 12 volt units, and a stainless steel exhaust system was added as standard.

Previously the Lynx had a divided front step arrangement, but the new model opted for a single full width entrance step, 305 mm above the ground. DiPTAC features became standard, with the option of either a gradually ramped or stepped interior floor layout. Other detailed improvements were made to the seating and interior trim. The first example entered service with Halton Borough Transport, a particularly loyal National and Lynx customer.

While 1990 had been a year which the industry wanted to forget, forecast registrations for 1991 were even worse. Leyland Bus was turning out to be an unfortunate investment for Volvo, and steps were therefore taken to try to stem the losses. In January 1991 Leyland Bus was split into two distinct operating divisions.

Rodney Swarbrick, a long-standing Leyland manager, became head of the Leyland Bus Body Division, with responsibility for all body related activity at Workington including the design, development and manufacture of single and double-deck bus bodywork. His staff included a small team which was actively working on new single-deck bodywork.

A few months later Tommy Svensson came across from Sweden to take control of the Leyland Bus Chassis Division, with responsibility for the Lynx II underframe, Olympian and Volvo B10M chassis. Ivan Wheatley commented at the time: "We decided to split the functions at Workington into two separate businesses because there are two distinct missions for the operations there. We could best achieve our targets by allowing each business to develop its own role.'

Caldaire Holdings continued to modernise its fleets, taking its 100th Lynx in February 1991. This brought the age profile of their fleets down to six years, a commendably low level by national standards. At the same time, Caldaire ordered a further 29 Lynx, for delivery during the year. Caldaire estimated that the new Lynx buses gave them a 20% saving in operating costs. This was achieved through improved vehicle availability and consequent savings in the size of maintenance facilities and the number of people employed in them.

Having taken the decision to confine the Lynx to the British market, Volvo Bus Corporation started looking to the future. Market research had shown a strong preference for aluminium framed bodywork on larger buses, because of resistance to corrosion and lower unladen weight. This was particularly true on double-deckers but was also relevant to full size single-deckers, despite the excellent durability of the steel framed National. Too many operators had suffered bad experiences with other makes of steel framed bodywork, especially MCW products in the period from the mid-1970s. On the other hand, builders like Alexander had produced very durable aluminium framed bodies. Those factors, taken together, were enough to sway their opinions.

The short term remedy was the decision to permit independent bodybuilders to build on the Lynx underframe, to the requirements of Leyland Bus on structural integrity but, while draft agreements were being discussed with certain bodybuilders, there would appear to have been second thoughts.

The bodybuilders were deeply concerned about investing very large sums in stress-testing structures which they would have to design specially for the Lynx underframe. Within weeks VL Bus & Coach was predicting a further fall in orders; selling the Lynx as an underframe would inevitably have diluted the number of orders for complete buses from Workington. Negotiations were gently stalled.

The medium to longer term plan was fascinating. Volvo had a wholly owned subsidiary, Saffle, in the town of that name, about 130 miles north east of Gothenburg. The factory had a capacity of about 150-180 bodies a year, built in aluminium, but in fairly antiquated premises, which meant that buses were shunted from building to building during the manufacturing process.

Saffle persuaded the Volvo Bus Board that it could build nearly twice the number of bodies each year, with the same labour force, provided a new assembly hall was approved. At the same time, as part of the exercise to reduce man hours,

The wide easy entrance of the Lynx. This is a Mk 2 version with the extended front end, which was designed to accommodate the possibility that the radiator might need to be relocated to the front, so that future build might comply with more stringent engine noise and emissions legislation.

Ivan Wheatley driving the first Workington built B10M off the line.

Top left and clockwise

The rear end of the Lynx 2 was little different from the original Lynx, but one distinguishing feature was the sight glass for the water level, on the offside rear corner.

Deregulation and denationalisation brought a flurry of bright new liveries. A Lynx 2 for the Caldaire subsidiary, Yorkshire Woollen, awaits delivery at the plant.

Lothian was the only operator to take a two door version of the Lynx. One of the batch is seen on handover on the esplanade of Edinburgh Castle.

A Lynx 2 in the fleet of Fishwick of Leyland, immaculately turned out as always with this operator.

Hovairs were used to convey B10M chassis in the Workington Plant during the dock assembly process.

London Country North West, a former subsidiary of NBC, bought a batch of all Workington Olympians before selling out to neighbouring Luton & District.

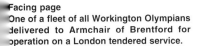

Facing page
One of a fleet of all Workington Olympians delivered to Armchair of Brentford for operation on a London tendered service.

Saffle undertook to design a new method of assembling bus bodywork, using aluminium extrusions.

The Body Division at Workington was involved in these plans almost from the start. This created an interesting conflict in approach to the project. Saffle was trying to advance from its old traditional ways. Workington had to pull back from its much more automated methods.

Saffle developed several extrusions, but early calculations suggested that the finished body would turn out to be rather heavy. For, instance, where the British market normally worked with aluminium panelling about 1.6 mm thick, the Swedish market called for 2.5 mm, especially on the offside.

While there might not have been a problem with the extra weight on single-deckers, it soon became apparent that the Saffle system could not be applied to double-deckers or for that matter to midibuses, where unladen weight was more critical. Workington was always pushing Saffle hard, trying to obtain prototype material almost as soon as it reached the Swedish factory.

The Volvo B10B made its debut in 1992. One of the first with Berkhof bodywork was exhibited at the RAI Show in Maastricht in the Autumn of 1992.

The problem of weight was addressed by Workington looking at lighter extrusions for certain parts of single-deck bodywork and for most of the upper deck on double-deckers.

Development work proceeded at a rapid pace. In September 1991 the new body project was signed off by the Board of Volvo Bus Corporation, with the intention that the body would be built on the new corporate rear-engined chassis, which was in the final stages of development, and was soon to be launched as the B10B.

The recession in Britain was proving particularly deep seated and stubborn. Although Volvo, including Leyland, comfortably retained its dominant share of the British market, the number of registrations was greatly reduced. Order levels continued to fall. A further 117 redundancies were announced at Workington in June 1991.

The Bus Body Division lost just over two-thirds of that total, because it was totally dependent on the domestic market. The Chassis Division had the benefit of Olympian orders from Hong Kong, which took 185 of the 298 Olympians built in 1991. Even so, it had to lay off 36 temporary workers.

An all Workington full-height Olympian with two door layout which was delivered to East London, a subsidiary of London Buses.

Further rationalisation was inevitable. On 17 June 1991, it was announced that Volvo planned to consolidate all its UK bus and coach activities, including engineering and manufacturing, under the control of one company, Volvo Bus Ltd, headed by Sandy Glennie, with headquarters in Warwick, and with effect from 1 July 1991.

The component manufacturing facilities at Farington, which reported to Volvo Components at Skövde in Sweden, were put up for sale with the incentive that any new owner could expect continuing business from Volvo Bus.

The Leyland name would remain on all current products, but new products in the course of development would be sold only under the Volvo name. Considering that Leyland had killed off AEC, Albion, Bristol, Daimler, Guy and others, some sections of the trade press got very worked up about the loss of the Leyland name. The people who mattered most, the operators, did not seem concerned and were reassured that they could still expect to get parts and service for Leyland products.

In characteristic fashion Sandy Glennie hit back strongly, warning the industry not to indulge in nostalgia. In a direct response to 'Coachmart', which in fairness the magazine published, he said: "We, hard-pressed managers in a crisis industry, have no time left for nostalgia. Volvo has invested millions of pounds in Leyland Bus, investments in products and facilities, in addition to trading losses. Many of the losses stem direct from outdated policies of using expensive low volume components produced in labour intensive plants running well below capacity. We have to take reasonable steps to correct this imbalance and we are doing so."

He went on to say that the single organisation of Volvo Bus Ltd would be much better placed to face the challenges of the future than two parallel businesses ever could be. There would be major benefits to customers in terms of a smoother supply of vehicles, parts and service.

The Leyland name lived on, in various products, and in bodywork. In some ways it was surprising that Volvo did not put everything under the Volvo name soon after the takeover, especially as the Leyland name was also being used by DAF on trucks. The main reason for the delay was the need to ensure that the parts business for Leyland buses and coaches was retained.

Concern about the Leyland name helped to conceal the fact that Volvo wanted to sell the component manufacturing facility, which employed nearly 500 people. Many of the products of that plant were being built in low volume, including spare parts for non-current models. Volvo had decided that the future depended on using high-volume low cost units shared with the truck range, and that the Farington Components facility would benefit from being sold to an organisation which would be better able to develop the business and broaden the range of products and customers.

That left only a small number of design engineers and other staff on the Farington site. By this time Jim McKnight and his engineers were working closely with their colleagues in Sweden and were taking responsibility for sections of several projects.

The Volvo powered Lynx 2 of Nottingham City Transport, which appeared at the UITP Conference and Exhibition in Stockholm in 1991.

This arrangement suited Volvo Bus Corporation, partly because skilled design engineering and development costs in the United Kingdom were approximately one-third of those prevailing in Sweden.

In July 1991 the prestigious biennial UITP Conference and Exhibition was held in Stockholm. With many of the world's leading bus operators attending Volvo Bus Corporation put on an impressive display. Apart from the fact that the event was being held in Sweden, Volvo's long standing rival, Scania, was celebrating its centenary.

The large Volvo stand included an all-Workington Olympian in the familiar red livery of London Buses, although it subsequently entered service with Capital Citybus, registered J135 PVC. It was the first Workington Olympian to be built to London's standard two door layout.

The other Workington exhibit was the second Volvo engined Lynx to be built, destined for Nottingham City Transport, an experienced user of both Volvo and Leyland products. At this very important show it was reassuring to see that the Leyland models looked very much an integral part of Volvo's bus and coach range. That was soon to change.

CHAPTER FOURTEEN

'The Saddest Day of My Life'

In October 1991, Larserik Nilsson moved to a senior public relations post within Volvo Truck Corporation. His successor as President of Volvo Bus Corporation was Björn Larsson. Another career Volvo man, he had considerable experience of the bus industry. Among his previous appointments he had been Managing Director of Saffle, Executive Vice President of Volvo do Brasil, which continued to build the B58 in large volumes, and before that, resident representative in countries like Iran.

The parent Volvo Group was heading for its first loss in 70 years of trading. The recession was hitting several key world markets and sales were falling. Larsson quickly took stock of Volvo Bus Corporation, ordering a temporary moratorium on investment in any new projects. Every part of the organisation was put under the financial microscope.

As so often happens in these circumstances the instruction almost coincided with the unveiling of a new mid-sized bus and coach chassis, known initially as 'B6R', but soon simplified to 'B6'. Volvo had noticed an increasing demand for light but robust long-life models in the 8.5 to 10 metre sector.

For a large corporation with strict engineering disciplines, Volvo reacted very quickly and developed a chassis using an impressive percentage of components from the high volume FL6 truck range, along with air tanks, electrics and the driver's binnacle from the B10M.

It was a measure of the durability of the new chassis that, in articulated truck form, the components could run at gross weights up to 31,000 kg, while the B6 was rated at a maximum of 11,500 kg. A six litre TD63 engine, developing 180bhp, was mounted vertically in line at the rear, driving forward through a choice of Allison or ZF automatic gearboxes, or a ZF synchromesh unit. Air suspension was fitted as standard.

Initially the B6 was built in Steyr Bus, a company owned 70% by Volvo Bus Corporation and based in Vienna. Steyr, a very old established company, had never built more than 150 units per annum for the small and specialised Austrian market. Within that small volume they built three or four different chassis, including a trolleybus.

In the British market, even before the launch, Volvo picked up a massive order for 200 B6's from Stagecoach Holdings. It was announced that the first 50 chassis would be built in Vienna. Thereafter the proposal was that chassis for the British market would be assembled in Workington on the proven docking system.

Volvo thought quite seriously about offering the B6 as a complete in-house bus from Workington and made preliminary studies on the possibility of building a suitable aluminium body. Since the new Saffle system was too heavy for this size of bus, alternatives were investigated, including Alusuisse, which already had British licensees in the shape of Wrights of Ballymena and, subsequently, Optare. Perhaps the loyalty of Stagecoach to Alexander and the sheer size of the initial order threw this proposal off balance for a critical period.

Volvo owns 70% of the Austrian builder, Steyr Bus. A Steyr trolleybus is seen here in the city of Salzburg.

The mid-size Volvo B6 chassis, designed for bodywork up to 45 seats. At one time it was proposed to assemble this chassis in Workington, but production for world markets is now carried out at the Irvine plant in Scotland.

Björn Larsson's critical review of Volvo Bus Corporation placed considerable attention on the British subsidiary. Workington needed well over 1,000 units a year to break even. There was no sign of an end to the British recession, nor any hope that volumes would rise anywhere near the break-even level.

In the autumn of 1991 Volvo Bus had tried to stimulate the British market by aggressive pricing and imaginative financing. At the BCC Show in October Volvo announced that Stagecoach would take 70 all-Workington Olympians in what was widely believed to be a leasing deal. Certainly Volvo's tactics were giving severe palpitations not only to competitive chassis manufacturers, but also to the few remaining bodybuilders.

It was therefore a great surprise when Volvo announced on 6 December 1991 that the British subsidiary was to be restructured, in an attempt to eliminate substantial financial losses, by bringing the cost of the company's operations into line with the size of the market, which was forecast to remain at severely depressed levels. All employees were told that demand for heavy duty buses had dropped by almost 50%, even from the poor levels of 1990.

Volvo said that it could no longer bear the losses being incurred by Workington and announced that the factory would be closed, with the progressive loss of all 370 jobs. Production of the Lynx, for which there had been ambitious plans only two years before, would cease on completion of current orders, which included a small number of stock vehicles. The same would apply to Olympian bodywork, of which only 51 were built in 1991. Both models desperately needed volume and it simply was not there.

The intention was to transfer the Chassis Division to Irvine during 1992, to become the world centre for B6 and Olympian production. The plans to assemble B6 at Workington were dropped. It would go straight to Irvine.

There was sufficient space at the Scottish truck factory to set up separate facilities for bus chassis assembly, using the docking system. It required an investment of £2.4 million at Irvine and created 50 jobs, some of which were offered to employees willing to transfer from Workington, with company assistance.

The original plan was to transfer chassis production during the summer of 1992, but that was later put back to March 1993 because it was decided to update the Olympian, including offering a Volvo engine as an option to Cummins. It also made sense to incorporate other standard Volvo parts, wherever possible, in order to keep costs down. That exercise cost over £3 million, but ensured that the Olympian could comply with forthcoming legislation and retain its position as the world's most popular double-deck chassis.

Workington had assembled 258 B10Ms in 1991. Borås took over responsibility for assembly for the British market for 1992 but the intention was that B10M would also go to Irvine, after the plant had reached regular production volumes with B6 and Olympian.

It was a devastating blow to Workington. Sandy Glennie, who had been in charge of the operation for less than six months, said: "This action has been brought about by events entirely outside our control, including the dramatic effects of deregulation of the bus operating industry. It is being taken with extreme reluctance and only after all other possible alternatives have been fully investigated. It is the only course in the current climate that allows the Company to consolidate its position and to maintain viable bus chassis production in the UK.'

In a meeting with the trade press on Monday 9 December 1991 in the Post House Hotel at Crick, it was confirmed that the decision had been taken only days before. Sandy Glennie had told the staff and workforce at Workington on the previous Friday and the story had broken in the national press on the Saturday, normally the quietest day of the week for business news.

The decision to close Workington was irreversible. There was no prospect of bridging the gap between even the most optimistic sales forecasts and the factory's production break-even point. Chassis assembly needed space but was not labour intensive.

The decision would benefit the much more compact Irvine factory, because 1,500 bus chassis would be added to the 4,000 trucks produced each year, making a welcome reduction in overheads. The closure of Workington would help the independent British bodybuilders to survive. It also reprieved the remaining activities at Farington.

As far as the British market was concerned Volvo had decided to concentrate on doing what it knew best, building chassis. Bodybuilding expertise existed in other parts of the Corporation, and that could help Volvo in its relationships with British bodybuilders. For instance, Saffle's newly developed bodywork system could be available to British bodybuilders, presumably under a licensing arrangement.

Glennie said that the acquisition of Leyland Bus had given Volvo a direct trading relationship with practically every bus operator in Britain, and some valuable overseas contacts. It had put Volvo firmly into first place in the important British market, and provided an excellent team of engineers. There was also a healthy parts and service business, although it was becoming difficult and costly to find suppliers to make small volume production runs of parts for some of the older and nearly obsolete Leyland models.

Despite the valiant attempt to salvage something from the closure announcement, the atmosphere was very sad. The man who had led Volvo to such success in the British market quietly admitted that the previous Friday had been "the saddest day in my life." Minutes later, as if on cue, the lights in that part of the hotel went out and a sorry little group stumbled out into the dark December evening.

Volvo Bus Corporation put a brave face on events. There was no mention of the enormous losses incurred by Leyland, but they must have been at least £15 million in 1991. In total, it has been reliably estimated that the purchase price of Leyland Bus and the accumulated losses since 1988 were around £100 million.

A large part of that was due to factors beyond the control of Volvo, including but not limited to high warranty and rectification costs on buses and especially the Sprinters, the cost of financing and disposing of the stock built up during and just after McKinnon's reign, and the other undisclosed special deals done by Leyland Bus before Volvo bought it. The recession was certainly another major factor.

There was a predictable political outcry from certain quarters, notably from the local MP, Dale Campbell-Savours, but registrations of new buses had fallen so steeply that Workington was an anachronism.

It had survived in artificial circumstances for much of the 1980s because the Government had grudgingly pumped money into Leyland Bus. It had diversified into projects on the back of hopelessly optimistic forecasts. Some of those ventures on their own lost millions.

One can understand Volvo's reasons for buying Leyland Bus when it did. Perhaps the rising domestic market in 1988, and the resurgence of the Hong Kong business encouraged the Swedes, but they were soon hit with massive rectification costs on the Sprinter trains.

As the recession bit, and the market went into the steepest decline since the Second World War, Volvo took the knife to Farington in a bid to make Workington viable, but at the end of the day even the mighty Volvo realised that Workington was beyond reality.

There were those who thought that it would have been better to have closed Irvine and transfer all Volvo assembly in the United Kingdom to Workington. Either way, it would have cost money to transfer truck production to Cumbria or bus production to Irvine, and truck production was running at four or five times bus levels in a lower cost plant. Bodywork was a lost cause, and the Irvine plant was much more in tune with the order levels being received and anticipated from the market. There is no doubt in my mind that Volvo made the right decision.

After the closure announcement had been made manufacture of bodywork ceased on fulfilment of orders on hand, including a small number of Lynx which had been built for stock. The few bodied Olympians were sold early in 1992, but it was late summer before the last Lynx was registered.

The plan to move Olympian production to Irvine was delayed, not just by the re-engineering exercise, but by the winning of two major export orders. Citybus of Hong Kong ordered 85 three axle Olympians, following a successful tender to operate several routes. Singapore Bus Services decided to expand its double-deck fleet by taking 200 three axle Olympians, its first three axle buses. Alexander won both bodywork contracts.

The greater complexity of these chassis and tight delivery requirements made it logical to keep Workington open for these contracts and a smaller one for ten three axle Olympians for China Motor Bus. Just after that decision was taken, the Larkfield garage of Strathclyde Buses suffered a major fire, which destroyed many elderly Atlanteans and a few Ailsas. Fortunately, the insurance policy was on a new for old basis.

The fire occurred at a fairly critical stage in plans by the management and workforce to buy out Strathclyde Buses, and the Secretary of State for Scotland insisted on a revaluation of the business to take account of the much higher value of new buses.

Several manufacturers competed for the business, but Volvo won an order for 52 Olympians. Strathclyde specified the combination of Cummins engines and Voith gearboxes, which had not been built on the Olympian for several years. Again, the

logical decision was to put this order, later increased by three, to Workington, thus keeping a limited number of jobs open until final closure in July 1993.

The decision to keep Workington open a little longer prompted various local initiatives. Cumbria County Council wanted Volvo to take on a smaller factory in the area and the Chief Executive of the West Cumbria Development Agency promised 'substantial cash aid if it stayed in Workington.'

Unfortunately Campbell-Savours carried on sniping at the company. He told the local 'Times & Star' newspaper: 'Having spent many hours ringing round the world to the company's customers I was, and remain, convinced that they should keep the plant open and get on with the business of re-developing Workington.' He went on to say that if there was 'a major uplift in the bus market, Volvo would have to keep the site going.'

Maybe some of this was his way of communicating concern to his constituents, but his trumpeting took a more sinister turn in February 1992, after Volvo signed an agreement with Jelcz to build buses in Poland. Claiming that Volvo had signed the deal to build cheap buses for the European market, he told the local newspaper: 'They may think that they can fool the people in the bus industry but they must ascribe to the people of Workington a little bit more intelligence.'

He failed to realise that the purpose of the Polish agreement was to build buses for the domestic and

An Olympian chassis on the dock assembly system at Workington.

neighbouring markets which badly needed more modern and reliable vehicles. To him a bus was a bus. He did not distinguish between different models and markets. Poland is just across the Baltic from Sweden. It had been a good market for Volvo trucks for international haulage for many years and had previous experience of collaboration with western European manufacturers, including the engine deal with Leyland in the 1960s.

Once again, though not culpable like the Conservatives for the fate of British bus industry, it is yet another example of the general ignorance of our politicians and their regular failure to be properly briefed before pontificating on any issue. Campbell-Savours went on to predict that 'within five years there will be an invasion of buses from Europe because the British bus industry will have been wiped out!" He withdrew from any involvement with the factory one week before the 1992 General Election, telling the loyal union representatives that he had other things on his mind!

It is to the great credit of the workforce at Workington that their attention to quality did not falter during the fairly lengthy reprieve from closure. Productivity was excellent. In the company's internal 'Ailsa News' in June 1993, Sandy Glennie wrote: 'Our colleagues at Workington are steadily turning out export Olympian chassis to high quality standards, in spite of being in a run-out situation and we extend our thanks to Ken Hargreaves and his group there.'

In fact, the quality audit was among the highest recorded at any Volvo plant, due to the docking system and the attitude of the workers. It was also a nice personal touch to mention Ken Hargreaves, who was the longest serving person at Workington and who finally had the sad task of supervising the decommissioning of the factory.

It has to be said that the Workington workforce was unique in the British commercial vehicle industry. In the early days they took on a variety of tasks when much of the industry was constrained by demarcation. They were willing to learn new skills, and they adapted magnificently when the factory diversified into different models in the 1980s. They took the highly mechanised production of the National, the much more traditional assembly of the Titan, diversification into railcars, the change from rivetting to welding, and Volvo's dock assembly system in their stride.

Volvo offered these people the opportunity to move to Irvine, presumably with some overall limit on numbers. In fact, at the time of writing, only three men took up the offer. Two were Scots, so it was not so hard a decision for them. Only Ian Lister was a native Cumbrian, and he did not relish the prospect of long term unemployment. That said a lot about the local community. It was tight knit and people who had been so willing to get to know new skills were clearly not willing to get to know new surroundings!

On the engineering side the Olympian was updated to incorporate a much higher percentage of Volvo components. Designated 5380 internally, but still keeping the 'Olympian' name in the market, the new model had as standard the same engine as the B10M, but in transverse vertical form, with the Cummins L10 as an option.

There was no place for Gardner, once such a force in the bus industry. In fact the new Olympian was unveiled in March 1993 and a few weeks later Gardner said that

With the original factory bench-mark in the background, a sad little group poses by the last Olympian. They are, left to right, Gerry Fowler, Personnel Manager, Mrs Doris Caldicott, Supplies Manager and Ken Hargreaves, Plant Manager.

The very last Olympian chassis, number 21080, built at Workington and awaiting delivery to Singapore. The photograph was taken on 8 September 1993, when contractors had already boarded up ground floor windows.

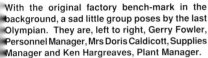

Olympian chassis underway at Volvo's new Bus Hall in Irvine, Autumn 1993.

the legendary 6LXB would cease production because it could not be made to comply with 'Euro 1' limits on emissions. The LG1200 engine could comply, but it was almost unknown in the market.

The Olympian's rear axle remained, but with Volvo hubs, brakes and drums. Further standardisation was achieved by using a Volvo front axle, air tanks and steering components, plus the same driver's binnacle and electrics as the B10M. All these measures resulted in substantial cost savings, and will simplify stocking of spare parts in the future.

The Irvine Bus Assembly Hall was opened in March 1993, building the B6 and the Olympian on the well tried docking system. The appointment of receivers at Leyland DAF Trucks the previous month had raised considerable concern about the reputation of the Leyland name. There were no protests when the Olympian became a Volvo model, indeed the only Volvo bus with a model name.

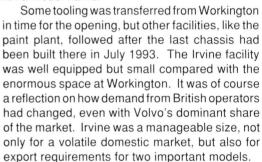

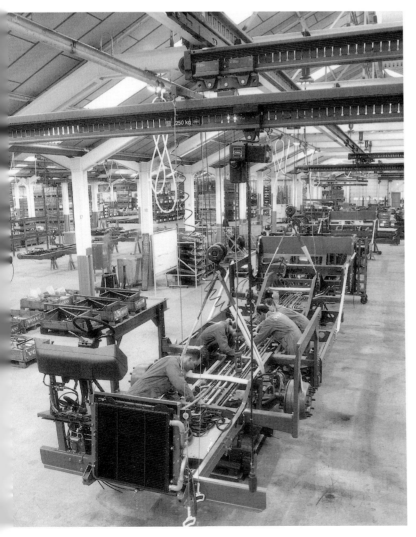

Some tooling was transferred from Workington in time for the opening, but other facilities, like the paint plant, followed after the last chassis had been built there in July 1993. The Irvine facility was well equipped but small compared with the enormous space at Workington. It was of course a reflection on how demand from British operators had changed, even with Volvo's dominant share of the market. Irvine was a manageable size, not only for a volatile domestic market, but also for export requirements for two important models.

Throughout the period after the closure of Workington was announced there was a resilience about the Volvo people. At the opening of the Irvine Bus ^ssembly Hall it was refreshing to see that the old buoyancy had returned. All the talk was positive and forward thinking, because this was a facility which was lean enough to respond quickly to variations in specifications and model mix in a deregulated domestic market, yet equally capable of building to the higher specifications likely to come from export markets.

Those who are unfamiliar with the recent history of the British bus industry, especially since the Transport Act 1985, will accuse Volvo of closing Workington. While it is true that Volvo turned the lights off and closed the door, they kept the plant running probably by as much as four years longer than any alternative owner could have managed.

In September 1993, Volvo and Renault announced plans to make a full scale merger, with Volvo having 35% and Renault 65%. That would have brought about a substantial excess of manufacturing capacity to the western European industry and represented a threat to the remaining British operations. In December the merger was called off – one national newspaper described it as

An Olympian chassis being fitted out at Irvine. Ian Lister, second from the left, is the Cumbrian who transferred to Irvine from Workington.

French arrogance and Swedish insularity! In truth the real reasons were the difficulty in putting a valuation on a state-owned company and Volvo's fear of loss of independence. Even so, at the time of writing, the 45% cross shareholdings in the respective commercial vehicle operations remain, and some kind of liason in the future cannot be ruled out.

Looking back at Workington, it has to be said that the plant, such a showpiece in its day, was created in almost artificial circumstances under the impetus of a political party which wanted to modernise the nation's bus fleet, so that it could take its rightful place in combatting the congestion which, even at that time, was largely attributed to private cars.

Twenty years later, and with the United Kingdom's car population having increased from twelve to over twenty million during Workington's lifetime, it was closed largely due to the policies of another political party which had done its level best to destroy the bus industry and the concept of providing a high quality public passenger transport service.

There is growing awareness that the world cannot continue to consume fuel at the present rate. City dwellers are telling pollsters that they want to live in an environment which is not clogged with cars and pollution. By the end of this decade we will see many measures to combat the intrusion of cars in larger towns and cities.

Before that can happen there must be efficient public transport of a standard which will compare favourably with the private car. Light rail is not necessarily the answer, because it is extremely expensive. Greater Manchester installed a system with 26 twin-car trams at a cost exceeding £125 million, and serving a fraction of the population. The same amount of money would have paid for replacement of almost all of GM's double-deckers, serving the whole community!

The bus is coming to be recognised as a low cost form of public transport, not just in this country, but even by such authoritative bodies as the World Bank. Yet the domestic industry can barely cope with order levels prevailing at the time of writing.

There will be a number of candidates for the description 'Last Leyland Bus'. At the time of going to press this Alexander (Belfast) Olympian for Dublin Bus seems set to be the last one into service4 in the British Isles.

If the bus boom comes, as some predict, it will need a factory of the scale of Workington to meet demand. That is one of the saddest aspects of this story. The Conservative party cannot and will not understand public transport. Neither can it plan and implement long term industrial strategies.

Even mighty international corporations cannot live in hope. Nor can they predict phenomena like Margaret Thatcher and her wilful neglect of the country's manufacturing base. No other country which considers itself to be an important industrial nation would have done the damage she did. The Germans, whom she often looked on grudgingly as a model for some of her policies, would never have behaved in that way. The French, whom she frequently treated with contempt, would never have done so much damage to so many basic industries. No wonder we have a balance of payments problem in this country!

Margaret Thatcher might have kept two thousand people in the Falklands, but she lost four million people in manufacturing industry in the United Kingdom during her premiership.

In that respect she too was, and still is, beyond reality!!

CHASSIS PRODUCTION 1981-1991

OVERALL PRODUCTION FROM ALL FACTORIES

FACTORY	1981	1982	1983	1984	1985	1986	1987	1988	1989	1990	1991	11 YR TOTAL
WORKINGTON	439	372	830	870	624	337	75	197	390	376	646	5156
FARINGTON	965	1308	1440	1197	777	656	790	1000	835	462	115	9545
CH ROE	0	4	29	27	0	0	0	0	0	0	0	60
BRISTOL	636	457	0	0	0	0	0	0	0	0	0	1093
GUY	1100	512	0	0	0	0	0	0	0	0	0	1612
TOTAL	3140	2653	2299	2094	1401	993	865	1197	1225	838	761	17466

WORKINGTON PLANT CHASSIS PRODUCTION VOLUMES 1981-1991

	1981	1982	1983	1984	1985	1986	1987	1988	1989	1990	1991	11 YR TOTAL
TITAN BU	145	301	242	197	0	0	0	0	0	0	0	885
NATIONAL BU	294	71	64	53	33	0	0	0	0	0	0	515
OLYMPIAN BU	0	0	514	578	563	293	0	0	0	51	298	2297
ROYAL TIGER BU	0	0	9	37	0	0	0	0	0	0	0	46
LYNX UF	0	0	1	0	8	2	0	0	0	0	0	11
ROYAL TIGER	0	0	0	5	20	12	20	0	0	0	0	57
LYNX COMPLETE	0	0	0	0	0	29	55	195	389	264	90	1022
B10M	0	0	0	0	0	0	0	0	0	61	258	319
OTHERS	0	0	0	0	0	1	0	2	1	0	0	4
TOTAL	439	372	830	870	624	337	75	197	390	376	646	5156

FARINGTON PLANT CHASSIS PRODUCTION VOLUMES 1981-1991

	1981	1982	1983	1984	1985	1986	1987	1988	1989	1990	1991	11 YR TOTAL
ATLANTEAN BU	449	293	364	183	20	5	0	0	0	0	0	1314
ATLANTEAN CKD	0	0	0	0	0	40	0	0	0	0	0	40
OLYMPIAN BU	0	0	0	0	16	345	331	423	375	364	0	1854
LEOPARD BU	250	147	0	0	0	0	0	0	0	0	0	397
LEOPARD CKD	62	20	0	0	0	0	0	0	0	0	0	82
TIGER BU	204	618	759	628	376	216	343	437	260	98	95	4034
TIGER CKD	0	4	35	126	133	24	48	38	8	0	0	416
SWIFT BU	0	0	0	0	0	0	36	102	192	0	20	350
VICTORY BU	0	0	0	2	1	0	0	0	0	0	0	3
VICTORY CKD	0	0	282	248	223	26	0	0	0	0	0	779
RANGER BU	0	0	0	2	0	0	0	0	0	0	0	2
RANGER CKD	0	0	0	0	0	0	32	0	0	0	0	32
UTIC KITS CKD	0	226	0	8	8	0	0	0	0	0	0	242
TOTAL	965	1308	1440	1197	777	656	790	1000	835	462	115	9545

CH ROE PLANT CHASSIS PRODUCTION VOLUMES 1981-1984

	1981	1982	1983	1984	4 YR TOTAL
ROYAL TIGER UF	0	1	14	4	19
ROYAL TIGER	0	3	15	23	41
TOTAL	0	4	29	27	60

BODY PRODUCTION 1981-1991

OVERALL BODY PRODUCTION FROM ALL FACTORIES

FACTORY	1981	1982	1983	1984	1985	1986	1987	1988	1989	1990	1991	11 YR TOTAL
CH ROE	152	123	93	115	0	0	0	0	0	0	0	483
ECW	503	408	302	246	243	281	30	0	0	0	0	2013
WORKINGTON	439	372	306	254	53	41	75	215	465	303	141	2664
TOTALS	1094	903	701	615	296	322	105	215	465	303	141	5160

CH ROE BODY PRODUCTION VOLUMES 1981-CLOSURE (1984)

	1981	1982	1983	1984	4 YR TOTAL
OLYMPIAN	12	120	78	91	301
ATLANTEAN	140	0	0	0	140
ROYAL TIGER	0	3	15	24	42
TOTAL	152	123	93	115	483

ECW BODY PRODUCTION VOLUMES 1981-CLOSURE (1987)

	1981	1982	1983	1984	1985	1986	1987	7 YR TOTAL
VRT	358	0	0	0	0	0	0	358
OLYMPIAN	119	253	302	246	243	281	30	1474
ATLANTEAN	23	0	0	0	0	0	0	23
TIGER/LEOPARD	3	155	0	0	0	0	0	158
TOTAL	503	408	302	246	243	281	30	2013

WORKINGTON BODY PRODUCTION VOLUMES 1981-1991

	1981	1982	1983	1984	1985	1986	1987	1988	1989	1990	1991	11 YR TOTAL
NATIONAL	294	71	64	53	33	0	0	0	0	0	0	515
ROYAL TIGER	0	0	0	4	20	12	20	0	0	0	0	56
LYNX	0	0	0	0	0	29	55	195	389	264	90	1022
TITAN	145	301	242	197	0	0	0	0	0	0	0	885
OLYMPIAN	0	0	0	0	0	0	0	20	76	39	51	186
TOTAL	439	372	306	254	53	41	75	215	465	303	141	2664
RAILBUS	0	0	38	6	94	98	26	58	0	0	0	320

BRISTOL PLANT CHASSIS PRODUCTION VOLUMES 1981-1982

	1981	1982	2 YR TOTAL
OLYMPIAN BU	265	428	693
VRT	261	0	261
LH	10	0	10
RE	95	0	95
OTHER	5	29	34
TOTAL	636	457	1093

GUY PLANT CHASSIS PRODUCTION VOLUMES 1981-1982

	1981	1982	2 YR TOTAL
VICTORY CKD	824	512	1336
VICTORY BU	275	0	275
OTHER	1	0	1
TOTAL	1100	512	1612

LEYLAND BUS CHASSIS PRODUCTIONS VOLUMES

	1981	1982	1983	1984	1985	1986	1987	1988	1989	1990	1991	TOTAL
UK BU												
DOUBLE DECKS												
TITAN	145	301	242	197	0	0	0	0	0	0	0	885
VRT	261	0	0	0	0	0	0	0	0	0	0	261
ATLANTEAN	308	185	193	41	0	0	0	0	0	0	0	727
OLYMPIAN	258	417	441	488	445	352	39	414	288	233	113	3488
TOTAL UK D/DECKS	972	903	876	726	445	352	39	414	288	233	113	5361
COACH & GENERAL PURPOSE												
LEOPARD	250	147	0	0	0	0	0	0	0	0	0	397
B10M	0	0	0	0	0	0	0	0	0	61	103	164
OTHER	105	18	0	0	0	1	0	0	0	0	0	124
ROYAL TIGER	0	3	15	28	20	12	20	0	0	0	0	98
ROYAL TIGER UF	0	1	23	41	0	0	0	0	0	0	0	65
TIGER	204	618	751	623	370	216	343	410	240	98	95	3968
TOTAL UK COACH & GEN PURPOSE	559	787	789	692	390	229	363	410	240	159	198	4816
SINGLE DECK BUS												
NATIONAL	294	71	64	53	33	0	0	0	0	0	0	515
LYNX	0	0	0	0	0	29	55	195	389	261	90	1019
MIDI	0	0	0	0	0	0	36	102	192	0	20	350
LYNX UF	0	0	1	0	6	0	0	0	0	0	0	7
TOTAL UK SINGLE DECK BUS	294	71	65	53	39	29	91	297	581	261	110	1891
GRAND TOTAL UNITED KINGDOM	1825	1761	1730	1471	874	610	493	1121	1109	653	421	12068
EXPORT BU												
DOUBLE DECKS												
VICTORY	275	0	0	2	1	0	0	0	0	0	0	278
ATLANTEAN	141	108	171	142	20	5	0	0	0	0	0	587
OLYMPIAN	7	11	73	90	134	286	292	9	87	182	185	1356
TOTAL EXPORT D/DECK BU	423	119	244	234	155	291	292	9	87	182	185	2221
SINGLE DECK BU												
TIGER	0	0	8	5	6	0	0	27	20	0	0	66
OTHER	6	0	0	2	0	0	0	2	1	0	0	11
LYNX U/F	0	0	0	0	2	0	0	0	0	0	0	2
LYNX	0	0	0	0	0	0	0	0	0	3	0	3

	1981	1982	1983	1984	1985	1986	1987	1988	1989	1990	1991	TOTAL
B10M	0	0	0	0	0	0	0	0	0	0	155	155
TOTAL EXPORT S/DECK BU	6	0	8	7	8	0	0	29	21	3	155	237
EXPORT CKD												
DOUBLE DECKS												
ATLANTEAN	0	0	0	0	0	40	0	0	0	0	0	40
TOTAL EXPORT D/DECK CKD	0	0	0	0	0	40	0	0	0	0	0	40
SINGLE DECKS CKD												
LEOPARD	62	20	0	0	0	0	0	0	0	0	0	82
B21/52	0	11	0	0	0	0	0	0	0	0	0	11
UTIC	0	226	0	8	8	0	0	0	0	0	0	242
VICTORY	824	512	282	248	223	26	0	0	0	0	0	2115
RANGER	0	0	0	0	0	0	32	0	0	0	0	32
TIGER	0	4	35	126	133	24	48	38	8	0	0	416
LYNX UF	0	0	0	0	0	2	0	0	0	0	0	2
TOTAL S/DECK CKD	886	773	317	382	364	52	80	38	8	0	0	2900
GRAND TOTAL EXPORTS	1315	892	569	623	527	383	372	76	116	185	340	5398
GRAND TOTAL UK & EXPORT	3140	2653	2299	2094	1401	993	865	1197	1225	838	761	17466
DAB UNITS	150	166	142	155	179	198	165	136	85	0	0	1376

LEYLAND BUS BODY PRODUCTION

	1981	1982	1983	1984	1985	1986	1987	1988	1989	1990	1991	TOTAL
DOUBLE DECKS												
TITAN	145	301	242	197	0	0	0	0	0	0	0	885
OLYMPIAN	131	373	380	337	243	281	30	20	76	39	51	1961
ATLANTEAN	163	0	0	0	0	0	0	0	0	0	0	163
VRT	358	0	0	0	0	0	0	0	0	0	0	358
TOTAL D/DECKS	797	674	622	534	243	281	30	20	76	39	51	3367
SINGLE DECKS												
R TIGER	0	3	15	28	20	12	20	0	0	0	0	98
LYNX	0	0	0	0	0	29	55	195	389	264	90	1022
NATIONAL	294	71	64	53	33	0	0	0	0	0	0	515
TIGER/LEOPAR	3	155	0	0	0	0	0	0	0	0	0	158
TOTAL S/DECKS	297	229	79	81	53	41	75	195	389	264	90	1793
GRAND TOTALS	1094	903	701	615	296	322	105	215	465	303	141	5160
RAILBUS	0	0	38	6	94	98	26	58	0	0	0	320

SOURCE MATERIAL

The illustrative content of this volume is, as mentioned in the Author's Introduction, largely taken from material issued over many years by Leyland. Doug Jack, John Senior and Alan Townsin have drawn heavily on technical, sales and marketing publications, in addition to making use of Ron Hall's department in his capacity as Leyland's Photographic Manager until his retirement.

The BCVM archive helped in verifying facts as did the Technical Centre records. Others within Leyland have provided financial and production figures, technical extracts and an extensive collection of press cuttings recording many key events. More recently Volvo's records have been examined and their photographic archive has been most useful.

The following books, trade journals and newspapers proved helpful in the preparation of *Beyond Reality* and thanks are due to the authors and publishers –

The British Bus Story – Turbulent Times (Townsin - TPC)
The British Bus Story – Late 'Seventies (Townsin - TPC)
National Bus Company 1968-89 (Birks et al - TPC)
The Leyland Bus (Jack - TPC)
Castle Diaries 1964-70 (Castle - Weidenfeld & Nicolson)
The Motor Makers (Adenay - Collins)
Mercedes-Benz Last Wagen und Omnibusse 1886-1986 (Oswald - MV Stuttgart)
Scania – 100 years (Scania)
Volvo: Sixty Years of Truck making (Olsson - Förlagshuset Norden AB)
British Rail Fleet Survey (Haresnape - Ian Allan)

The company histories of Alexander, AEC, Park Royal, Charles Roe and ECW published by Transport Publishing Company were very useful.

Trade magazines and professional papers included –

Bus & Coach
Bus & Coach Buyer
Coach & Bus Week, formerly *Coachmart*
Buses
Commercial Motor
Motor Transport
Bus Ride (USA)
Modern Railways

Institution of Mechanical Engineers – papers
Design, produced by the Design Council
The Financial Times
The Times
The Times & Star, Workington
Leyland Guardian
Lancashire Evening News

REJUVENATED NATIONALS

The Leyland National single-decker is likely to be around for many years to come – certainly well into the next century. Recently the value of the corrosion-free structure has been recognised by companies prepared to invest in refurbishment. The illustration shows Western Travel's 'National 3' which has had a DAF engine installed together with full renovation of all other mechanical units and a full renewal of interior furnishings. East Lancashire Coachbuilders of Blackburn also offer a rejuvenated model of the National – the Greenway – and their product involves considerable restyling of the basic vehicle as well as the installation of either Gardner or Volvo 'green' engines. It seems likely that a life in excess of thirty years will be achieved by such vehicles, thus matching that of the remaining London Transport Routemasters.

INDEX

Note: Names are listed as they were known at the time of involvement in this story and might not necessarily include subsequent knighthoods or enoblement. Bold entries indicate illustrations.

158